DON'T ASK FOREVER:
My Love Affair With Elvis

DON'T ASK FOREVER:

My Love Affair With

ELVIS

A Washington Woman's Secret Years with Elvis Presley

BY

JOYCE BOVA

AS TOLD TO

WILLIAM CONRAD NOWELS

KENSINGTON BOOKS

KENSINGTON BOOKS are published by

Kensington Publishing Corp.
475 Park Avenue South
New York, NY 10016

Kensington Books is a trademark of Kensington Publishing Corp.

ISBN 0-8217-4616-2

Printed in the United States of America

"A man like me sees a woman, he knows, damn it. . . .
(A) man like me knows when a girl is right for him."
—Elvis Presley to Joyce Bova

UNTIL IT'S TIME FOR YOU TO GO

Yes, we're different, worlds apart
We're not the same
We laughed and played at the start
Like in a game
You could have stayed outside my heart
But in you came
And here you'll stay
Until it's time for you to go
Don't ask why, don't ask how
Don't ask forever
Love me, love me, love me, love me now

From the never-released demo album inscribed by Elvis: "To Joyce, with love." Presented to her on August 16, 1971, marking two years to the time they met.

And six years, to the day, before Elvis would die.

For Janice.

My special thanks to Elise Donner, my editor, for her expertise and friendship.

Prologue

I stood there amidst all the mementos assembled in the Authorized Elvis Presley Traveling Museum, staring at one particular photograph.

"That's Bobby Gentry there with The King." The museum's founder, Jimmy Velvet, looked from me to the photograph and back again to me. "Leastways, they told me it was her," he said, shaking his head.

For him, it was a moment of mild confusion. For me, it meant being swept back in time by a flood of emotions I had kept dammed up for nearly fourteen years.

Jimmy Velvet interrupted my reminiscence with him and Elvis's stepbrother, David Stanley, with an invitation to join him and his wife and kids for a bite to eat, which turned out to be several hours of exchanging stories. Listening to Jimmy, who with his museum had dedicated his life to preserving the memory of Elvis, talk about the star's tragic end and the scattering of the entourage I had come to know those many years ago, it struck me that, with all due respect for his efforts, Elvis's spirit transcended all tangible attempts to keep it alive.

While I myself had preserved a few material objects from my

years with Elvis, what really remained of our love were my special, heartfelt memories, memories that until this day, I had shared only with the person closest to me, my sister, Janice.

Let me explain. I have been a staff member of the Armed Services Committee of the United States House of Representatives for twenty-five years now. At the time I was involved with Elvis, I was quite young, and quite a junior member of the staff. Consequently, I was very discreet about my relationship; only close friends on and off the Hill knew. And no one but Janice knew the whole, bittersweet truth. Janice, my big sister by twenty minutes—my identical twin. The bond between twins is very likely to be special, but the one between identical twins has no parallel. Janice is my mirror image, my other self—and I am hers. No wonder she was the only one privy to my relationship with Elvis, himself a twin.

Later, as we were about to part, Jimmy Velvet pulled me aside.

"You're the one, Joyce," he said, taking my hand. "The one who should really write a book about Elvis."

That night, I dug out the diaries I had kept during those years with Elvis. Immersing myself once more in that magic time, I felt a weight lift from my heart. It came to me then and for the first time that sharing my Elvis with the world would act as a catharsis, as the revelation of any whole, unvarnished truth must be.

The next week, a card came from the museum. "Now I know why Elvis loved you," it said. It was signed, "Jimmy Velvet."

I was deeply moved. Jimmy Velvet's card made me aware of the hundreds of millions of people whose lives have been touched by the music and warmth and excitement of Elvis Presley. I can only hope that my memories of him, finally shared with you, will do the same.

Chapter One

It was the summer of nineteen sixty-nine, a summer in which women wore bouffant hairdo's and miniskirts; a long, hot summer of riots and burning draft cards; of the My Lai massacre and of Neil Armstrong's walk on the moon; the summer of the Manson Family murders and the first summer of Richard Nixon's Law and Order Administration. It was the summer Mary Jo Kopechne drowned on Chappaquiddick Island and the summer of Woodstock. It was the summer Elvis Aaron Presley and I fell in love.

The months prior to the summer of nineteen sixty-nine were grueling ones for all of us at the House Armed Services Committee. The My Lai disclosures were tearing the country apart, and my subcommittee on investigations was naturally at the eye of the storm. By the time my vacation rolled around, I was exhausted from working at fever pitch for months. I racked my brain for the perfect place to seek relief from an endless mountain of paperwork on chains of command, ultimate responsibility, and military cover-ups. An overload of reality if ever there was one—so where better to escape than the mecca of *un*reality?

Las Vegas.

AnnMarie Wade, a friend from the Hill, decided to come along with me. Her strawberry blond hair made me look darker and more Mediterranean in contrast as we stepped off TWA's flight from Washington that fateful evening, the 16th of August 1969.

Actually it was on our third night in Vegas that fate really began to take a hand. We were staying at the Dunes and the hotel had arranged ringside seats for us to Paul Anka's show. When Mr. Anka suddenly dropped to one knee right in the middle of "Put Your Head on My Shoulder," AnnMarie and I were eye to eye with the performer.

"How about sharing with the rest of us what you just whispered to your girlfriend," he said to me, thrusting the microphone into my face.

I was already too embarrassed to utter a word, but just then, the blazing spotlight swung around to hit me full in the face with its blinding glare. I felt my cheeks flush bright red.

Paul Anka leaned closer. "If you won't tell the audience, how about telling only me?" He covered the mike with his hand.

"All right," I whispered in his ear. I would have told him practically anything to get off the hook and get that spotlight out of my eyes. "We met Anthony Newley backstage after his show last night, and I just told AnnMarie that I wished it had been *you* instead, that's all."

He drew back and gave me a look that I should have known was coming had I time enough to think how my words had sounded. Still, in all fairness, he let me off the hook by standing up and smoothly announcing, "Oh, sure, I'll sing 'God Didn't Make Little Green Apples' for you." Very decent of him. But it didn't stop me from feeling like a twenty-four karat fool on exhibition.

I was up and out of my seat before the curtain fully shut, AnnMarie trailing in my wake. The two of us were barely a stride from the exit when I felt a hand on my shoulder. I turned to find a short man in a blazer, out of breath, but doing his best to smile at us.

"My name is Ron Stewart and I work for Paul Anka. . . ." Before we knew it, AnnMarie and I were accompanying him backstage.

"Well . . . here she is." Paul Anka smiled and rose to greet us as Ron Stewart escorted us into the singer's dressing room. "The young lady who knew the next song I wanted to sing was 'Little Green Apples.' "

"That *was* awfully nice of you," I conceded.

"It's all right. I put you on the spot out there and you were a good sport about it."

"Well, I really would like to explain. What I meant to say—"

"About Newley? Let me take a wild guess. After you saw his show, one of his people appeared and asked you backstage?"

"Right." I nodded. "But he barely listened to our compliments about his performance before he started telling us that young women shouldn't be alone in Las Vegas and asking us to go sailing with him today."

"And you sensed it could turn out to be one of those sails a girl might have to swim back from?"

I smiled. "His tone seemed definitely to imply that he had more than just a friendly cruise on Lake Meade in mind."

"I know I'm shocked," said Paul Anka, "but just out of curiosity, how exactly did you answer him?"

"We just told him," said AnnMarie, "that we had other plans."

With that out of the way, we made small talk. We told him our names and where we were from and about our work on the Hill. He was easy to talk to, with a tendency to tease, so that when we declined a second drink, he smiled mischievously. "Mmm, I wonder how exactly you'll answer me . . . I don't have a boat on Lake Meade, but I *would* like to take you to dinner tomorrow night."

"Oh, really, now—" I began.

"Both of you." He gestured to include AnnMarie.

"Sorry, but it's impossible," I answered. "We're going to see Elvis Presley tomorrow night."

"Now, that *is* impossible . . . unless you have VIP reservations?"

"We've done all right so far," I said defensively. "We'll probably get in."

"The difference is, I can *guarantee* it. Professional courtesy, you know." Somebody called out that it was time for him to get ready for his next show, and when he turned back to us he said, "Your names will be at the showroom entrance . . . the VIP reservation line. Afterward, wait for me in the lounge. Remember, now, I'll expect you there . . ."

All the way to the new International Hotel that next night, the 19th of August, AnnMarie and I could *feel* the excitement. It seemed to pulsate in the thin desert air. Even now, if I stop and think back I can feel it, a palpable, physical force seeming to emanate from the ten-foot-high neon signs that everywhere blazed out the words: ELVIS NOW!

Naturally, the hotel that was hosting him could not be outdone in a town that prides itself on big and blatant, so the International's marquee was a trillion kilowatt monument, 5 letters that lit up the heavens:

. . . E . . . L . . . V . . . I . . . S . . .

We passed through the heavy glass doors, entered the lobby, and were greeted by images of Elvis everywhere. Posters and larger-than-life pictures decorated every wall and encircled the pillars that supported the ceiling. We walked on toward the showroom and saw that every conceivable space was devoted to huckstering The King: there were Elvis toys and puppet Elvises; Elvis mugs and Elvis drinking glasses; pennants, T-shirts, balloons and novelty clocks; utensils and stuffed animals. Every kind of gimcrack and geegaw one could imagine had been fashioned in his image like religious icons.

Even more daunting testimony to Elvis's presence was the length of the line outside the showroom. I pointed out to Ann-Marie that we would have a heck of a time circumnavigating it even to find out if Paul Anka's name was as potent as he claimed it was. Besides, we had a feeling that if we tried to walk to the front of the line, we'd run the risk of being lynched by the mob ahead of us.

"Too bad." AnnMarie was adamant. "Ever since I can remember, Elvis has been the object of my fantasies. Tonight, I don't care about anything but getting in to *see Elvis.*"

At that moment, a man who had been walking up and down the line approached us. "Good evening, ladies," he said. "My name is Chick and I'm with the International. May I ask how long you plan to be in town?"

"Probably not long enough for us to get to the front of this line," I observed.

"It really is a ridiculous situation," he said, smiling. "But I might be able to solve that problem for you."

"Great," we chorused.

"Now, how would you both like to meet Elvis?"

"Here we go again," I said, throwing my hands in the air. "Did he say what I thought he said?"

"Let me guess," AnnMarie answered. "After the show, for a drink in his dressing room?"

"Well, no." Chick raised his eyebrows. "Now. Before he does his second show."

"Well . . ."

"Joyce, what do you mean, 'well'?" AnnMarie was glaring. "I told you, this is Elvis Presley, who I have been crazy about since I was a kid. What are we hesitating for?"

Probably because I'm suspicious of real life when it keeps threatening to turn into fantasy, I wanted to say. But I didn't. I just followed AnnMarie who was following Chick, through the first door he opened and down a long, brightly lit corridor that led into a maze of hallways. "I don't think we should expect too much this time," I remarked, trying to keep things in perspective. "There'll probably be a long line of fans ahead of us and we'll be lucky to get a smile and a handshake."

"That's okay with me," she replied. "I'm just wondering how we'll ever be able to find our way back without a guide!"

It was seeing the armed guards that finally brought what was happening home to me. I had to ask myself: Did guys pop up like this all the time to inquire politely if you'd like to tête-à-tête with a star? Where was the catch? There had to be one . . .

Chick was knocking on a closed door. It was opened by a rather ordinary-looking, middle-aged man. "Ladies," Chick said, ushering us inside and closing the door behind us, "this is Vernon Presley."

I could see immediately that Elvis's daddy hadn't his famous son's flair; the way he slouched off to the side, seeming to fade into the woodwork, made him seem physically smaller than he actually was. He had thick, full, gray hair and wore an open-collared shirt with dark, wrinkled slacks and a sport coat. It was clearly not *his* DNA that carried whatever genes had given Elvis his flamboyance. I heard him ask AnnMarie something about the dress she was wearing as Chick led me across the room to a heavyset, Italian-looking man.

"Joyce, this is Elvis's 'right arm.' Joe, meet Joyce. I thought she and her friend would like to meet Elvis."

"Joe Esposito," the man said, putting out his hand. "Nice to meet you, Joyce . . . ?"

"Bova. Did you say Esposito? I thought Elvis's men were all from the South," I kidded, knowing from his flat, midwestern accent that he wasn't.

"They are, Joyce. I just happen to be a good ol' boy from south Chicago. How about you?"

"I'm a westerner, myself, Joe. West Baltimore, that is."

"And Italian, too."

"How did you ever guess!"

He laughed. "C'mon, I'll introduce you to some genuine good ol' boys."

The West boys, Red and Sonny, were definitely the genuine article, cut in the stereotypical mode the public had come to associate with the Presley "Memphis Mafia." Cousins rather than brothers, each was in his thirties and of a size and demeanor that left no doubt as to either their intention or their ability to fulfill their roles as Elvis Presley's sworn-to-the-death protectors. Sonny even mentioned in the course of conversation that Red had started "kind of looking out" for Elvis back while they still were attending high school in Memphis. Both West boys were extremely polite in the southern tradition, "Yes, ma'aming" and "No, ma'aming" me from word one. But I couldn't help noticing that their eyes never ceased flicking around the room, that they never relaxed their hard, watchful stares above the warm, country smiles.

Charlie Hodge, on the other hand, was a complete doll. He may have hailed from Alabama, but his droll, dry, mischievious manner was pure leprechaun.

"Oh, no," he protested a minute or so after we were introduced, "I don't go as far back with Elvis as Red does. Fact is, I first met Elvis in the army. A couple of thousand GIs and Elvis Presley. We were both pfc's back then, except that in the minds of an awful lot of the population of the country, the young female half, especially, Elvis ranked somewhere just slightly higher than the Commander-in-Chief. Which couldn't've made things easy for him. But, you know, he handled it well . . . plus he must've took a liking to my guitar pickin'. Else I wouldn't be here tonight talking to a pretty lady. Notice you're carrying 'round an empty glass; let me get you a refill."

As he walked away, AnnMarie waved me over to where she was still talking with Vernon. An enormous, gruff-talking man barged ahead of me to mutter something to Elvis's dad. Vernon Presley introduced him as Lamar Fike and I observed that like

Red, Sonny, Joe, and even Vernon himself, this Lamar also cast periodic glances at a closed door on the other side of the room. You didn't have to be Sherlock Holmes to deduce that it was Elvis Presley they were expecting. It was a familiar sight to me; Washington crawls with people whose careers depend on anticipating the next move, mood, and whim of the powerful men they serve.

Before long, I caught *myself* shooting glances at that door. And since I didn't have the excuse of being an employee, I had to face the fact that this must be the residue of adolescent hero-worship. To paraphrase: you can take the woman out of her teens, but you can't completely take the teen out of the woman. I was an Elvis Generation kid and standing in that room, I could feel the carpet of my hard-earned Washington sophistication being yanked right out from under me by the idea of seeing him in the flesh.

I can't claim surprise as a factor in the shock tremor that soared up my Richter scale when that door finally did open. It was Elvis Presley I was prepared to see come through it and it was Elvis Presley who *did* step through it—and into the room so close to me I could have reached out and touched him.

But what I wasn't prepared for was how beautiful he was.

Beautiful. That was the word that leapt to mind. Not just physically attractive or handsome, which he was, but something more, something instinctual. He inspired in me not so much desire, but a mixture of curiosity and awe, like what you feel when you see your first tropical sunset or when you come unexpectedly on snowflakes falling silently in a moonlit forest of pines.

Chapter Two

I don't remember any longer who actually introduced us. But I do remember and can still feel as if it were yesterday, the touch of his hand as he reached out and took mine.

"It's a great pleasure to meet you," I told him. Not exactly memorable first words to Elvis Presley but I did have the excuse that I was mesmerized by those intense, incredibly sexy eyes that even offstage seemed to sparkle and glow beneath his long, thick lashes. Not easy to take your eyes off this man, I warned myself.

Not that he seemed to want me to. Still holding my gaze with his, he acknowledged that it was a pleasure to meet me, too, in a voice so sweet and sincere that my knees got all wobbly and I gratefully accepted the chair he led me to. I watched him drop gracefully into one he pulled up alongside. He crossed one bell-bottomed trouser leg over the other. "You know, Joyce Bova," he said matter-of-factly, "you're a beautiful girl." I was nowhere near regaining my composure when he went on, "You're not from around here, are you . . . from Vegas?"

His question broke the tiny flash fantasy I'd slipped into: all my teenage girlfriends suddenly materializing en masse to gape at their old pubescent playmate being called beautiful by Elvis Presley.

"No, I'm not." I returned to reality, or what was passing for it at the moment. "I'm from Washington, D.C. . . . at least that's where I work."

He nodded. "You're not in show business, then." He turned away, interrupted by a small mob of fans and well-wishers swooping down to gush their fullsome praise all over him, but turned back almost immediately. "Pretty thing like you, ya mean to tell me you're stuck away in some government office?"

"Well, I guess . . . If you think of working for Congress as 'stuck away.' "

"Congress, hunh? How about that. Anything I might've heard of?"

"The House Armed Services Committee? Actually I work for the Investigations Subcommittee."

"Yeah? Sounds like that could be pretty fascinating work."

I started to say that I was new and still getting the hang of it, when Joe Esposito called, "Time to get ready, boss!"

"Yeah, man . . . okay," Elvis answered. I began the "good-bye" I assumed would now end "the time I met Elvis Presley." Instead, he reached for my hand. "That work you do . . . it sure does sound interesting."

Was I crazy or did he *not* want to let me go?

"I'd really like to hear more." He smiled again, this time looking intently into my eyes. "Would you like to see the show again?"

"Uh, actually we haven't . . . uh . . . but we've been looking forward to—"

"Looking forward? Dint ya just come from it?"

"No . . . we . . . uh . . . ." I knew instinctively that there was no point in mentioning Paul Anka. ". . . AnnMarie and I made arrangements to see the *second* show," I explained.

He let go of my hand, stood up, and pointed to Joe Esposito.

"Joe," he said, indicating first me and then AnnMarie. "Put them in my booth."

Then he turned and faced me.

"Will you come back after the show?"

"An act of Congress couldn't keep me away," I dared to say. And was rewarded with the notorious curled-lip grin.

"Joe will get you right afterward and bring you back, honey."

With that "honey" ringing in my ears, I followed Elvis's "right arm," gathering AnnMarie along the way. On the hike back to the showroom, I filled her in on what had taken place with Elvis and she was still shaking her head in wonder as we were escorted past the waiting throng and deposited in a red velvet booth directly at center stage. Before he left us, Joe Esposito told the waiter who had materialized almost immediately that the rule about not serving people during the performance was to be relaxed in our case.

The instant we were alone in the booth, AnnMarie leaned close. "Joyce, what do you think is going on here? Should we pinch ourselves, or what?"

I had to laugh. "I'm not really sure," I admitted.

"Well," said AnnMarie, good-naturedly, "I hope he realizes you're not just another pretty face."

"Who knows if he really even thinks *that*. Anyway, all I want to think about now is enjoying myself. That's what we're here for."

I turned my attention to the enormous, packed house and was just about to make some thoroughly innocuous comment on the broad age range of his audience when Elvis, without any announcement or introduction, strode onto the stage.

The sight of him onstage brought it all back: My rock 'n' roll years—dancing to "Don't Be Cruel" at the Catonsville Teen Center, hearing once more the rustle of my crinoline, feeling the raspiness of my cardigan against my hot, damp neck, floating across the dance floor, enraptured by the pure, raw energy raging from deep inside Elvis's heart and soul. He'd shimmered with such mesmerizing sexuality that by comparison, his rivals seemed as dim as the objects in the room you first enter after gazing into the summer sun.

Now, just as effortlessly as he had dominated my teen years, Elvis dominated the vast, intimidating International showroom. There was a great, collective gasp, followed immediately by silence. Then came the screams of delight and anticipation, the women in the audience going slightly out of their minds, leaping to their feet with wild, shrill, erotic cries. Their eyes wide and shining, they emitted little animal yelps that seemed to come from deep in their throats. There were women of all ages carrying on like this—not just teenagers, but full-bodied, mature women, even graying matrons—all of them going berserk, screaming, crying, jerking spasmodically like Shakers or Holy Rollers. They seemed possessed by the same kind of religious fervor in their devotion.

I wouldn't have thought it possible, but the screams actually rose in pitch and volume when Elvis launched into, "That's All Right, Mama." The lyrics were lost in the rising crescendo of adulation. But that didn't really matter to his people: Hearing the words to songs they knew by heart did not mean as much as paying homage to the singer in the only way available to them.

Elvis responded to us with a mix of appreciation and amusement. I say "us" because even though I wasn't as outwardly demonstrative as most others, in my mind and heart I had melded and fused into that shrieking, ecstatic mass of humanity—and become a fan again. Elvis had the power to make you a fan again at any age, that was obvious. I had had no problem in falling under his magic spell and half becoming that starry-eyed teenager, racing once again to the record store for his latest release. I may have worked on Capitol Hill for the Congress of the United States, but that night I was a skinny, breathless adolescent all over again. Even with a full orchestra blaring and thousands of people jumping up and down and screaming their lungs out, I felt that everyone in that vast room must have been able to hear my own heart pounding above it all.

By that point Elvis was truly into it, his boundless energy manifesting itself in somersaults and one karate move after another. Each one brought down the house. The applause was incessant now as he moved closer to us, the once-notorious pelvis gyrating wildly . . .

Until, in the midst of one of the grinds, he halted abruptly, looking not only surprised, but chagrined.

"Oohhh!" I laughed out loud before I could catch myself. "He's split his pants!"

"Do you think he meant to?" AnnMarie whispered.

"If it *was* staged," I answered, "I can only say that it was very effective!"

Meanwhile, Elvis had casually backed offstage and quickly changed his pants without missing a note. He returned to launch into, "Love Me Tender." At one point during the song he came to the edge of the stage and knelt down before a group of women fans, again of all ages, frantically clustered at the edge of the stage in desperate anticipation. They shrieked and pawed and kissed while Elvis kept that crooked little smile of amusement through it all.

As the crowd around me climbed to new heights of hysteria, I had to fight to keep from feeling smug and superior. Knowing that the subject of this frenzied outpouring of love and adoration had chosen *me* to be with him after the show was a major head trip. Which led me to another insight: it was a trip that could get pretty complicated. Here was a man who was the object of a million female fantasies, a man who had spent his adult life having women throw themselves or their intimate apparel—or both—at his feet. It occurred to me that, not unreasonably, he just might be expecting more than I was prepared to deliver.

It was at this moment that AnnMarie chose to lean over and shout, "I'm not going back with you to see Elvis."

"What? Why not?"

"Paul Anka, remember? We promised to meet him in the lounge? Well, I'm going to."

"Couldn't you . . ." I had to raise my voice even louder above the screaming, whistling, and foot-stamping that signaled Elvis was bringing his performance to its climax. ". . . Please come back with me, even for a few minutes?"

Beneath her head of light curls, AnnMarie's small, pretty features twisted into a thoughtful frown. "All right." She nodded. "But just for a few minutes."

It took only seconds for his eyes to search the room and find me.

"Well," he asked, "what did you think of the show?"

Under the circumstances a natural enough question, but somehow, coming from the show himself, it threw me for a loop. As I hesitated and gulped in response, he impulsively reached out and took my hand. There was an intensity to that grip and I thought, wow, he cares what I think or, at least, what people think. He really wants to *know*.

"Well," I stalled, "you've really put me on the spot. I don't know what to say. Except that you were wonderful . . . incredible . . . fantastic. In a word, magnificent."

He let go of my hand and gave me the curled-lip grin. He turned delightedly to his "boys" and shook his head in mock concern. "I don't know how Joyce and I are ever going to be friends," he said, "unless she learns to show some enthusiasm."

He drew the usual big laugh and I laughed along with them. "I'm just glad you weren't expecting some high-powered critical analysis," I said.

"All the critical analysis in the world never beat one word, truly felt, spoken from the heart."

"Well," I responded, "I truly never felt anything so exciting, never imagined until I actually was there that anyone, even you, could project that much energy."

"*Positive* energy." He smiled, put his arm around me, and patted my shoulder.

I looked up at him and just said quietly, "I was truly moved."

He smiled and took my hand in his once again. It was as if he felt a need then to take us out of what, for him, must have been an all too familiar routine: Star beaming modestly while female fan gushes all over him. He indicated the record playing on the stereo and said that he liked Dusty Springfield very much.

"I try to shy away from hearing just my own music. You know, got to listen to what the other guys are doing."

"The *energy* you put out up there on that stage . . ." I blurted, my thoughts reverting back to his performance. "I don't see how you can withstand such a pace."

"Clean livin', darlin', clean livin' and down-home cookin'." He grinned. "Although, if the truth were told, I sweat out about seven pounds a night." He put his arm around me again and walked me over to an empty chair.

Just then, two expensively dressed men and women came into the room and Elvis excused himself and went over to them. I heard him respond to one of the men's introductions with the same old-fashioned good manners he had just shown me.

Left to my own devices, it was suddenly brought home to me that I didn't really know anybody else there.

"Joyce—"

Except, of course, for AnnMarie, who had made a beeline for me the second she saw Elvis excuse himself.

"Joyce, I really have to go soon."

"I know."

"I mean *we* really should go."

"I know."

"Well, let's go then, okay?"

I shook my head. I was torn. I didn't want to just hang out, one more star-struck girl trying to eke some reality out of her fantasies. But he *had* put me in his booth, and it was *his* idea that I come backstage after the show, and he'd even remembered my name . . . Damnit, I had to stop kidding myself! There are things that just don't happen in real life. But still, I couldn't quite bring myself to say the words that would take me out of that room. Out of his life.

"Joyce?"

"Just a few more minutes. Please."

I looked over at Elvis. As if he'd received my silent message, he glanced up and made a little comic pantomime of peering at me through the wall of well-wishers surrounding him.

AnnMarie saw it, too. "More has happened than you ever could have expected, Joyce. He has a truly disarming way of dealing with us earthlings," she added pointedly. "But you would be better off leaving right now."

"Can't have pretty girls going thirsty."

I looked around and there was Charlie Hodge, holding two glasses out to us.

I gave a "what-can-you-do" shrug at AnnMarie's impatient frown, took the glass from Charlie, and found a chair for myself. As soon as I had, I spotted Elvis heading straight for me, nodding politely to the people vying for his attention, not being rude, but not stopping, either—not until he got to me.

"Looked like you were getting ready to take off on me," he said, the curled-lip grin spread across his handsome face, a face that would probably be described as sculptured if he were a hero in a gothic romance.

"Well, to tell you the truth . . ." I began hesitantly, and was almost immediately interrupted by the appearance of an elderly lady being escorted into Elvis's presence by some of his entourage. She was one of those Elvis mega-fans, and I saw in her unheralded arrival the excuse I needed to bow gracefully out of the scene. For she carried countless albums and full-to-bursting scrapbooks and with her strung together bundles of memorabilia, she resembled nothing so much as some kind of archival bag lady. Elvis showed an immediate fascination for her wares, and I started to get up so she could have my seat—only to have him take hold of my arm.

"Hold up there, darlin'," he said, gesturing for another chair. "You never know, you might find some of this ancient history from before you were born kind of interesting."

A pretty irresistible combination: flattery about my age, insistence on my company, and self-deprecatory humor. I sat back down to enjoy a nostalgic feast of pictures, wirephotos, articles, and clippings.

The items the lady produced from her grab bag went way back, back to the days when Elvis had his initial success with his first record, the now legendary, "That's All Right, Mama," a song he'd recorded with two local boys, Scotty Moore and Bill Black, for Sam Phillips's Sun Recording Company. A yellowed clipping said that it had sold 30,000 copies and brought Elvis so much fame, he was interviewed on a local radio station. Another article related the forming of the Blue Moon Boys with the addition of drummer D.J. Fontana, and told how the four young musicians were appearing in places where country and western stars of the time like Eddy Arnold and Hank Snow also played. And then, Elvis was delighted to see, there was a little piece about his second successful record release, entitled "Good Rockin' Tonight."

He also laughed good-naturedly at the expense of the self-appointed guardians of the nation's morality who had tried so hard to crucify him back then for what they considered his "immoral music."

But I think he got the biggest kick out of a piece from some show business columnist of a few years later proclaiming that a new singer was "taking the country by storm" and would soon "surpass Elvis Presley." The columnist went on to say that it would "be a good and healthy sign for our country's teenagers when the gyrating Mr. Presley is replaced as their idol by the clean-cut, well-groomed, and decently mannered Fabian."

Elvis shook his head ruefully: "That was then and still is *now,* about the most stupid thing a so-called 'responsible' commentator could make up to say 'bout two dudes who were basically just entertainers. But they always tried to lay up the bad vibes against my music."

There was a chorus of assent from the others and I realized for the first time that they had all more or less been deferring to my position with Elvis. They were not the sort to be unaware that Elvis Presley had zeroed in on me as if the rest of that room full of people did not exist.

"Honey, what do you think of that?" He was still shaking his head over the clipping. "That the way you felt back then 'bout me and Fabian?"

"No way." I leapt loyally to the bait. "My friends and I never thought that for a second." My response set him off and it dawned on me that unquestioning devotion wasn't just something that stroked his ego—he *mainlined* it.

"Boy, I was a saint compared to what they have today," he went on. "I was never vulgar. Did you ever listen to the words in some of those Rolling Stones songs? And that uh, whatsis name? David Bowie? He is some kind of weirdo, man."

An old photograph of himself from around the time he went into the army caught his eye and he singled it out. "Whoa, man, look at the baby fat on that."

This observation inspired the scrapbook lady to lean her bland, dumpling-dough face close to mine. "That was just before you met him in Germany, Priscilla dear," she cooed, her eyes glittery with excitement.

I felt my face flush. Before I could reply, Elvis, with that easy grace that came so naturally to him, said simply, "No, this is my friend, Joyce."

The scrapbook lady nodded and, gathering up her treasured relics, paid me a parting compliment: "You are a beautiful girl, Priscilla."

Elvis just squeezed my hand and smiled at me, a warm,

reassuring smile that let me know that it was okay, that *he* knew I wasn't Priscilla.

Actually, if the truth be told, I was feeling pretty self-assured and sophisticated at that moment. I had kept my cool while the superstar of the epoch treated me like someone who mattered to him, referring easily and naturally and spontaneously to me as, "my friend, Joyce."

I realize I run the risk here of sounding like a celebrity rag calling for the canonization of a star for simply behaving like a normal, decent human being. But Elvis's behavior really wasn't an act; I'm used to *that* from congressmen. He was as down to earth and genuine as I'd always imagined he'd be.

I had been an Elvis Generation kid, no doubt about it, still in grammar school at St. Agnes during those years the scrapbook lady chronicled so faithfully, when he'd first blazed out of Memphis, Tennessee, and torn across the American scene like a meteor. "The white boy who had the Negro sound and the Negro feel," Sam Phillips, who owned Sun Records, had called him. The first singer to mix the black and white sound. And I had grown up in the Baltimore that had been the first southern city to mix black and white kids in its schools.

Elvis's hand, a ring glittering on each of the long, strong fingers, shook me gently out of my trance.

I jumped up, asking, "Did my friend leave?"

Elvis nodded. "But we've hardly talked," he said. "I want to know more about you."

I sat back down.

"Well, what would you like to know?"

"Many things."

"To tell you the truth, I would rather you did the talking," I said, "especially about your life and everything."

"Oh, we'll get to knowing each other, darlin'. But there is one thing I'd like to know right now. You *are* Italian, aren't you?"

"Sicilian . . . both sides."

"I knew it. I could tell. You see I can tell a lot of things. I have a kind of power to see things . . . oh, I don't mean just about things like that. It's actually a kind of sixth sense, ya know what I mean?"

He actually did appear to be serious, so I refrained from pointing out that given my dark hair and complexion, you didn't have to be clairvoyant to guess my ancestry.

"Let's see," he continued. "I can see you have a European quality, a womanly quality about you. But you're also ah . . . ya know, a sweet girl, too. I can tell. I know it. It's a rare thing. I bet you're quite unique, Joyce."

Sure, I was tempted to say, I'm so unique that lady mistook me for Priscilla, your wife. Instead, I just replied, "Actually, there are two of me, if you want to know."

"Of course." He smiled. "All of us have two natures, especially fem—"

"No," I interrupted. "I mean literally, physically." I smiled back. "You see, I have an identical twin sister."

He stared at me.

Then I remembered. Elvis was a twin himself. He had been a star for so long that certain autobiographical details were no longer fresh in my mind.

"My little brother, Jesse Garon, died when I was born," he said now. "You know, they say the twin who survives lives on carrying the qualities of both, of the one who died as well."

At first, I thought I had upset him. But as he went on it seemed that he drew comfort from my revelation, as though it had created a kind of bond between us.

"Do you miss her a lot?" he asked. "I mean, when you're away from her, like tonight?"

"To tell you the truth," I replied, "all through this entire evening I kept thinking how much I wished she were here to share each incredible moment with me. Actually, she was supposed to come to Vegas with me. But, of course, I know she knows how happy I am."

"How do you mean?" he asked.

"Well, it's hard to explain, exactly, but Janice and I have always had this capacity to feel the other's emotions no matter how many miles separate us from each other. Especially whenever one of us is feeling extreme sadness or joy."

He looked at me without saying anything for what seemed a long time. In reality, however, it was probably no more than a matter of moments until he spoke.

"Joyce," he said, "would you come up to the suite later and have dinner with me?"

This definitely was messing with my mind.

Part of me was dying to accept, of course. I mean, let's be serious about this. Dinner with Elvis? Not too many events on the old social calendar can match that. Unfortunately, the rest of me was turning out to have cold feet. Things were just happening too fast.

"I'm sorry," I said. I felt extremely vulnerable and a little like a child who had bitten off more than she could chew and now has to spit it out on the table in front of everybody. "But Ann-Marie and I promised to meet some people after the show."

"Really? No you didn't. You don't sound like you mean it."

"I really don't think I can . . ."

"Is this some guy? Y'know, I can tell . . . some guy you maybe just met . . . while I . . . and you . . . uh, have spent all this time here talking and gettin' to know each other."

His blue eyes were suddenly piercing. "Why don't you try telling me the truth."

Of course, the truth was that I was afraid. Because he was Elvis Presley and I was just plain scared. Having dinner with a man you've just met, in his hotel room, is a rough enough choice under any circumstances. But when the man was *Elvis Presley?* That was not just taking on a man; that was jumping into the vortex of the whirlwind.

However, I was not about to tell him that, and when I didn't make any attempt to answer his question, he put his arm around my shoulder and gently but firmly took me out of the general commotion and off into a corner together. He tilted my chin up to face him and said, "This time, goddamnit, I expect you to tell me the truth. We've been talking nothing but truth—you and I—all night. Up till now."

"All right," I said. "You're probably going to regard this as very unsophisticated reasoning for 1969, for being in Las Vegas, for being who you are in show business and . . . and . . . whatever, but you said you wanted the truth. Well, the truth is that I would love to have dinner with you. Very much. But I just can't help feeling that you probably pick out a different girl to be with each night and that this night it just happens to be me. And that's not what I want. I adore you, but no, thank you." I waited, almost afraid of what he might say to my honesty.

"You mean you can't believe that I just simply enjoy your company? That all I want is to get to know you better?"

One of his guys called over to him then about changing the Dusty Springfield album but he just waved him off and went on. "Besides that, it's ridiculous. You ought to realize it's not physically possible for me to be with a different girl every night and still do what I do up on that stage."

"There's also the fact that you're married."

"What does 'married' have to do with this?" he asked indignantly. "I just want to be with someone I can talk to . . . ya know? Besides, I know what kind of girl you are, even if you don't think I do. You should realize that with you I would have to be a perfect gentleman."

He paused, and then without warning, his face took on the sweetest, gentlest expression—almost cute, if there is a way to be cute and commanding at the same time. "And that's a promise."

That last line did it, of course. I caved in like a freshman congressman confronted by Tip O'Neill. Elvis would either honor his word or he wouldn't, and my every instinct told me he was a man of his word. Why, then, had I been so reluctant? My fear, naturally, had more to do with me than it did with him, and a lot of that had probably been instilled through the terribly strict Catholic upbringing Janice and I had endured. Our mother, who had been a dancer and a beautiful, vivacious woman when she was young, had for some reason tried to impose a relentlessly repressive regime throughout our entire adolescence.

I think it was partly her own experience of rejection and neglect that made her act that way. Our father was a sergeant on the Baltimore Racket Squad when we were growing up. Between the enormous demands his work made on his time, and the disparity between his view of life and hers, their resentment and bitterness grew until the marriage was one in name only. It was not an example that encouraged Janice or me to enter easily into a relationship.

Early on, I picked up my father's skeptical view of the world. (It is a tendency that has stood me in good stead during my years in Washington.) I say, "picked up" rather than "learned" because teaching us was not in his makeup, really. He was one of those fathers who would give his children anything, except his time. But his liberal, hands-off parenting was a welcome contrast to our mother's strict discipline.

Still, Janice and I always felt that the music and rhythm in our souls came from her. Without that feeling for music, it is unlikely I would have been there in Las Vegas that night to meet Elvis—or to be asked to what would probably turn out to be just a nice, quiet dinner. Definitely a memorable moment in my life, but the kind of event that winds up as the story you're famous for boring the grandchildren with. Nothing more.

Chapter Three

Ithink maybe I was always like that," Elvis was saying. His voice brought me back to the present. One arm draped casually around my shoulder, he was talking while he watched an entire second wave of visitors coming in.

"Yeah," he continued, "anything I ever wanted, I just have to have it. Anything I like . . . uh . . . seems I just can't get enough of it."

"Like Dusty Springfield?" I kidded. The same album of hers was still playing on the stereo.

"I really do like her style a lot."

"I do, too, and I was curious about what singers you enjoy, but don't you think it's about time to put on an *Elvis* record?"

"Haven't you heard enough of him for one night?" he asked, flashing the disarming smile.

"Never," I blurted out. "Right now I feel that I could see your show every night and then go home and listen to your albums until dawn."

"Every night? The *same* show?"

"Well, you do make changes from time to time, don't you?"

"He sure does," Charlie Hodge wisecracked as he passed by

with a gaggle of young, attractive, and giggling girls he had ushered in. "And sometimes they're even the ones we've rehearsed."

"Just remember," Elvis came back at him, "that one of them changes might just be a particular gee-tar picker." He turned back to me. "Now, honey, were you putting me on, too?"

I solemnly raised my right hand. "I swear I have never been so moved."

I could tell from his face that I had struck a responsive chord. He started to speak, but before he could say a word, he was whisked off to meet someone and I found myself standing alone in a roomful of strangers in a strange city (which is still how you might think of Las Vegas even if you'd lived there your whole life.)

Of course, I actually was acquainted with one person there. Only he happened to be Elvis Presley. Talk about strange!

I found a chair and tried not to look or feel too much like a bump on a log while I watched Elvis submit to one of the ritual obligations demanded by his position: the laying on of hands (and mouths) by his fans to demonstrate their loyalty. It must have started to make me nervous. I remember having the distinct feeling that the room was closing in on me, while the people in it seemed to get further away. I took out a cigarette.

And Elvis, spotting my action from halfway across the room, slipped out from under all that heavy flattery to swagger over and light it for me. I knew he was trying to make me feel not so left out and I truly appreciated the gesture. It was the kind of sweet, simple, considerate act that seemed to be instinctive with him. There was a basic niceness about him that contradicted the popularly held view of superstars and their inflated egos.

The fact that he had no qualms about showing small kindnesses in front of his court of sycophants seemed to me to confirm the down-to-earth genuineness of the man. When I thanked him for the light, he gave my shoulder a reassuring, comradely pat before returning to the gaggle of gigglers. I sat and suffered, watching him endure at their hands an interminable period of the most repellent simpering and fawning, throughout which his courteous good humor and cheerful decency never once flagged.

Until Paul Anka walked in.

The diminutive Canadian was accompanied by a young blonde woman of so classically molded a beauty that it drew all eyes to her instantly, and kept even me from noticing for a moment the other person with them.

That other person was AnnMarie.

Now, I wasn't surprised she had kept our original commitment and gone to meet Paul Anka; I was, however, very much surprised that she had brought him back to Elvis's dressing room.

I was not the only one paying attention to the newcomers. "It was Anka, wasn't it?"

I looked over and caught a hint of disdain in Elvis's curled-lip grin. I timidly shrugged my shoulders and gave a weak little nod of my head.

Elvis fixed me with a stare, raised one of his eyebrows and said, "All along, those 'people' you 'promised to meet'—it was Anka?" He shook his head. "Impressed with Anka, hunh."

I wanted to say I wasn't impressed with *anyone* just because he was a star, but for the moment I could only hold my tongue.

Elvis greeted Paul Anka warmly but with, I detected, just the right touch of reserve to remind him who was the star of stars and who was only the satellite. It was the first inkling I was to have that even though the "just folks" element in his makeup was genuine, Elvis Presley was never unaware of his status nor the public role it required him to play.

AnnMarie took me aside then to explain why she had returned. Unfortunately, I wasn't listening. Out of the corner of my eye I had noticed the beautiful blonde woman make a beeline for Elvis. This left Paul Anka with little to do except pay attention to AnnMarie, an option he seemed to find appealing, and continued to pursue when Elvis beckoned us all over to join him.

Elvis did have me sit next to him; Paul Anka was on my other side, and AnnMarie was positioned on the other side of Anka. The blonde woman, disdaining all this complicated choreography, nonchalantly draped herself around the chair on Elvis's right.

A five-way conversation was thus inaugurated among us, which turned almost immediately into a three-way conversation, as the blonde woman had words and eyes only for Elvis, and made no bones about monopolizing our host. Being an impeccably well-bred young lady, I naturally did my best not to overhear any of the remarks they exchanged.

Unless I was actually doing my best *to* overhear them. I suddenly found myself in an awkward situation, caught between wanting desperately to eavesdrop on their conversation and wanting equally (if not desperately) to conduct myself like a worldly, confident woman. I felt I had a right to eavesdrop since this new arrival on the scene definitely looked like she was putting a move on Elvis. That was okay with me—I had no claims on him—but if she was going to replace me on that dinner date, I wanted to know in advance so *I* could do the canceling.

I wouldn't have blamed Elvis if he had made the switch. The woman was exquisite, no question about it—although I thought it could be considered pushing it a little that she wasn't wearing any shoes or stockings with her long, slinky black gown. But I wasn't going to nitpick. I felt I could be big about things. After all, it wasn't *my* idea to have dinner with him.

To put things in their proper perspective, until a few hours prior, this man had been no more to me than a voice off a hunk of spinning vinyl. He had been a sound emanating from the radio, a phantom flickering across a screen. I'm not denying the excitement and appeal those images had held for me during my formative years, nor am I even trying to deny there was still some carryover of that excitement and appeal into my adult life. How could I? I have already pointed out how the memory of that initial impact enhanced the experience of meeting him now and seeing him perform live.

Nevertheless, I felt I had always been the kind of person who could differentiate between image and substance, between fantasy and reality. Finding myself caught up in a situation that threatened to obliterate the thin line between them triggered my basic survival instincts and made me super-cautious.

What I am driving at is simply that since I had managed to live twenty-four years, eight months, one week, and several hours without ever imagining I would *meet* Elvis Presley, I knew that I would certainly be able to live the rest of my life equally as well if it turned out that I didn't have dinner with him.

For one thing, I had not enjoyed being mistaken for his wife. Not that I wasn't well aware of how gorgeous Priscilla Presley was, but somehow it had bothered me and I just didn't feel like being gracious about it.

My mood wasn't lightened any by the first fragment of the Elvis–blonde woman conversation I did catch, either. It was a proposition, pure and simple. That stunning woman informed Elvis she wanted to stay the night with him.

I began racking my brain for a graceful exit line.

"So you stood me up for Presley, right?"

It was Paul Anka, with a not particularly graceful entrance line. One that was designed to send me a little zinger of guilt.

"Funny you should say that." My retort was sharp. I was annoyed. Not with him, even though his interruption prevented my hearing Elvis's response to the woman, but with myself. Because, in spite of my resolve, my heart had already begun to ache, wondering what Elvis's answer would be.

"Because when you walked in here," I continued, "Elvis accused me of wanting to stand him up for *you.*"

Paul Anka's mouth opened, whether in astonishment or just to respond, I never found out. Before he could say anything, the blonde woman's charming voice, French-accented and husky with sex, totally captured my attention.

"I think there is only one best way to discover . . ." was all I heard her murmur before she knelt on her chair, leaned over and whispered in Elvis's ear.

Elvis shook his head. My ache subsided.

She slid off the chair. When she stood up, she seemed to do it in waves, each one more sinuous with carnal promise than the last.

"In France," she said, "there is a saying: 'Even the most beautiful woman cannot offer more than she has.'" She smiled and was gone.

She had walked right past me and this, together with having, for the first time, heard her voice clearly, finally combined to send a recognition signal to my brain. I was amazed I hadn't known her straight away. I had seen at least three of her pictures: *Umbrellas of Cherbourg, Repulsion,* and *Mayerling.* Some people were already calling her the most beautiful woman in the world. Catherine Deneuve.

"What do you suppose she whispered to Elvis?"

The expression on Paul Anka's face was all too innocent. "What do you think?" he asked, barely bothering to hide his amusement.

"I think it's embarrassing," I replied evenly. "And probably Standard Operating Procedure in this world. But you would know more about that than I would."

"Touché," he conceded and turned for consolation to Ann-Marie.

My thoughts drifted to what kind of consolation *Elvis* might be expecting now, in spite of his protestations about just wanting to have dinner and his only desire being to get to know me. I mean, I have always had a reasonably high opinion of my talent for making interesting table-talk. Compared to the ultimate favors of Catherine Deneuve, however, this pleasant little attribute would seem to finish a distant second even if I were a combination of Bertrand Russell and Groucho, Chico, and Harpo rolled into one.

Especially to a man who was used to having women drop like flies at his feet! Unless . . . hold on a second! Didn't that phrase contain the clue? Wasn't it possible, I thought, that Elvis Presley might be satiated with easily available women? That it would be a welcome change of pace for him to have a casual meal with a woman who *wasn't* blatantly offering herself to him? I began to examine the possibility that he had singled me out because he could tell that although I was a lady, I was also a good sport, the kind of down-to-earth woman he could relate to, and who wouldn't turn out to be just another heavy-breathing fan, panting to thrust herself up against his golden glow. There was one more factor as well. It occurred to me as I saw him send Joe Esposito an almost imperceptible signal. Based on everything I had experienced so far, I sensed that Elvis preferred being the aggressor and pursuer, and that he felt he was both charming and adept in that role.

By this point, The King's retainers were already circulating throughout the room and requesting, with extreme politeness, that everyone leave.

I took a shot at standing up in waves, too—and managed to make each one sinuous with the promise of stretching, as my foot had somehow managed to fall asleep while every other nerve in my body had been drawn taut as a bowstring!

Poised on one foot like a flamingo, I watched Elvis say his goodbyes. He dealt with the cloying homage paid him by adapting a special humility toward those who praised him so lavishly to his face. As though a screen of heartfelt and humble "Yes, Sirs" and "Yes, Ma'ams" might act as an antidote against the near toxic levels of flattery to which he was constantly exposed.

He turned then and our eyes met. We had both made promises. I would keep mine and have dinner with him. As to his promise of being a gentleman, my thinking it through had helped me regain my composure and calm my insecurities in that area.

I walked over to him.

The suite of rooms occupied by Elvis and his entourage on the twenty-ninth floor of the International Hotel invested the words garish and ostentatious with new meaning. The rooms were designed in unbelievably vivid splashes of color. Elvis walked me through the entire setup. The bedrooms, not surprisingly, were the most outlandish, and that barely begins to describe them. Each had an enormous, round bed and a mirrored ceiling. Their total effect was somewhere between an Edwardian bordello and a harem out of the Arabian Nights. I certainly had never seen anything quite like it.

I wound up barely touching any of my food that night. I think it was because I felt so foolish when I realized that the tête-à-tête dinner I had envisioned, the idea of which had so threatened me that I saw it as compromising the complicated sense I had of my own self-worth and independence, was in reality nothing more decadent than hanging out with "the guys" in the suite's dining room and munching hamburgers.

And "munch" Sonny, Red, Joe, Charlie, Lamar, and Vernon (along with a man I hadn't met previously, Gee Gee Gambill) did—with gusto.

"Hey, Joe." Elvis, two huge hamburgers to the good, had obviously decided it was about time that he began to "induct" me into the group a little. "Did you know Joyce is from Washington?"

"I know that, 'E,'" Joe acknowledged. "And I know she works on Capitol Hill."

"Yeah? But you don't know *who* she works for, do ya?" Elvis turned to me. "Tell 'em the name of that committee, honey."

"Well, I work for the Armed Services Committee, on the House side."

"Isn't the head of your committee kind of famous, Joyce?" Charlie Hodge asked.

"Didn't you tell me you actually worked for an *investigating* committee?" That was Elvis cutting in. Had I known then what I learned later about his interests, I would not have been surprised at his remembering that detail.

"Yes, that's right. I'm flattered you remembered," I added before turning back to Charlie. "I *am* actually attached to the Investigating Subcommittee of the House Armed Services Committee. And you are probably thinking of Mendel Rivers who is the chairman of both the full House Armed Services Committee and my subcommittee, as well."

"He's some colorful figure, ain't he!" Sonny West interjected. "And quite a drinker, I hear."

"He does have a reputation, I have to admit." I was surprised at how they had taken Elvis's lead and made me the center of conversation. All the more so since my own work seemed pretty ordinary compared to what they were a part of.

"You know," I said, "a lot of us have begun to refer to Washington as 'Hollywood East'—and I think some of those congressmen up there actually believe it!"

Amidst the laughter and general agreement that followed, Charlie Hodge said, "Yeah, if E could act as good as most of the politicians I've seen, we could have almost as many Oscars here as hamburgers."

With that Elvis planted his booted foot on Charlie's chair and sent it and poor Charlie sprawling, to the near-hysterical amusement of everyone, especially Elvis.

"Hey, did *she* ever win one. . . ?" Lamar Fike piped up. "An Oscar?"

"Who's that?" Vernon asked.

"That French babe. Downstairs, you know, the one didn't have no shoes and . . ." Lamar's deep, slow southern drawl trailed off under the withering looks being shot him by Sonny and Red West. Looks designed, I think, to keep me from being embarrassed. I was touched.

"Uh, Joyce . . . what about President Nixon?"

I looked over at Elvis. It was charming to see him looking kind of apprehensive. Just like any guy on his first date with a girl might be if another girlfriend was brought up and he wanted to change the subject. "I really like the President," Elvis added. "Did you ever meet him?"

"Not yet." I smiled. I turned back to the others. "No, I don't think she ever won an Oscar," I said. "But she sure is awfully beautiful," I added, figuring I could afford to be magnanimous and get everybody off the hook at the same time.

"Maybe to some people that kind of look is beautiful," Elvis said, jumping on my line with both feet. "But, you know, I've always thought brunettes were much more beautiful than blondes."

"Makes perfect sense to me," I said, matter-of-factly.

Well, that really broke him up. He laughed so hard that he nearly choked on his third burger.

Watching him carry on, it occurred to me that I would definitely have to watch myself. It had nothing to do any more with worrying about being put in a compromising position. I was long past that concern. Now, it was only *myself* I had to worry about. Probably it is only *ourselves* we ever have to worry about. If I were going to wind up compromised, it would be because I had done it to myself.

I was not awed by him. I knew myself well enough, even then, to know that part of his appeal was due to the same superficial "glamour" that many of the men I had already met in the political arena possessed. I enjoyed the excitement they were capable of generating, but, in my heart, I considered "climbers" who fed on and thrived in the limelight, merely diversions who were not, ultimately, to be taken seriously. For me to truly take a man seriously, he had to be deeper. Both more subtle and yet, at the same time, of greater substance.

On that first meeting, I saw that Elvis embodied many more of the qualities I'd always sought in a man. He was an incongruous mixture of flamboyance and homespun simplicity. Throughout the evening, I had found him direct, down-to-earth, and genuine. He had never talked "at" me, always with me. I began to feel that even had this man not been the fabulous ELVIS PRESLEY, the "King of Rock 'n' Roll," his effect on me would have been the same.

It was a little before five o'clock in the morning when my last reserves of energy gave out and I told Elvis I thought I should be leaving.

"Thank you for a wonderful time."

"Will you come back another night, Joyce?" I was aware that he had reached over and taken my hand, but even more aware that his eyes, looking deep into my own, were reaching for my heart. "There's a lot more we have to talk about. We didn't get too good a chance tonight."

"I'd love to," I said.

"Great. How about—"

"Why don't you call me and . . . uh . . . invite me."

"I just did." He seemed genuinely nonplussed.

"I meant . . ." I looked away from his eyes. "Properly."

His lip curled in amusement. "Etiquette, hunh? Silly, 'course I will. I'll call you about, uh, seven-thirty Friday night. That's the Dunes Hotel you're at, right?"

I smiled and nodded.

"Gee Gee," he called. "Take Joyce down and see her safe into a cab."

As soon as I walked into my hotel room I grabbed the phone and began to dial Janice. And then, I stopped. It was too early. It wasn't the time of day, either. Janice would not have minded being wakened, just as I wouldn't have, were our roles reversed, no matter what the hour.

I meant that it was too *soon*, even though it had always been our custom immediately to get in touch with each other if anything important happened. This time, somehow, it was different. It was a combination of circumstances, really. I knew my sister as well as she knew me and I could anticipate her excited response . . . and her questions. The problem was that I had no answers.

I called her anyway.

Although I find it slightly embarrassing to admit this, I never once left my room that Friday. I was afraid Elvis might telephone early and I would miss his call. The closer it got to seven-thirty, the higher my anxiety rose. At last the phone rang—at exactly seven-thirty. With all the cool I could muster, I picked up the receiver, cleared my throat and said, "Hello?"

Of course I recognized the unmistakable semidrawl instantly, my pulse quickening at the words: "Could I please speak with Joyce?"

I took a deep breath. "Who's calling?"

"Elvis."

I couldn't resist. "Elvis *who?*"

There was a moment of silence, then a chuckle. "You're a silly little girl."

It was the perfect icebreaker. Elvis explained the arrangements he had made for AnnMarie and me to see the late show. And for me to have dinner with him once again afterward.

That night all the preliminaries—beginning with Emilio, the obsequious maître d', bowing and scraping us past the long waiting line and into the showroom with the words, "Yes, indeed, Miss Bova. We have been expecting you"—went off perfectly. Once again, ensconced in "his" booth, oversized, cushiony, covered in red velvet, and with a commanding view of center stage, we were informed that the rules prohibiting service during the performance would not apply to us.

Still, those preliminaries were only preliminaries. And that night even the show was something of a preliminary. Even though I enjoyed Elvis's performance even more than I did the first time, I knew that everything was only leading up to that moment when I would be with him once again.

The very second he went into "Can't Help Falling in Love with You," which signaled the end of the show, Joe Esposito appeared. To take me, this time, to the actual dressing room where Elvis was changing. He grinned when I walked in, looking especially pleased with himself as though he knew he had given a great performance and was waiting for me to agree. He would have had trouble stopping me. Since I now felt it was an accepted fact between us that, as far as his music was concerned I had no credentials as a "serious critic," I didn't worry about how unoriginal and subjective my comments were. I just gushed.

Beaming with delight, Elvis finally managed to get a word in edgewise. "Glad you liked it. It was for you."

It was definitely a drag having to share him with everyone who had been waiting in the sitting room. Once there, Elvis went through his rituals with the fans. The second part of his performance, it occurred to me. Elvis couldn't stop being Elvis just because the curtain had dropped.

As though he sensed how eager I was to be with him without being part of a mob scene, Elvis cut his postperformance duties down to a minimum that night and we were soon back in the dining room of the lavish suite on the twenty-ninth floor.

Once again it was the cheeseburgers he was famous for that we ate off the expensive china, but this time the guys in the entourage drifted in and out while Elvis held center stage. He told one story after another, amusing everyone immensely, especially me. He was a surprisingly effective storyteller who knew how to make his point with economy, insight, and humor. I say "surprisingly" because it must have been obvious to him that his audience on these occasions was a captive one that would never accord him anything but enthusiastic appreciation. Nevertheless, he never let himself get careless and sloppy in relating his tales, but took pains to employ the brilliant sense of timing and pace he had developed as a stage performer to ensure that his delivery was as effective in private as it was in public. I think it was observing this facet of his personality that led me to first realize that the "Elvis" aura was (or had become), to a great extent, his true self. He *was* his image and that image, of course, was both "ELVIS" and Elvis.

When, at one point, everyone else present seemed to get up and exit as if on cue, it made me a little uneasy. It seemed like such an obvious male strategy move. His choosing that precise moment to declare once more that during the show, "I was singing just to you," did nothing to dissuade my feminine intuition from its conclusion that I was being seduced. Subtly, perhaps, even charmingly and romantically—in an awkward sort of way. I put my glass of Pepsi down on the dining-room table.

"Can I ask you something?" I had decided to take the bull by the horns.

"Anything," he said.

"What exactly am I doing here? I mean, why *me?*"

He took a moment before answering. "Why *not* you?"

"You mean it's going to be somebody, anyway, so as long as I was there with whatever it is you happen to like in a woman, or at least some of it . . ." I stopped and spread out my arms, the palms of my hands up. "That just goes back to what I said when you first asked me to come up here."

"No, it's not a thing of there's *got* to be some girl *this* night. It's not like that at all. Trouble is . . . it's kind of hard to explain. It's been a long time," he said, "since I've felt so comfortable with a woman. I mean I have sort of a way about knowing things. You'll understand . . . you'll see what I mean when you get to know me better . . ."

My God, I thought, "get to know him better"! Could this really be happening to me?

". . . But Joyce, you have to be honest with yourself. Like what you said there before to me was a part-truth."

"When? What did I say?"

"That you were *there*. With what I look for in a girl. A man like me sees a woman—he knows, damn it."

"Knows what?"

"Well, not everything, not right away. But a man like me knows when a girl is right for him."

"What if he's already got a woman?" I asked.

His face changed and for a second I thought he was going to be angry with me for saying that. But he just looked at me and then said, "It doesn't matter what *he's* got or hasn't got . . . what I'm sayin' is, c'mon, *you* gotta know what's right for you."

"You live it all the time, don't you?"

"What do you mean? Live what?"

"I don't know, being Elvis Presley, I guess. The magic, the power. You can do things other people can't."

"Does that bother you?"

"It could. I never thought about it until now."

"Then let me put your mind at ease. I'm not 'The King' or any of that stuff they publicize about me. I'm just a man."

He reached over and poured himself a glass of water from the pitcher on the table. I wanted to believe him, but a part of me still remained guarded. I was also aware that I was being charmed. And yet I was willing to submit to the magical moment. Up to a point.

I didn't really think that it could be more than that—a moment. "Elvis, I may be naive in a lot of ways," I blurted out. "But I know what powerful egos . . ."

"It's not an ego thing, Joyce. It's just that I . . . like you . . ."

"It always comes back to 'why me'?"

"Only time can answer that question, Joyce."

There wasn't anything to say to that. There wasn't any deep love in my heart for him really. Not yet. I looked at him, but he seemed suddenly distracted and I realized he was listening to a radio that had been left playing. An announcer was saying that Jerry Lee Lewis was appearing down the street at the Landmark Hotel.

Elvis got out a local publication and showed me an article in which Jerry Lee Lewis was quoted as saying that he and Elvis were good friends. Elvis was obviously annoyed. "You know, that boy and me have never been friends."

It was about then that I heard the radio announcer say that it was five A.M., which meant telling Elvis I had to leave or chance missing my plane back to D.C.

When I did, he excused himself for a moment, but seemed lost in thought when he came back into the room. He remained silent as he walked me to the door. Then he blew my mind one more time. "Joyce, don't you think you could stay for a couple more days?"

"Elvis, don't . . . please. What I mean is . . . I'd love to, but I can't. Really."

"Give me one good reason why not?"

"Well . . . uh . . ." There I was again, groping for a sensible answer not only for him, but for myself.

"Come on, Joyce. I won't take no for an answer."

This was the first glimmering I had of Elvis's stubborness, the first clue to the fact that he could not accept another person not doing what he wanted them to—and at the exact moment he wanted it done.

"We need to get to know each other better; we need more time." His tone had changed and now he was almost pleading.

"Elvis, that's what *I'm* saying. This has all been too quick for me."

"That's not good enough. You know you can manage one or two more days."

"Believe me, I would love to, but the Congress of the United States doesn't recess for me." The truth was that I really did not want to stay. I had already taken in as much as I could handle at one time.

Elvis frowned, then abruptly altered the focus. "The other night when I mentioned the investigating committee you work for in front of the guys, I noticed you changed the subject. Was that because you're working on something secret?"

"Not really. Although I only started on this committee a few months ago and I'm not absolutely positive as to what is classified and what I can safely talk about."

He nodded. "That's another thing. How old are you?"

"Twenty-four, why?"

"I was just wondering how somebody I didn't think was twenty-one yet could be working for the Congress?"

I opened my mouth to tell him he was putting me on, but no sound ever came out. He had covered my mouth with his own. For the first time I felt the softness of his lips. He kissed me again and again and, hearing the elevator coming up outside, I felt its silken purr could easily be emanating from somewhere inside of me.

"Would you give me your phone number at home?" he whispered finally. "I want to call you and see you again."

I scribbled my number hastily on a piece of paper and when I folded it into his hand, he replaced it in my palm with a small ring, its exquisite diamond set in beautifully wrought gold.

"So you won't forget me."

"I'll never forget you, or this moment."

"I'm not going to give you the chance."

I stepped out into the wee small hours of the Las Vegas night, the night that never ends. And reminded myself that not only must all good things come to an end, but most of them never even begin.

Chapter Four

I was not satisfied with one brief moment of magic. I was a sleepwalker who could not wake from her dream. My normal, day-to-day life back in Washington seemed dull, stale, and predictable. It had never been that way before. My work on Capitol Hill had been important to me, always vital and interesting, never just ordinary drudgery.

But now . . .

I told myself over and over that I had to put things into perspective, had to view what had happened in Las Vegas in the harsh light of reality. The trouble was that reality—or common sense, or any conventional wisdom by whatever label—could only tell me that I would, of course, never hear from Elvis Presley again, that he had probably already forgotten ever meeting me. It was a dose of reality too harsh for me to swallow. My only antidote against it was a secret vision held in my deepest heart, my vision of the Elvis I had gotten to know personally. It was a vision of a man who had opened himself to me. For whatever reason, he had instinctively allowed me to see, had wanted me to know that he was different from the way all the others seemed to perceive him. Admittedly, all I had to support this wisdom of the heart was an intoxicating cloud of memory on which I now floated as if still breathing the heady atmosphere of the Vegas Strip. Images from those nights haunted me: Elvis onstage and singing for me; Elvis smiling at me from across the room; his lips moving ever closer to mine. . . .

At the end of a hectic week, a week that began with a Department of the Army communication advising us that even as our investigation of the "My Lai incident" continued, the army itself was about to set in motion the landmark court-martial of Lt. William Calley, I was taken to dinner by the man with whom I had experienced my first love affair. You may have heard of Duke Ziebert's; it has a reputation. It is one of the places in Washington where people go to impress or are taken to be impressed. The man who brought me did not get what he wanted. Surprisingly, it was marriage. Flattering, but that train had left the station. He couldn't know it, but he was one love too late.

Bringing me home, he hesitated a second. I could tell he had hoped I would say something before shutting the door. But there wasn't anything to say. I certainly didn't love him and I didn't hate him, either. Usually I am a woman of extremely intense emotions. If I give myself, I give myself heart and soul. My feelings are too focused to be spread around and there was only one man on whom I was focused.

I was latching the door when the phone rang. I looked at the clock. It was almost two A.M. In some strange way I knew it was Elvis. It was too perfect, but it also had to be. For anything ever to make sense between us, it would always have to be like a fairy tale. I was still standing there transfixed while the rings reverberated over and over through the dark, empty rooms, the urgency of its sound filling me with . . . what? I wasn't sure. I jumped and grabbed the receiver. "Hello?"

"Hello." A soft, semidrawl. *The* soft, semidrawl. "Is this Joyce?"

"Elvis . . . it *is* you."

He laughed. "Who did ya think it was, Eddy Arnold?"

"I guess I didn't really believe you would call."

"It's been tough, honey. They've got me in California now . . . got me doin' a bunch of things. But what are you doin'? I think about you a lot. You still runnin' the government?"

"It's still running, anyway. Probably more in *spite* of me. Actually, I just got home."

"Hey, it's gotta be real late out there. What's a little gal like you doin' out so late?"

"Nothing special." I sensed an undertone and, making sure my own tone was casual, added, "Just out to dinner with a friend."

"Friend?" he snapped right back. "What kind of friend? You got a boyfriend or anything like that, do ya?"

"No. Nobody special, no boyfriend."

With that settled, we somehow seemed to pick up right where we left off in Las Vegas and kidded and made small talk and carried on for what seemed like hours. Suddenly, he said, "You know I want to see you."

"Me, too. I want to—"

"I mean I want you with me now. I want you to come out here to California."

Before I could answer, I heard my sister at the door and had to ask Elvis to hold on while I let her in. As soon as I picked up the receiver again he asked, "You mean your twin's there? Put her on the phone, I want to meet her."

"No problem." I laughed. "I told her it's you and she can barely restrain herself from ripping the phone out of my hand."

"She sounds just like you," he said when I finally got the phone back.

"What did you say when she said she didn't believe it was really you?"

"I didn't say anything . . . just sang her a couple bars of, 'She's Not You.' "

"I knew it. I knew you were singing to her. You know something? You're awfully sweet for a superstar."

"Well, you just remember that, Joyce." He laughed. "And you remember I want you out here. I'll call you soon."

"Good night, Elvis." I put the phone down.

Janice was looking at me. "Good night, *Elvis?*" She shook her head.

"I know, it's wild. Do we need to talk, or what?"

"Well?"

"Well, for openers, he wants me out in California with him."

"Is that what you're going to do?"

"I don't know what I'm going to do. How can I leave now with the workload we have?" I got up and went over to where I'd left my cigarettes and lit one. "Two minutes off the phone with him and already I'm driving myself crazy."

"You're not trying to tell me you think anything can come of this, are you?"

"I don't need any more questions, Janice, just answers."

"Elvis Presley is no answer, that's for sure. He's just a more complicated question."

"I don't know. I showed you the ring he gave me. That's something, isn't it?" Even as I said it, I knew how lame it sounded, but it was the only counter I could think of to all that common sense being thrown at me.

"Oh, stop. He probably has a collection of them that he hands out. Something like that is meaningless to him."

"I'm going to bed."

Where I tossed and turned and watched the dawn come up. Maybe my sister was right, maybe I was kidding myself. Maybe I should forget it, I told myself, gritting my teeth as I lay there in the semidarkness. Did I really want to open myself up to the kind of hurt and rejection that seemed inevitable in trying to have a romance with Elvis Presley?

I got up and padded barefoot into the kitchen. I poured a little milk into a saucepan and put it on the stove. Too bad I'd never really developed a taste for booze; it probably would have done a better job of helping me relax than milk. When it was warm I emptied the saucepan into a glass. I had made up my mind. There was no point in tearing myself up over this idea of his that I should join him in California. I just wasn't up to pulling off something like that. For a lot of reasons. Most of them not exactly conducive to reinforcing the image I had of myself as sophisticated and independent. Still, I had to be true to me, even if that me was exhibiting symptoms of being a scared young woman.

Back in my room I sat on the edge of the bed and sipped slowly at the warm milk while putting myself through something I imagined women had done since the first Cro-Magnon man asked a Cro-Magnon woman to try his lifestyle on for size. I tried to figure out if the chemistry between Elvis and me was strong enough for something to really come of it. One big plus we had going for us, besides the obvious physical attraction, was a kind of basic palship. I could tell it meant a lot to him that his guys accepted me. He was impressed by my capacity to remain every inch a lady and still be comfortable just hanging out, the only woman at dinner with that macho entourage of his. It also seemed to me he sensed right off the bat that I just plain *liked* him as a person. He knew I wasn't after anything, that to me he was separate and distinct from "ELVIS." For his part, he had responded in kind, been genuine and down to earth, never trading on his stardom or allowing it to get between us.

I sat there by myself in the dark and thought and dreamed and fought that lonely battle we fight against our own insecurity, against the icy inner terror that freezes your guts and makes you shrink back from the big scary world out there, that makes you scrunch yourself into a tight little ball of fear. I silently shouted down the little voice mocking in my ear, asking who did I think I was, didn't I realize I was just an ordinary little Italian girl from Baltimore? No, that wouldn't matter to him, he knew he was just a 19-year-old poor, white trash kid from down south when he was magically transported to a hermetically sealed fantasy world that both protected and almost muffled his song. Besides, he'd already decided he could allow me at least to glimpse the surprisingly fragile human being who lived inside "ELVIS."

And I wanted it to happen. I wanted it all to happen. I was falling in love with him and, despite anything my sister could say, despite any misgivings of my own, despite all logic and common sense, I wanted Elvis to love me. At that moment, sitting there in my darkened bedroom in my little apartment, unknown and only half believing, deep down inside the feeling swept over me that this impossibly absurd, incredible thing could, no . . . *would* be.

Ironically, I first had to persuade him that I couldn't possibly leave work and fly across country to be with him right then and there. I'm afraid I did such a good job of impressing him with my unavailability that it was the middle of December before he called again. It was apparent that evening, however, that not only his usual good humor had returned, but even his interest in my work. It seemed he could barely wait to dispense with the usual amenities before inquiring, "Your committee's the one workin' on the stuff I'm seeing on the TV about the My Lai thing, right?"

"That's us, all right," I concurred. "You should see our office. It's been a real zoo. There've been reporters and cameras and different media people all over the place every day."

"Hey, that's real interestin' . . . and my girl is in the middle of it. What's really goin' on, anyway?"

"Well, Representative Mendel Rivers who is the chairman of—"

"Of your committee, I remember you tellin' us that night. Go ahead."

"Okay, what he's done is just appointed Congressman Hebert from Louisiana to head a special subcommittee that will conduct an in-depth investigation of the entire matter."

"So when is that gonna happen?"

"I'm not really sure," I admitted. "They're just getting started with the first of their preliminary interviews. They do plan to start their formal interviews within the next few months, though, so until then there's not much more I can tell you."

"Well, you'll have plenty of time to bring me up to date then, won't you?" Elvis promptly interjected.

"No," I said, not sure whether he was kidding or not. "All the interviews are being conducted in executive session, meaning behind closed doors. They're supposed to be absolutely secret. Leaks from any of the staff are punishable by death by firing squad. It will be the same with the hearings, the press and public strictly excluded; anything I might possibly learn from being on the inside I couldn't tell you."

"Couldn't tell *me?* Couldn't tell ol' Elvis . . . not even if he asked you nicely and promised to never, never repeat . . ."

"Elvis—"

He laughed. "I'm just kiddin', honey. You know I wouldn't want you to get in trouble or anything with the government because of me."

"There *is* one thing I can tell you . . . it's already been openly discussed in some of the newspapers here. One of the reasons the special subcommittee was set up is that the army failed to produce the information and witnesses Chairman Rivers had requested."

"You know, Joyce," Elvis said, his voice serious, "I have great respect for the Congress but I really think they ought to leave those guys over there alone. They were just doin' their job and tryin' to stay alive. It's gotta be hell for those boys. Now half the country talks about 'em like they were the enemy and the Viet Cong were the good guys. Let me tell you, Joyce, a lot of people in this country got screwed-up ideas about right and wrong."

It didn't seem that getting into a long-distance political debate with Elvis at that point in our lives could lead to anything positive, so I changed the subject to what was really on my mind.

"Elvis, when am I going to see you?"

"Honey, I'm sorry, I know it's been months. But you know that I did ask you to come to me in California."

"Isn't there any way you could come here?"

"It's just impossible. They got me so busy I don't even know what I'm gonna be doin' from one day to the next. Joyce, I'm always thinkin' of you, you know that. We've got to get together just as fast as I can get these things goin' on here straightened out. I'll call you and let you know soon. Really, it'll be okay. Why don't you think about it and be prepared to come out here?"

In the following days there was plenty to occupy my thoughts. To begin with, my twin had gotten herself engaged to a handsome young man from Italy. I had the usual misgivings of any protective sister, misgivings which were heightened by my concern about the ability of two people from such different cultures—American and Italian—to make a life together.

A less serious interlude occurred at a cocktail party held by a local radio station to introduce the newest addition to their staff, the legendary—or notorious—deejay, Murray, "the K," Kaufman.

My girlfriend, Katharine, who also worked on the Hill, happened to be dating the guy who flew the traffic helicopter for WWDC and it was she who invited me. To make a long story short, the "K" took an instant shine to the two of us and for the next couple of months we got to go to any number of opening nights and similar show-biz events through his contacts in the music industry.

These were impressive, no doubt about that; almost as impressive as he made them sound in the boastful, self-aggrandizing monologues about his glory days in the Big Apple that he was prone to launching into at the drop of a name. You might not be surprised that a man who could proclaim himself the "Fifth Beatle" could also get on my nerves at times with his self-centered soliloquys. So much so that even though Murray was neither a real close friend nor family, I decided to tell him about the events of the previous August.

"Elvis! No kidding?"

It impressed him all right, but even as I took some satisfaction from stopping him in his tracks with the magic name, I regretted it even more. It was almost like taking something sacred in vain.

"What happened?" he asked, his curiosity obviously growing. "You'd better be careful there, Joyce," he added, revealing by the look in his eye and his intonation as much as by the words themselves, the direction in which his curiosity was inevitably headed. Realizing my mistake, I made up my mind to close that avenue off then and there.

"Actually, Murray, it was a big nothing," I fibbed. "A girlfriend and I met him backstage and we had some cheeseburgers in his suite with a bunch of people. And that's all there was to it."

Over the next couple of weeks the preliminary interviews wound up and, with the special investigating subcommittee about to commence formal hearings, the pace of work in the office accelerated past incredibly busy to purely frantic. There was also the furor and excitement generated by the initial appearance of the accused officers, Lieutenant Calley and Captain Medina, along with famed defense attorney F. Lee Bailey. All of which led to yet another 12-hour day and my conking out that night as soon as my head hit the pillow.

The telephone rang.

"Joyce, that you? Your voice sounds funny."

"Oh, Elvis—you are just what I needed. The perfect antidote to the killer day I had."

"They wearin' my little girl out? Must be that My Lai thing, hunh? How's it goin'?"

"All I know right now is that I am more tired than I ever thought it was possible for any one human being to be."

"Then that's it. You are going to take a break. There's times when a person just has to get away. You are going to come out to California and spend some time with me."

"Oh, Elvis, I can't now. I would give anything to be able to;

I'm worn out from these long, frantic days. But if I left while all this was going on they really would shoot me."

Elvis changed the subject this time, and a bit abruptly, too. I knew that every occasion I used my job as an excuse not to see him caused him to become annoyed with me.

"Elvis," I broke in, wanting to show him that I understood and that it wasn't my fault, "I know you think that there's no obstacle too great to overcome, but this *is* the Congress of the United States I work for, you know."

"Nobody knows it better'n me, honey," he said.

Years later, when I found out he had been the highest individual taxpayer in the country for a number of years, I remembered the way he had said those words and wondered if he was thinking about the millions we had levied from him.

"I just don't want my pretty little girl to play *too* hard to get," he continued.

"You know I'm not doing that."

I said it with a little deliberate coyness. We both knew there was some truth to his accusation. But I rationalized that Elvis, an occasional burst of annoyance notwithstanding, seemed to enjoy the pursuit of me almost as much as I was enjoying being pursued.

Wrong rationalization. Very wrong.

"Joyce." His voice cut sharply into my thoughts. "I've made up my mind. You're coming out here tomorrow. I'll take care of all the arrangements."

"I can't . . . Elvis, you know I can't. If you can arrange for me to come out there," I grumbled unreasonably while trying to sound reasonable, "I don't see why you can't come *here.*"

"Now this is getting ridiculous," he snapped back. "No way can I do that. I have things I have to do here. Damn it, Joyce, I've asked you I don't know how many times now to meet me. Maybe you're just not interested."

"Don't say that. You know it's not true. But I can't. I don't know how I can explain it to you any more clearly."

"Why'nt ya try . . ."

Without waiting to figure out if he meant try to come out there or try to explain more clearly, I blurted, "Anyway, what about your wife?" and could have bitten off my tongue.

"We've been all through that. I don't know what else to say."

"I'm sorry, neither do I."

"Then I don't *have* anything else to say. 'Cept goodbye."

There was a click and I was left holding the phone, in my stomach a sick, empty feeling.

Bringing up Priscilla was lame. I knew it and I knew he knew it.

No, it wasn't really a question of adultery. It was a question of me. I was afraid, of course. But was I simply afraid of him, of what he would expect of me? Or was I afraid of the weakness he brought out in me, the vulnerability?

On more than one occasion he had assured me that his marriage was nearing its end and that I need not worry about it. The question that remained was giving myself to him heart and body and soul. It was the only way I could ever envision myself with him, but a commitment to Elvis would not be like a commitment to any other being. Could I make it and still remain the strong and independent woman I also felt I must be? Lying there in the dark that night I knew the only way I would find out was to try. Just as I knew that if I were ever to see him again, I would have to be the one to make it happen.

Chapter Five

It was Elvis making his long-heralded return to the International Hotel in Las Vegas that gave me my opportunity. I would make my unheralded return at the same time. It would mean returning to where we first met. It would mean knowing once and for all whether Elvis and I were illusion or reality. It would mean sucking in my gut and swallowing my pride.

It would also be too heavy a trip to make alone. In my experience, twins are uncomfortable doing things alone. In fact, just having been *born* a twin might have been a factor in Elvis's needing that tightly knit entourage of his. The West boys, for instance, were more like brothers to him than employees. Anyway, my twin had gone and married the handsome but jealous young man from Italy and so I asked Karen, one of my closest friends on the Hill, in her place. It wasn't until we were cruising 50,000 feet above the green and brown parquet floor of the Southwest that I ventured to tell Karen she could be in for more than she had bargained on. She took it philosophically; the sheer excitement of meeting Elvis Presley apparently overcame any hesitation she might have had about being thrust without warning into my romantic adventure.

Unfortunately, after we had landed and were finally unpacked and settled into our room at the Dunes, I turned into a jellyfish. All my determination, every ounce of will I had summoned to propel me across the continent, drained right out of me the instant I picked up the room phone to call him.

"Suppose . . ." I stalled, receiver in hand. "Suppose he's still angry?"

"Well," said comely, soft-spoken, sensible Karen, "isn't that why you're here? To show him there's no reason anymore for him to be angry?"

"But maybe I'm acting like a jerk, chasing after him like this." I sat down on one of the beds. "I don't say this conceitedly, Karen, in fact, maybe something like this proves I *am* a jerk, but I've never chased after a man in my life."

"Honey, this isn't *some man* you're talking about. This is Elvis Presley."

"Then maybe the great Elvis Presley is the jerk! Why couldn't he be big enough to apologize for the attitude he took the last time we talked?" I put the phone back down.

Karen shook her head. "People have to be given an opportunity to apologize. Especially men."

"I thought you just said Elvis wasn't a mere man."

"Unless you think *he's* going to phone *you?*" She tempered the sarcasm by picking up the phone and gently depositing it in my lap.

"He could be with another woman, you know."

"I think I know you well enough, Joyce, to say that if you really felt that, you would never have come out here in the first place. It's not *another* woman that's the problem here. The only woman you're scared of being with Elvis is *you.*" She plucked the receiver from its base and held it out to me.

I hesitated a second—and then dialed.

"Joyce? That you? Where are you?"

I recognized Joe Esposito's distinctive Chicago accent the second I heard it. "Right down the street, Joe. At the Dunes."

"Hold on."

I did, feeling the adrenaline begin to pump.

"Joyce?"

"Elvis." And pump!

"Why didn't you let me know you were coming?"

His tone was sharp. Was he angry? "I wanted to surprise you."

"Well, you sure did, darlin'."

He wasn't angry. He was happy. Happy to hear from me.

"You must be psychic, honey; I was just about to call you."

"You were?" I wanted him to detect my glee.

"Yeah, silly. But you can't be giving me such a hard time." I could actually envision the twinkle in his eye. "But you can make it up to me."

"How?"

"By comin' to the show tonight . . ."

I covered the mouthpiece of the phone with my palm and whispered to Karen that he wanted to see me. She was smiling broadly.

"What? I'm sorry, I didn't hear what you said."

". . . and afterward comin' back to be with me."

"Okay, Elvis. But . . . I have someone with me."

"Am I finally goin' to get to meet that twin of yours?"

"No, it's my friend Karen."

"Well, you bring her of course, baby. Now . . . you know Joe'll meet you in the lobby first and . . ."

At ten-thirty on the dot Joe opened the door to the dressing room and Elvis turned and saw me. Our eyes met and a split second later I was in his arms. "You're even more beautiful than the last time I saw you," he breathed as we clung to each other. "You don't know what it means to me, baby, havin' you here. But"—He pulled his head back and slipped me the curled-lip grin—"it sure took you long enough."

His arms tightened around me and the warmth and strength

of him made me feel secure and sure that whatever delays and doubts there had been were now in our past.

Later, while we were watching the show, Karen leaned over to talk. "It's incredible," she whispered. "When you told me on the plane I was, well, skeptical is too strong a word, but you know, I did think maybe you were exaggerating a little? Only you actually played it *down*. I mean the way he was so excited to see you. And he's . . . he's so . . . so . . ."

"What?"

"So damned attentive to you," she breathed. "I think you really are special to him."

Seeing Elvis perform onstage did nothing to diminish Karen's enthusiasm. Once we were backstage again, she gushed with the best of us. I waited until she finally began to run out of superlatives before I pointed out, "Elvis, you were no less spectacular than when I saw you the last time, but wasn't there something missing? I don't mean from the music. Didn't you omit the somersaults, for instance?"

He nodded. "It was getting too much for me. Hell, I would wind up losing ten pounds a night. You've seen how I gulp down all that Gatorade."

"I know, I know. I mentioned it to Janice and the next time we were in the market she took a bottle of the stuff down from the shelf and showed me the label. Tons of chemicals. She said it tastes even worse than it reads."

He laughed. "You tell her I work too hard keepin' this body of mine in shape to *ever* put anything harmful in it. Hey! Let's call her up. What d'ya say, honey? Why don't you get her on the phone?"

I didn't say anything. I was already too busy dialing her number. It would be pretty late back home, but I was counting on Janice being too excited at hearing from the two of us together, to really mind.

Over the ringing I could hear Elvis asking Karen if she knew Janice. "She is really something," he said. He turned back to me.

"How about that time she got me to sing to her over the telephone?"

Just then I heard her sleepy voice in my ear.

"Janice, are you awake?"

"You got her?" In a flash Elvis was at my side reaching for the phone. "Maybe she'd like to hear an encore?" he asked.

"Joyce, what's wrong?"

"It's all right," I said into the mouthpiece. "Everything's just great. It's just that Elvis wants to talk to you."

"Hi," Elvis said, taking the phone. "I hope this time you'll believe it's me without making me have to prove myself."

I couldn't hear what Janice replied, of course, but whatever it was caused Elvis to beam from ear to ear with pure delight. Which was really nice to see, the man who had captured my heart having a great time talking with the person I'm closest to in the whole world. I moved onto the arm of the chair so Elvis could sit and talk in comfort. I looked around and noticed the room was filling with well-wishers, celebrities, and friends. Some of the boys had begun to regale Karen with their stories of Elvis and Charlie Hodge turned to me. "Joyce, I was just telling your friend here about how we none of us ever know where E is gonna come from on that damn stage. He'll do anything to catch us off guard. He has even hid behind the drums and sneaked out from there."

"Then I'm disappointed," I kidded. "Every time I'm here he just walks onstage from the wings like a normal person."

"Now hold on there." Huge Lamar Fike was grinning. "Nobody has ever said the man was normal."

"Oh, yeah?" Elvis was not about to let that go by. "I just do them things 'cause I wanna be sure you're on your fat ol' toes!" he yelled, handing me the phone.

"He is something, isn't he?" I said into it.

"I have to admit he's even more charming than I thought he'd be. Joyce, you just be careful!".

"Good sound advice. But careful isn't really what I flew all the way across the country to be."

"Well, try anyway."

I had to smile. "Don't worry, Older Sister, you just get the rest of your beauty sleep. Not that a person with a face like yours really needs any."

"Thank you, person with a face like mine."

"Good night, honey."

"Oh, Joyce, if only I were there. Just to—"

"Don't worry," I interrupted. "The important thing is I know I have your moral support in my heart. We're always there for each other in spirit and—Janice?"

There wasn't any response at first, only muffled sounds that could have been whispering. Then, finally, Janice's voice, very faint: "Joyce?"

"What? What happened? Is something wrong?"

"Nothing. Everything's fine. Just remember I love you, too. Bye."

"Janice! What's going on? Please . . . tell me."

But the line was dead and Elvis had hold of my arm.

"C'mon, honey, I want you to meet some people."

We cut through the mob that had gathered, Elvis parting them like the Red Sea. "I can't believe you and your sister." He shook his head. "Your voices even, you have the same voice and everything."

"If she hadn't just got married, she would be here now. You have no idea how much she wants to meet you and see you perform in person."

"She let a little thing like getting married stop her?" he teased.

I tried to smile and Elvis began introducing me, starting with Ricky Nelson, whose wife Elvis said was the daughter of a famous ex-football player.

"And this here . . ." He finished up with a little flourish, as he introduced the last one, a tall, Waspishly lean man with cool, unblinking eyes, impeccably tailored, and fashionably tanned. "This here is Mr. Jim Aubrey, the head man of MGM."

I shook hands with the man who I remembered the gossip columnists referring to, when he was president of CBS, as "The Smiling Cobra" and then directed my attention to Karen. She didn't seem much interested in the men there who were interested in her, and for the most part we talked together while Elvis tried to divide his attention among all his guests until it was time to go up to his suite.

Karen had to use the powder room at the last moment and we turned out to be among the last to arrive on the thirtieth floor, now completely redone as one lavish suite for Elvis & Co.

"Is it usually this crowded, Joyce?" she asked looking askance at the mob scene all around us.

"No," I said, even more surprised than she.

We thought we would circulate a while by ourselves—might *have* to, in fact, if Elvis was once more going to try to pay every one the right amount of attention. Instead, he came right over to me. His nervous energy level seemed, if anything, to have actually escalated since he'd come up to the suite. I could feel the tension in him when he took me by the hand and sat me down next to him and put his arm around me. He began telling stories and talking nonstop, often using my presence to underscore a point he wanted made.

"Y'see, Charlie," he called out at one point to his long-time rhythm guitarist, "Joyce says she loved the way I did 'Hound Dog' tonight."

"Well," Charlie Hodge shrugged. "So did the audience."

Elvis, his fingers tapping on the arm of the sofa, nodded rapidly several times. "Y'know I can always tell when it's right."

"Elvis," I observed, wanting to go with the flow of his energy, but to keep it upbeat because it seemed powerful enough to overflow and go wild, "you seem more pleased than ever with how you performed tonight."

"You know why that is, honey?" He had bounced up off the sofa.

Startled by his vehemence, I stared up at him, shaking my head. "No."

He leaned back down to me: " 'Cause I came out of it alive."

"What are you talking about?"

"Y'know, it's actually a good thing you *haven't* been around these last couple of days. You won't believe what's been goin' on. First, somebody called the hotel the other day and told them I was gonna be kidnapped. Then somebody called Joe and said I was gonna . . . uh . . . they were gonna blow me away."

I just kept staring; I knew my mouth must have dropped open.

"That's right, honey," Elvis went on, "next we got one of them souvenir menus, y'know, with my picture on it? It'd been sent to the hotel, but with a gun drawn on it, pointed at my head."

"Wh . . . What did you do?" I stammered, visions of the Kennedys and Martin Luther King racing through my head.

"We had to call in the FBI."

He shook his head and sat back down.

"Ain't it a bitch? Some crazy man gonna kill me to make a name for himself!"

He jumped back up.

"Y'know, Joe and Daddy and the management here tried to get me to cancel my shows, but I figured we scared the sonofabitch off with the FBI and extra security and all."

He sat down again and put his arm around me and called Red and Sonny West over.

"Hey, man." He gestured to them. "Tell Joyce. You guys were really scared, weren't ya?"

"That's right, E," Sonny said while Red nodded in agreement.

"Joyce, y'know, ol' Sonny here, he was going to jump in front and take the bullet for me, weren't you, man?"

"If I had to, E."

"Honey, did you or . . . uh . . . do you think anybody in the audience heard me when I said 'the fuckin' bastard should go ahead and shoot now'?"

"I didn't hear anything," I declared. "Or hear anybody commenting. And Karen didn't mention hearing anything."

"Naw." Red West shook his head. "Nobody heard ya, Elvis."

"Well." Elvis was on his feet again. "I was ready for him, ya know what I mean?"

"Elvis," I said, reaching up for his hand, "won't you sit by me?" I had noticed backstage that his face looked marked up, as if he had been scratched but now, as whatever had been daubed on to cover them wore off, it became really obvious. I was hoping to calm him down and, having already sensed how readily he responded to genuine care and attention, felt that dealing with those scratches might be the best way. "Let me have a look at those, honey, please? Honestly, they seem more than superficial to me. Was it some of those crazy fans trying to grab and kiss you?"

"Was it?" He turned to Red and Sonny again. "Hey, that was a sick audience down there tonight, hunh? Did you see the old lady in the front row? Her big, ol' fat husband had to *hold* her down."

Once the West boys nodded their agreement—as usual, as everyone did—he brought his attention back to me.

"And, man, those . . . uh . . . goddamn girls over there on the side. Shit, they were clawin' and grabbin' at me like there was no tomorrow. They're the ones got my face a mess. I mean, they were wild. I wanted to yank 'em clear out of their seats and throw 'em all the way up into the balcony. It's a good thing you were right there, Red, or they would've had my clothes."

Then, just when I thought he had finally calmed down, he was up again, striding over to look into one of the wall mirrors.

"Damn," he muttered, examining his face more closely. "If I work here another month, I'm gonna need plastic surgery."

I walked over and stood by the windows and looked down

on a glittering panorama of Las Vegas with the lights of the nighttime city below and the desert stretching beyond into the night. I could still hear Janice's voice on the phone. I knew there was something wrong no matter what she said to reassure me. I should have called her back.

"What are you thinking about?" Karen had come up alongside me.

"Oh, different things. That Elvis was on the floor below last time I was here." It was difficult making small talk but I wasn't ready to talk about what was really on my mind.

"I've been thinking, too," Karen said. "About you. You and him."

"Oh?" I looked back down at the strip, wondering how many souls down there were discovering that inside the glittering casinos they were lost in the *real* desert. Not knowing what was happening with my twin was making me feel a little lost myself.

"You know, Joyce, most of the females in this galaxy would give anything to change places with you tonight."

I turned and looked at Karen then. She was looking past me and beyond, back into the suite. I followed her gaze around past the crowded bar, skimming over the huge living room and adjacent dining area and kitchen only to stop dead at the door just to the right of the foyer. The entrance to Elvis's sanctum sanctorum, his suite within the suite. And the place Karen—and I—were really thinking of. His bedroom.

"Do you really think you can handle it? Handle all this?" She shook her head slowly from side to side in wonder. "I mean, well . . ." She shrugged. "He is bigger than life, isn't he?"

"Karen," I said sharply. "If he can handle putting up with me, I can certainly handle 'all this.' As for his being 'bigger than life,' then I'll have to get a little bigger myself," I added, in an attempt to tune out my concerns about Janice and concentrate on myself.

Karen looked puzzled. " 'Put up with *you*'? You mean because the two of you are—I don't mean to sound like a corny song title, but—from such different worlds?"

"Something like that." I glanced back out the window. "That doesn't seem to matter to him," I said finally. "In fact, it seems to be what he wants. And needs."

"But, Joyce, once you brush away the stardust?"

"How would I do that?" I had to smile. "How do you take the stardust from Elvis Presley? And why would I want to?"

"You know, Joyce," she said, laughing, "you're right." She seized my hand in both of hers. "Forget all the stuff I just said. It's obvious he's crazy about you, anyway."

"Joyce!" Elvis was motioning to join him by the stereo. There the moths, as usual, were forming around his flame, eager to bathe in a star's reflected light. A record was playing over and over and to show him I hadn't forgotten, I said, "It isn't Dusty Springfield this time."

"Anne Murray." He nodded. "Thinkin' I might just record that myself someday. It's a great new song called 'Snowbird.' "

"If you keep it playing over and over like that I'm going to start feeling it's a great *old* song."

He laughed. "You know I can't get enough of it when I like something." His voice got serious and he took my hand. "Or someone."

"You're making me blush," I said as he sat me down alongside him. "But it's the same for me."

"Yeah?" he asked playfully. "Ol' Elvis your favorite singer, li'l darlin'?"

"Always. Janice and I swore by you from the first notes of 'Love Me Tender.' She's even more loyal than me. When we were invited to an Engelbert Humperdinck show, she actually scolded me for wanting to go," I said, tongue-in-cheek.

"Proves she has good sense." Elvis got the round of uproarious laughter he always got for anything even mildly humorous. I knew I should have dropped it right then, but thinking of Janice made me race on relentlessly with the story, as if by invoking her name, her image in my mind would be a talisman that could somehow safeguard her happiness.

"You haven't heard the best part. Afterward, at the reception, guess what they played? 'Release Me'! *Your* album!" I started to laugh, but then realized none of the others were joining in.

Because Elvis wasn't laughing. Not at all.

"You went anyway, hunh? Even though your sister was against it?"

"Wait!" I was taken aback by his tone of voice, but couldn't stop myself from plunging ahead. "You haven't heard the very best part. The minute I heard the song that was playing, heard that it was *you* singing, I blurted out for everyone to hear: 'Oh, you're playing my favorite singer!'"

I paused and looked around. They all, even Karen, were watching Elvis.

"Well, everyone *did* hear," I persevered. "Especially Engelbert Humperdinck himself, who immediately informed me that, and I quote, 'Elvis shouldn't try to sing my songs.'"

"Why that sonofabitch!" Elvis leapt from his chair. "I was singing that song way before anyone even heard of Engabertel Humferdinkel or whatever the hell his name is. And what were you doing with a guy like that, anyway?" he demanded, turning his full wrath on me.

"I told you. I went to his show. I was just one out of a whole group of people at the reception, that's all."

"Well, damn it, Joyce, it could have been something where that wasn't 'all.' You gotta learn to be less trusting with these show-business people trying to impress you."

As often happened with Elvis, I didn't know what to say and so said nothing. There was ironic humor in Elvis Presley, of all people, chastising me for being in a situation where a star could make romantic overtures to me, but that irony obviously was lost on him. I didn't laugh because that might hurt his feelings and, of course, none of the others would dare. Also, let's face it; I was extremely flattered by his outburst. As Karen, who had looked on silent and saucer-eyed, put it in a whisper:

"God, Joyce, he was actually jealous."

As if to prove her right, Elvis came over then and, politely excusing himself to Karen, took my hand and led me to one of the seating areas in the huge living room. Never letting go of my hand he sat us down on a sofa and drew me close to him. That was when I felt his leg quivering.

"Elvis? What is it?"

"Happens sometimes, baby. When I'm windin' down after a show, y'know?"

I didn't think anyone else could see it. I only knew because he had pulled me tight against him. "You're sure there isn't something bothering you?"

"No." He shook his head. "Not really. So . . . uh . . . anything to this Humperdinck stuff?"

"Don't be silly, Elvis. You know the answer to that."

I sat back a little and looked at him. The tremor in his leg was now a lot more noticeable.

He noticed. "It's a back and forth thing," he said. "Part of the highs and lows, y'know? The cycles of havin' to get myself up to do the show, then comin' back down again after." He took his hand from mine and began to twist and turn each of the several rings he always wore. "Those entrances I make that they were talkin' 'bout before? I do 'em to keep from getting bored. That's why I change 'em. The same stuff every night, man! You know what I mean? Hey, those funky plastic angels they got hanging all over the showroom? I might just have one a them fly me onstage next time . . . in a tux. Like that crap they had me do on Steve Allen."

He had been speaking much faster than usual. He stopped abruptly and got up and stepped behind the sofa to signal his guys to begin clearing out the suite.

It was only moments later that I felt his arms come around me and heard him whisper, "I need you to be with me tonight, honey. Please go to my room. I promise I'll be right there."

I knew he was going to ask. Still, as much as I had been hoping it would happen, I felt a hot, nervous flush come over me. When I did not get up immediately, Elvis sat back down and looked deep into my eyes. I rose without a word.

Karen followed me out and I ushered her into the bedroom to tell her in private that I wouldn't be going back with her, but would be staying the night with Elvis.

"I figured you would." She nodded when I had finished. "He wasn't really sore about Engelbert then?"

"No, we straightened that out," I said, trying to usher her back out before Elvis arrived.

"Well, good luck," she said, heading for the door. "Joyce . . . ?" Karen hesitated, one hand on the knob. "Is everything all right? I mean, you seem a little, I don't know . . ."

"Everything's perfect." I smiled. "I'm just . . ."

"I understand—" she began when suddenly, the door was wrenched open from the outside.

"Well, did you tell her?" Elvis's voice was gruff. He seemed to stare right through me.

Unable to ignore a cue like that, Karen hastily thanked him for a wonderful evening and exited. He shut the door behind her and entered the bedroom.

I turned and walked to Elvis.

Chapter Six

"You stayin' or what?"

The four simple words struck me like a slap in the face.

"What?" I managed to gasp a single word.

"You're standin' there like you got one foot out the door." He marched right past me to the closet.

"How can you ask that *now?*" I had to stop for breath. I was so hurt my voice had broken and I was close to sobbing. He had never spoken to me that way before. It was as if he had suddenly turned into a stranger, flinging his words at me like a challenge.

But why?

Why at this moment of all moments, when I finally believed that he really wanted *me?* I stood frozen in that enormous, overdone room. The enormous, overdone master bedroom of the enormous, overdone suite the International Hotel had specially designed for him, and stared in disbelief. The piercing blue eyes stared back, hard and cold.

"What've we got here, darlin', a failure to communicate?" He shook his head. "I'm just usin' plain simple English."

Wham! Another slap in the face. "It wasn't just your words,

Elvis." I cleared my throat, knowing I had to pull myself together, to get across to him how he had made me feel.

"It was the way you said them, like you were sneering. Is that what you wanted? Were you trying to hurt me?"

"Hey, I thought I was doin' the askin' here?"

His tone was still harsh. My lip began to quiver and I bit down to make it stop, and to keep the tears out of my voice. "And I'm *doing* what you asked. How could you, of all people, doubt I was staying when you asked me to come to your bedroom?" My voice softened. I felt myself moving closer to him.

"Well, that didn't come as any shock, did it?"

"No. You know I wanted you to."

A part of me may have wanted to from the first, but my basic insecurity had kept me out of his bedroom until now. I'd had the standard sexually repressive Catholic upbringing not only at schools staffed by nuns, but also at home, which was staffed by a dad who was a sergeant on the vice squad and a mom who could have been. This seemed to bring out Elvis's romantic gallantry, inspiring him to kind of put me up on a pedestal and court me. Until now.

I stood there hoping he would stop rummaging around in his damned closet and say something, *any*thing, make a joke of it, laugh at my having overreacted. Then take me in his arms and tell me he had only been kidding.

I looked over at him and there it was—just a trace of the famous crooked grin. Maybe everything will be all right after all, I told myself. I felt my heart skip a beat. I reached out and took his hand and smiled into his eyes. I could still feel some of the dried blood on his hand where his fans had scratched him.

"It's just that I want it to be special with us, Elvis," I said.

"Then, little darlin', maybe you oughta calm down 'stead of actin' like you're perched on the edge of some big ol' cliff."

The accusing look had come back and turned the blue eyes to ice. "Well, you're kind of making me feel that's about where I am," I said and looked away only to find myself staring at the huge bed. Canopied and draped in green and white, it *also* had been placed on a pedestal, from which its regal expanse dominated the room.

"You always act like you got one foot out the door, always ready to run. You've gotta learn to put your trust in me. You didn't have any trouble trustin' Egghead Hungerdickle. No trouble at all makin' up your mind to go see him."

I didn't blow up and point out that going to someone's show was a little different from climbing into someone's bed. I reminded myself that this beautiful man in front of me had just gone through the terrible ordeal of performing with some lunatic threatening to shoot him onstage.

"Elvis, if I didn't trust you," I asked, "would I have come all the way out here from Washington to be with you?"

"You're like one of these 'liberated' women, worryin' so much 'bout who *you* are that you can't really see the man in front of your own eyes."

I was stunned by the force behind his words. Still, I had come this far and not to be honest with him was impossible. "Elvis, I know who I am . . . or, at least, who I'm *not*. I'm not some little starlet who gets caught up in the glamour and stardust and glitter of the kind of life you lead and winds up being your latest conquest, bandied about in all the gossip columns or—"

"Joyce," he said, and his eyes held mine so that I couldn't look away.

"Do you remember that first night, the night we met? I told you I wasn't into conquests and starlets and . . . uh . . . I think I've proved it, too. Now, you gotta stop acting like you know best, you gotta let me show you the real me, you gotta put your faith in me."

"Damnit, Elvis, you had to know I was ready to . . . to love you, really love you tonight. You scared me, Elvis. The way you changed so suddenly . . . like you didn't really care."

"You can't always be questioning me, Joyce."

"But I don't, Elvis, not usually . . . this time it was just that you turned so suddenly."

"There you go again. I'm tired of people tellin' me how I am, or how I'm not. How they think I'm different, how they think I change from one time to another. I'm always me. You got to believe in . . . in the things I'm able to see ahead for us."

"What does that really mean, though?" I had the bit in my teeth now, surprised at my own strength. "You say there are things you see ahead for us. But what place, really, is there for me in your life?"

I knew I should stop, that I was going too far, but I couldn't. "What 'us' can there possibly be when you—"

The way his face darkened, he must have sensed what was coming. But I couldn't hold back. The words were burning a hole in my gut.

"—when you have a wife?"

"This is ridiculous." He turned angrily away and strode across the room to the dresser. "I don't know what else I can say that I haven't already said," he muttered through gritted teeth.

I was watching him as though I were a spectator at an event, looking at something that was happening to someone else.

He ripped open one of the drawers. "If you're gonna stay, then stay!" he exploded. "And get this on and get into that bed." With that he stormed into his bathroom and slammed the door behind him.

I stood there stunned as my whole world spun crazily away from me, the black silk pajama top he had flung in my face still dangling from my shoulder.

I glanced wildly around that overblown, overdecorated room, noticing crazy things like the rug being a different color than the other rugs in the suite, while the realization dawned that it was ending between us—ending before it really began.

I didn't know what to do. A part of me wanted to go and pound on that bathroom door and demand . . . or beg . . . or what?

I brushed the silken, flimsy thing from my shoulder onto the floor and trod disdainfully across it on my way to the door. I yanked the door open and slammed it behind me as loud as I could. And hated myself for hoping he would hear it and come rushing out to stop me, arms outstretched, whispering words of . . . what? Of love.

That did it. I felt the first, solitary tear slide down my cheek as I reached the main door of the suite. Furious at revealing my hurt, I flung it open and slammed it shut so hard it brought the armed guard outside to his feet, his hand on his holster. Still blinking back the tears, I pounded the elevator button until the car finally came.

There was one consolation anyway. I had "walked out" on Elvis Presley. As the doors slid open and I stepped inside the Muzak cocoon, it struck me that this would probably go down as the most pathetic consolation in history. But someone was going to be told, even if it was the wrong someone. I leaned back through the still-open elevator doors and forced a smile I surely did not feel into the unwavering watchdog glare of the guard.

"To hell with Elvis Presley," I said.

The doors closed shut.

Chapter Seven

"Forget it ever happened, Joyce."

I had wasted no time in catching the first flight Karen and I could get back to Washington, but my sister, once she heard what had happened with Elvis, had wasted even less time in giving me her advice.

"Get him out of your system *now*."

Just seeing her there waiting in the airport had brought home to me how much I needed her, and I had begun pouring my heart out even as we embraced. All through the drive to my place she listened intently to every word of the events that had led to my grand exit. Between my sobs of despair and flashes of anger, she responded with the solace and sympathy that only she, from whom I can conceal nothing, could provide.

By the time we arrived at the apartment, my sister's logic seemed undeniable. And final.

"Just remember," she said as we stepped inside, "it's *his* loss. Not yours."

I needed that, too, her strength.

"He's the one who—"

"Right," I interrupted to reassure her. "Don't worry, Janice, I'm going to try to forget him."

"Try? Joyce, 'try'? Don't you mean you *will* forget him?"

"I mean there's no point in trying to kid myself," I said firmly. "You don't actually 'forget' Elvis Presley, not even after he behaves like a jerk who *should* be forgotten. If for no other reason than he can't be avoided—unless I'm somehow going to avoid the entire twentieth century of radio, jukeboxes, newspapers, magazines and television and spend the rest of my life as a hermit in a cave."

Janice smiled in spite of herself. "Well, just remember you got along without Elvis Presley for twenty-four years before you ever met him, and you'll get along just fine without him for the next twenty-four. And the twenty-four after that."

"Sure," I admitted. "Except I'll miss like hell how good he made me feel, even by just talking to him. But after last night . . ." I went into the bathroom, splashed some cold water onto my face and hurried back out to help her with my luggage. "Damnit, Janice, when he and I are together . . ."

"*Were* together, Joyce. You have got to forget about him, period." Her voice was stern, a "big sister" voice. "Of course the good times are going to be the hardest part to give up and to forget."

During the months to follow, my work kept me from dwelling on what had happened between Elvis and me in August. The atmosphere on Capitol Hill can be that intoxicating; you always have that sense of being at the epicenter of power, the place where the Movers and Shakers move and shake and, if you let it, or if you want it to, it can numb you to almost anything else that is going on in your life.

Just before Christmas I was looking over the Naval Court of Inquiry report on the *Pueblo* incident when my phone buzzed. I thought Diane was calling to remind me of my promise to help her with what she was working on for our investigation of the Defense Department's worldwide communications network.

"Wrong." She laughed. "There's an interesting-sounding man on the line who's looking to communicate with you."

"Who?"

"An unidentified man."

It was my turn to laugh. It's so easy to fall into the Washington jargon. "Did you say 'an unidentified man'? Is that like the 'unidentified sources' that are always being quoted around this town?"

"With one important switch; sources *give* information. This guy wanted some. First thing he asked was if you worked here."

That piqued my curiosity. I pressed the lit button.

"Is this Joyce Bova?"

"Who are you?"

"My name is Jerry Schilling. I'm a friend of Elvis Presley."

Whoa. That got my adrenaline pumping. I didn't say anything, though, and he went on. "It's because of Elvis that I'm calling. In fact, he's here in Washington. He's been . . . he wants to see you."

After the initial shock I gathered my wits. It couldn't be a prank, it really had to be . . . All my carefully nurtured resolve went out the window. Only one thing mattered—but I had to be sure, had to hear his voice.

"If he really . . ." I forced a note of skepticism into my tone. "Put him . . . put Elvis on the phone."

There was a brief pause and then I heard his unmistakable voice and I felt my heart begin to pound.

"Joyce . . . are ya there?"

"Yes, Elvis. I'm here." The words came out in a hoarse whisper. "Is it really you?"

"Yes, silly, who else could it be?"

"But why . . . how?"

"Before you say anything, I have something to say. I want to apologize."

"What?" I had to be hearing things.

"Are you listenin' to me? I'm tryin' to apologize. Don't hang up."

"I'm here, Elvis. I'm not going to hang up."

"Yeah, it's true. I wasn't myself last time I saw ya. And I came here to find you and to ask you to forgive me for the lousy way I acted."

That really threw me—no, it knocked me out of my socks. Contrition isn't something you expect from superstars. Their lifestyles don't encourage accountability.

"Did ya hear me, Joyce?"

"I think so. I mean . . . yes, I heard you."

He chuckled. "Meanin' you heard but you're not sure you believe. I wasn't myself that last time, honey. You got to remember those death threats I was gettin' then, and the FBI everywhere, agents hangin' around and all. . . . Man, it was just an unfortunate time."

"I know, Elvis, and I do believe you and it's really great that you were big enough to call like this and apologize. Of course," I said, trying to be cute with him, "I deserve it."

"You do." Another chuckle. "Now, after all the trouble I went through to find you here—"

"How *did* you find me here, anyway? I never gave you this number."

"Goddamn, it wasn't easy. I had Schilling here callin' all over Congress lookin' for ya.

"How long have you been here?"

"The first time, a few days ago. But then I had to go to California. I wanted to ah . . . oh, hell, baby, I'll tell ya all about it when I see you. Just tell me where to send the car."

I hesitated. Not because I didn't want to see him, but because it was all happening so fast I wasn't prepared for how *much* I wanted to see him. And frightened that I would be opening myself up to more heartache.

"Now?"

"I want the chance to make it up to you, now that my little girl forgives me. Don't you want to see me?"

"It isn't that, it's that I know you. When you say you want to see me, you always mean right that second. And I can't get up and just walk out of this office."

"Okay, I know that. Tell me where and when and the limo will be there. And, honey? I really want to meet your twin. Think she'd like to come?"

"*Like* to?" I laughed. "I think I might be able to twist her arm."

I got home before Janice that evening. She had recently moved in with me after only a few months of marriage to her husband, Vince. My concerns about the ability of two people raised in such different worlds to make a life together unfortunately were proving true. I had barely begun getting ready when I heard the door, and then her footsteps coming toward my bedroom.

"Do you know that after you phoned I spent the rest of the day thinking about this and—Joyce?"

"In here, in my bedroom."

She followed my voice in. "Are you absolutely positive you want to put yourself through a thing with him again?"

"Janice, at this point I'm not absolutely positive about *anything*. But he did come all the way here to apologize. That has to mean something."

"Everything means something, but does this mean the same thing to him that it seems to mean to you? What the heck are you doing crawling around down there for?"

"Damn, I must've thrown it away." I got up from where I had been rummaging on hands and knees in one of the cabinets. "That frosty brown eyeshadow he likes so much. I wonder if it could . . ."

Janice rolled her eyes heavenward. "You have the most amazing capacity for changing instantly from a responsible, adult female into a gushing pushover. He makes one little phone call . . . Whatever happened to, 'I'd be perfectly content never to hear his name again'?"

"If I said that, it was talk. This is life. And whatever happened to *your* philosophy of 'seize the moment, it may never come again'? Don't you see," I said, wanting Janice to understand. "All the excitement, joy, and passion, everything that makes life worth living— I left behind that night in Vegas. I've been blocking that truth out of my mind, but the second I heard his voice, it all came rushing back. Once I knew he'd come here, Janice, that he had come all the way here even after I walked out on him, well, I'll bet he's never done that before. It means a second chance for us to find out if it's really meant to be."

It was massive Sonny West, Elvis's genial, bearded body-guard who opened the door to suite 506 of the venerable old Hotel Washington. He did a double take when he saw the two of us, looking from Janice to me and back to Janice again, his broad, welcoming smile growing even broader. He ushered us in, at the same time calling out, "All right now, E, which one is Joyce?"

Elvis, already headed toward us with his arms spread wide, stopped and stared. "Damned if I know," he exclaimed. He looked at each of us in turn. "Hold on here, I do know." The curled-lip grin came. "I can tell Joyce by her smile, by the way she's smiling at me."

He strode across the hotel sitting room and wrapped his arms around me and kissed me. "Good thing I was right, man," he drawled. "Guy picks out the wrong woman in this spot and he could get slapped."

"Twice!" Janice couldn't resist teasing.

We all laughed and I introduced her to Elvis.

"Damn," he said, taking her hand. "I wouldn't have thought it possible for so much beauty to be in one family."

Janice, formerly the stern Big Sister, matched him compliment for compliment. "I wouldn't have thought it possible for you to be even more gorgeous in person than on the screen."

"That's nice to hear, 'specially the way I been feelin' these last days . . . not exactly 'gorgeous.' "

"What's wrong?" I put my hand on his shoulder. "You look wonderful to me." I smiled. "I love your outfit. Black really looks great on you. You know, the way it goes with your hair. . . . You're smiling. What did I say?

"Did ya ever hear of Tom Mix?"

"Who?"

"He was a cowboy star, back in the silent days. My momma used to tell me about him from when she was a little girl and saw some of his movies."

"Sure, I recognize the name, now," I said. "But I don't understand . . ."

Elvis grinned. "He had hair like mine, and the same way I do, too. He used to hold up his little brush and bottle of black hair dye and say, 'The Good Lord intended me to have black hair and I'm certainly not gonna blaspheme 'gainst the will of the Lord.' That's the story this old-time makeup man at the studio told me about him one morning while they were gettin' me ready for my scene."

By this time Janice and Sonny were chatting away like old friends on the other side of the room and Elvis had led me over to the sofa. " 'Course, Tom Mix dyed his hair cause it was graying," he said, sitting down and patting the sofa for me to sit next to him. "Which I don't."

"No, I guess everybody knows you just decided to change the color of your hair," I agreed. "You also like to change the subject," I kidded him. "When it's something you don't want to really get into, like what was wrong that you were feeling down?"

"Oh, that was nothin'. I just had a bad reaction from some medication that irritated my eyes was all."

I sat as he directed and he took hold of my hand and did his thing of looking directly into my eyes. He began to tell me, his voice so soft and mellow, it was barely above a whisper, how he had come to Washington to find me.

"It all started out," he confessed, "with this argument me and Daddy had. Then Priscilla got into it."

"Priscilla?"

"The whole thing was about business, really. Or money, which usually amounts to the same thing. It was an unfortunate situation and I had to get off by myself to weigh and analyze it. The Colonel came into it, too," he added.

He paused then and seemed to be brooding about something. Not knowing what else to do, I sort of prompted him by asking, "Colonel Parker, your manager?"

He nodded. "You know, my momma seemed to really like the Colonel," he said. "Ya gotta have trust, though. . . . Yeah, that was part of what Daddy and I fought about . . . the Colonel . . . There is lots of bits and pieces there . . . But I don't know, maybe Daddy was right. I mean about business and things of that nature . . ."

He stopped short again and seemed to have lost the thread of the point he had wanted to make.

When he started in again, although his voice remained quiet, it was obvious he still felt strongly about certain of the events that had set him off.

"Mostly, though, accusations were cast. Against me. That's where Priscilla joined in. That's where dollar signs flashed, with Daddy, too." I felt his hand tighten on mine. "I can't be put in that position," he said. "I can't be always looking over my shoulder."

He made a waving-away gesture with his hand as if to dismiss the unpleasantness once and for all. "I felt so down that I just had to get away," he said. "I knew I wanted to be with you, that I had to see you again."

I started to say something, but he shook his head to silence me. "It wasn't that easy a thing, either. I'd just walked out, ya see.

I don't think they, either one of 'em, believed I could do that, you know? Just walk the hell out, all on my own. And get myself a ticket and take the damn flight right here to Washington, by myself."

It was revealing, and a little unsettling, to hear Elvis Presley recount with unmistakable pride, a "feat" that most of his contemporaries would take for granted, and that millions of his fellow citizens, from teenagers to grandmothers, accomplished regularly without any fanfare. But at the age of thirty-five, a millionaire many times over, he had never been on an airplane by himself before this trip to Washington, and though it was, I suppose, a small thing, it brought home to me with a poignancy that events more far-reaching might not have, how different it was to be "Elvis." It was wonderful, of course, in the sense of being full of wonders other people could only imagine and envy, but it was also, in a lot of small but vitally human and meaningful ways that I would continue to discover, awful.

"That was a few nights ago," Elvis said, "but once I got here I could tell that finding you was gonna be a job for more than one man."

"Why didn't you just call me? Didn't you bring my home phone number with you?"

"No. I . . . uh . . ."

"You lost it didn't you," I said, and laughed because I could understand that happening easily enough.

"Yeah, I . . . no, damnit, Joyce, truth of it is, I threw it away. I was so damned mad after you walked out on me in Vegas that night, I tore it up and threw it away."

"Oh." I didn't laugh, but I could understand that, too. Maybe even better. "So that's how come you had to call me at the office," I said finally.

He nodded. "Right. Took another plane out of here and flew all the way out to California to get Schilling to help," he explained.

"And he was the one who found me and called me, this Jerry Schilling? Is he here?"

"I sent him back to California after I found you and got Sonny here."

"Elvis, it's just hard to believe that you made this trip to Washington just to find me. I mean, I'm sitting here, listening intently, but it's still hard for me to grasp. You say you had a fight with Priscilla and your daddy and you're here because of it . . . but I don't really understand that."

"Well," he said, his voice still very low, very soft, "I'm just trying to tell some of the things that led up to me coming here."

I pressed on, still confused. "I mean, I'm not sure I understand why you're here at all, why it's *me* you . . . you . . . you're with. You're married and you have a family."

I was beginning to hate the sound of my own querulous voice. I was also becoming more and more flustered. And I knew why. Deep down, it was obvious as hell and I didn't want to face it. I had almost blurted it out, almost asked him why it was me he *wanted,* but had chickened out.

The man had searched for me and found me, done things he had never done before in his entire life so that he could be with me, and all I did was continue to ask him for explanations.

The answer was so obvious: He wanted me.

This time we had come down to it for sure and it was high time that I decided once and for all whether I wanted him.

Elvis must have sensed my inner turmoil. He placed the tips of his fingers gently on my mouth, saying, "Joyce, don't be upset, just hold on and let me start at the beginning when we first met. I was immediately attracted to you, your looks, you know, the dark exotic type. But you were different." He had dropped his hand from my lips and put it in one of mine. "When we talked that night," he went on, "I could tell right away you were different. You weren't after an evening with Elvis Presley, if you know what I mean, you know, to brag to your friends and all. Like taking a souvenir home."

He was so sincere, so intent on opening his heart and soul to me, that I could feel even my deepest reservations melting.

The quiet comfort of the traditional, rather staid accomodations provided by one of the capital's oldest and most respected hotels was conducive to this. It was in direct contrast to the conditions under which I had seen him every other time—the turbulent atmosphere of Las Vegas, bursting with the nervous energy of his performance.

"Now, about Priscilla," he said at last, taking a deep breath after that long pause. "I guess you deserve an explanation there. I've known her since she was a little girl and I . . . uh . . . taught her how to dress and act and everything. She's a wonderful girl, but lately we're just drifting apart. We don't spend much time together. When I'm in Memphis, she's in California and, when I'm on the road, she's home takin' care of Lisa Marie. She's a good woman, but the marriage is about over, otherwise I wouldn't be here now."

At that moment there was a knock at the door and Sonny stood, saying, "Room service" as he went over to open it. Elvis leaned across then and, putting an arm around my shoulder, kissed my neck as though he were sealing a pledge with the gesture.

I squeezed his hand in response and then got up to help with setting out the soft drinks and snacks that had just been brought. Janice and Sonny now joined in and talked with us as we ate and drank, but Elvis did take the opportunity to make one last remark in his low, private voice: "That about answer your askin' how I came to find you here in Washington?"

I nodded. "I'm satisfied," I conceded.

"That's real good," he said, suddenly squaring his shoulders and chest and lowering his voice even more dramatically. "Now I can tell ya'll how it was I decided to call President Nixon."

"How you *what?*" Janice was staring, first at him and then at me.

"Yeah," he continued, "it was when I was flyin' back here with Schilling that I got the idea."

I turned to Janice and saw she was trying to muffle a laugh. "Elvis," I said, trying to keep my own face straight, "what idea? What do you mean, you decided to call the President? What for?"

"An appointment." He was deadly serious. "I figured if I could see him today, then—"

"Today?" Janice looked from Elvis to me. It had been years since she worked on Capitol Hill, but Janice knew as well as I did how difficult it was to get *any* appointment with the President of the United States, and that getting one immediately was virtually impossible. "C'mon, Elvis," she challenged, "you're making this up, aren't you? You don't have to impress us," she teased good-naturedly. "I'm already—"

"Shucks, ya can see right through me, can't they, Sonny?" The curled-lip grin spread and became a full, cat-who-ate-the-canary smile. He stood, marched across the room, took something from a table and turned to hold it up to us.

" 'Cept I wonder then, how I got this?"

It was a badge from the Bureau of Narcotics and Dangerous Drugs and it certainly looked to us to be the genuine article.

"Elvis," I said, "you actually met with the President?"

"Nixon, man," he said, nodding and pacing at the same time. "I knew he'd want to see me. He's a smart guy. I knew he'd be glad I wanted to help him."

He palmed the badge and sat back down alongside me, still extremely animated, glancing at the badge as he spoke.

"That sonofabitch, Finlator, man, he didn't want to give it to me, but Nixon, man, he made him."

"Finlator?"

"Met him first, the deputy director, told me I couldn't have it," he added, putting the badge away. "The President's a good dude, man. He knows I can get to the kids and tell 'em what's goin' on with drugs."

Chapter Eight

It seemed Elvis and I had barely begun to scratch the surface of all the things we needed to say to each other when I saw my sister looking at her watch.

"You know I hate to be the one to break up a party."

Elvis turned to look at her then and she smiled in apology. "But if I don't get back home and get some sleep I'll never be able to get up and go to work in the morning."

There was little doubt that so far we had all spent a nice, warm, chummy evening, a fun evening, but I was watching Elvis and when he turned back to me I could see there was *no* doubt in his mind that the night would belong to us alone. It would be *the* night.

"Will you stay here with me tonight?"

I can't claim I was surprised. I'd been waiting for and wanting it, too. But still, that it was Elvis Presley saying those words took my breath away and I found myself just staring at him.

"You know I've come here to show you how really sorry I am for what happened in Vegas." He moved in close then, his voice very low, very husky. "To show you how much I want to be with you." He took my hand and I squeezed his in return, smiling up into his eyes, still not answering with words. There was no need. Like all the best answers to all the best questions, he knew what it would be before he asked. And so did I.

"I'll need to get some things, though."

"Well, tell ya what." He beamed. "Let's all of us take your sister home first."

"That will be perfect," I said.

There had been a downpour and the Baltimore-Washington Parkway was wet and treacherously slick and we soon found ourselves in bumper-to-bumper traffic. A car had been hit and it had skidded across both lanes to end up perched at an odd angle off to the side.

"There's a woman lying across the seat." Elvis was leaning out the window, his face lit by the flashing lights of a police car. "Pull over, man," he yelled to Ben Guervitz, the limo driver. "I wanna see if I can help."

"Hold on, now, E, you sure you—"

Deaf to Sonny's protests, Elvis was out the door before the limo had even stopped, with me hot on his heels. I thought I might be able to help him and I didn't want to miss out on any extemporaneous, bonus adventure. Up ahead I could make out the shiny rain cape of a policeman. Elvis was heading directly for him, shouting.

"Officer, can I help with anything? I'm Elvis Presley."

The policeman turned and I saw the stunned expression on his face as he saw Elvis. He stood rooted to the spot, his flashlight shining up, drops of rain dribbling down from the peak of his cap past his staring eyes and wide open mouth. Elvis shrugged and left him standing there. He walked right over to the car and when I caught up to him I could see a woman, alone, sprawled across the front seat, and apparently conscious, her eyes open.

Elvis knelt down beside her. "Hi-ya. How ya doin?" he began in what he tried to make an especially cheery tone.

It was hard to know how dazed and disoriented the poor

woman was, but like the policeman she, too, just stared at him without responding.

"Are you in pain, ma'am?" Elvis asked finally, reaching out to touch her gently.

I could see her mouth working.

"Ask if we can get her anything."

"What is it, ma'am?" He touched her, again very gently.

"She's trying to say something."

"Just relax, ma'am, and tell me what you need."

At last the words came: "Are you . . . really Elvis Presley?"

"Uh . . . here comes the ambulance now," said Elvis, suppressing either a smile or look of amazement, I wasn't sure which.

I heard the siren myself then and saw that a second policeman had materialized to direct the traffic around us, waving the ambulance in with his electrified baton.

"You're going to be all right," Elvis announced, standing up.

I started back toward the car and almost bumped into Sonny who had come up behind while we were concentrating on the lady. Trotting through the heavy, wet mist, I couldn't resist a last glance at the first policeman. He was still staring. "Hey, miss!" he shouted. "What is this guy, some kind of nut?"

"Maybe," I called back, "but he also *is* Elvis Presley."

I got in with Sonny right behind me, but when we turned around we saw that Elvis had detoured to direct the other lane of cars around the accident before making his dash past the ambulance crew who by then were all out and gaping at him. He paused only to inform them, "It's okay, boys, I think she's gonna make it."

Looking into the expectant faces of my sister and Ben Guervitz, I just couldn't resist. "She's going to make it, all right," I seconded, "but when that poor lady first looked up and saw Doctor Elvis, she was sure she had died and gone to heaven."

They all laughed, and none harder than Elvis himself, who

had jumped in just in time to catch the punch line before we drove away.

He wouldn't take no for an answer when we arrived at my apartment complex. "No way, I've got to come up and see where you live, honey."

The apprehension I felt as the four of us climbed the stairs to my little third floor, garden-style apartment, apprehension about how my modest living accommodations would strike him compared to what he was used to, was immediately dispelled the moment I finished giving him the Cook's tour. With the wonderfully unpretentious air that came so naturally to him, he just smiled and said, "You've made a beautiful home, here, Joyce."

Coming back out of the bedroom with my overnight bag, though, I found him standing by himself in the middle of the living room just staring into the lights of the little Christmas tree we had put up. I wondered, inflicting some pain on myself, if the sight made him homesick for Graceland and his family.

"Can I get anyone something?" I asked, partly to break the serious mood.

Sonny shook his head. "No thanks."

"Maybe just a Coke?" Elvis answered. "You really do have such a nice place here," he continued, still looking around and following me toward the kitchen until he was distracted by the sight of my record collection.

"Thanks," I said, struggling with the ice tray.

"Glad to see ya have some good music here," he offered, picking his way through the albums.

"Oh, yeah, that's right, there is a lot of you, isn't there?" I brought him his Coke. "I told you I had good taste." I excused myself to get something I'd forgotten from my bedroom.

Once there, I walked over to the window, opened it, and looked out. Down below, the long, sleek limousine was waiting, its engine idling. I drew a deep breath of the cold night air. Waiting there for me. For us.

In the living room Sonny was now seated on the sofa and

Elvis had moved over by the sliding glass doors that led onto the balcony, listening to Janice extoll the pleasures of our little suburban abode.

"We really do like it here. Joyce even has a really good view of that grove of trees. You can see it when it's not dark!"

Elvis nodded politely, then, seeing me, asked where the bathroom was.

Janice took the opportunity to let me know that her misgivings about Elvis had been allayed, at least for the time being.

"I have only one regret, actually," she remarked as we heard the sound of the toilet in the bathroom.

"What's that?"

"That I didn't have nerve enough to ask him not to flush."

"Janice!" I could hear Elvis coming out.

"Think of it, 'Bov,'" she went on. "You know how fanatical Elvis fans are? Your bathroom could become a shrine."

"Good night, sister."

"I'm going to walk you down," she whispered, "and the password is: Seize the moment."

It may have been 2 A.M. but that didn't stop Janice, as Elvis and I climbed into the back of the car, from shouting:

"Wow! Elvis Presley in a limo! Can't you blow the horn to wake the neighbors so they can see us?"

"I think you just accomplished that little detail all by yourself." I leaned across and kissed my beautiful buffoon of a sister good night.

The ride back to Washington and the hotel passed in a hazy blur. The heater must have been on because I remember the side windows fogging, but mostly I remember the warmth of Elvis alongside me and the funny little spark that seemed to be going on and off inside that made me feel flushed and giddy, almost as if I were in a dream. This is going to be a very special night, I told myself, one of those nights you remember the rest of your life. The whole thing was intense, the anticipation, all of it, all magnified by who the man was, by the inescapable fact, drawing closer with each passing second, that I was about to make love with Elvis Presley.

Once we were inside the suite I excused myself to get ready. In the bathroom I undressed until I stood naked before the mirror. Was I too skinny? Or maybe too fat? I stared at my reflected image until I noticed every imperfection. All of a sudden my stomach began to flipflop. I drew a deep breath and tried to compose myself.

The tile floor was cold against the bare soles of my feet, and I shivered, slipping into the beautiful light blue satin nightgown I had borrowed from my sister's wedding trousseau. My hands moved to my breasts, barely brushing the delicate gown, but shaping it to conform to my nipples and then down both sides of my body outlining every curve, all the way down to the swell of my hips. I pressed in against my queasy stomach, trying to clench it and quell the nervous somersaults. I took another deep breath, said a silent prayer that I was doing the right thing and, closing the bathroom door behind me, stepped into the dim light and cool air of the bedroom.

I felt a chill through the flimsy nightgown as I walked slowly toward the bed. Why was I so nervous? In some ways I was young for my years and afraid my nervousness was apparent. Besides, there isn't any handbook to consult about making love to a world-famous celebrity, the object of a million women's sexual fantasies. It was one of those times a woman just has to hope she can handle the decision she has made.

Elvis was sitting on the edge of the bed and wearing red silk pajamas. He smiled and stood up when he saw me—an adorable smile that not only reassured me but also sent my temperature and heartbeat soaring.

He spoke first. "You're beautiful, Joyce."

"You are, too," was all I could manage to say.

"It was great meeting your twin," he offered, trying to put me at ease.

"It was great for *me* that you two hit it off. I knew you would and I know she had a wonderful time. It made me feel especially good that you wanted her to be here tonight."

"Well, I have to . . . uh . . . confess that I had kind of a motive there."

"What do you mean? What kind of motive?"

"Let's just say I understood that until your twin gave her, y'know, blessing to us, you . . . well . . . you wouldn't be able to give yourself to me."

He reached out and took my hand "Y'know?"

Things were moving fast. I could feel my heart starting to pound. I squeezed his hand with both of mine in silent agreement, then took them away, turned around and sat down on the edge of the bed.

I looked up to find him standing over me and smiling deeply and lovingly into my eyes. "Your twin is that other part of you, Joyce. The part that I lost, y'know, when I was born and my little brother, Jesse Garon, died. But I still have part of him inside me in ways. That's one of the reasons I understand. A lot of life has to do with changes . . . and with understandin'," he added.

When he didn't continue I wanted to break the silence and kidded him a little about whether he had actually come to Washington especially to see me as he claimed. "Or were you also planning to see the President all along?"

He held his palm up. "Swear I didn't think of seeing him till after I was here and couldn't find you. Like I said, it was on the plane coming back with Schilling that I got the idea 'bout Nixon. Started writin' a letter to him right then and there."

"Well, you *did* find me, that's the important thing. And I am truly glad that I got found." I smiled at him. "After all you went through to find me, I promise never to ask you again: 'Why me?' "

He sat down on the edge of the bed alongside me. I thought about how much I wanted to reach the man inside the glittering star. It could not be an ego trip for me; there would never be any reality in that. I would have to search out the real him—and remain me, somehow.

"You're my sweet, pretty little girl," he whispered and leaned over to put his mouth softly on mine. "You know I love you, you silly thing, don't you?"

I think I murmured, "No," once, but it might as easily have been "yes." It would be the last word I spoke aloud for a long time.

He pressed his lips gently to my neck. "If you really want to know 'why you'. . ." His voice came softly in my ear. "First off, you're a beautiful woman and you're a pure little girl, too, aren't you?"

I touched my fingers to his lips. I didn't need to hear any more. He understood and pulled me in tight to him.

"Joyce, I know this is new for you, but it's right, believe me."

My brain was whirling, but I knew it was no time to disillusion him with confessions. In a way he was right, it would be "new" for me—an intensity of passion never known by the good little Catholic girl who had stayed out of trouble and turned into the determined little career woman who was about to find plenty of it.

He moved me to the center of the bed, then stretched his body out alongside mine. Snuggling up to him, I put my head on his shoulder and then slid my leg over his. I was hungry for him, hungry for the whole experience, for the fullness of it. I was sure I had never known anything compared to what was about to happen.

We kissed and touched each other with soft, gentle caresses, on and on, making time stand still. There was just gentleness at first, our passions restrained, and still I wanted more, still more. He stopped and smiled. "You're really lovely. And so delicate," he murmured.

"Not too skinny?"

He chuckled. "You're exactly what I want. Besides, I happen to like skinny girls," he teased sweetly.

I loved his playfulness. It made me want him even more, but I fought to hold back my desire. He had to take the lead, and I knew that. Lying so close, I longed for him. My body ached for his, but I did nothing, not even speak. He sat up and leaned over me. I was putty in his hands, hands that cupped my face to kiss it, then stroked my hair. He nibbled at my neck and sent a shiver racing up my spine.

When he motioned for me to undress, I did so obediently—slowly and timidly—until I was naked in his sight. He looked at me, caressing me first with his eyes and then with his long, slim fingers. My eyes followed his hands as they moved over my body, exploring all of me. The temperature of the air in the dimly lit room seemed to rise with the heat of my body.

"Elvis," I whispered, "I want to feel you next to me."

I reached up and tugged at his pajama top, trying to pull it off. He resisted at first and I thought for a second I was being too aggressive. In another second I didn't care. He was rolling over on his back and pulling me onto him. I helped him unbutton and wriggle out of his silk pajama top and was reaching out to do the bottoms when I saw on his face a shy, almost boyish expression that was so unexpectedly charming and at odds with his public image, that it endeared him to me all the more.

Finally the bottoms also joined the heap at the foot of the bed. I could hardly believe it was happening, but he was completely bare now. I wanted to wrap myself around him and squeeze him as hard as I could. I pushed myself up off his chest and looked down to see the entire naked length of him.

Thin. God, he was thin, much thinner than he looked with clothes on. But there was a strength in him, too. A strength that suggested a power that went beyond mere muscle, sinew, and bone, that was derived from some deeper source, from the driving force that had made him, from his will.

"You *are* strong," I ventured, squeezing his biceps. This was the Elvis I wanted, and I pressed my chest back down against his, wanting his warm body against mine. He wrapped his arms around me, holding me tight. Our lips met in a kiss. I shuddered with the electric excitement of our embrace. I don't remember thinking or even breathing. I felt nothing, and yet I felt everything—all my nerve endings screaming with tension, his heart beating against my breast, his weight heavy on top of me.

Still, I wanted more.

Finally I moaned and was almost embarrassed by it. It was just that I wanted to show him that my body welcomed his—no, ached for his. There was no other word for it but happiness. It went beyond mere gratification. I experienced a sweet, soft, serene glow of real happiness. Our rhythms grew more intense, the surge mounted, and his final, muffled explosion filled me with a sublime joy.

Even though it had not happened for me, I knew he could make it happen and that this was the way love was meant to be.

A siren wailed outside in the cold, wet streets. I pressed my naked body against his, our passion beginning to cool and chill the sheets beneath us. The sun must have risen, but if it had, I just barely sensed it. The fervid sex that had made him famous had, in reality, been gentler, a sweet and tender passion.

I could hear the radio still playing faintly in the sitting room; just as there had been one playing the night he first kissed me. Poised in that twilight cosmos between dream and desire, I wondered if he heard it as well, wondered what visions music brought to Elvis Presley. Did it echo songs of timeless triumph through all the worlds and palaces he had conquered before me . . . who lay naked in his arms?

Chapter Nine

I slept fitfully. Through the remaining hours of the morning, I woke over and over to see him, Elvis Presley, lying beside me, and I would relive what had taken place between us. We had done it, finally done it, shared ecstasies and ultimate intimacies. I was content—but I was young, and hoped for still more, for a spiritual bonding that would match the physical. You could not miss the spiritual need in Elvis, even in the throes of passion.

When I woke for good I lay for a while just watching his chest rise and fall before I got up and walked to the phone.

They weren't thrilled at the office when I told them I was not feeling well enough to come in, sick days being frowned upon in the committee. I didn't care. I wanted to be with him for as long as possible.

About an hour later, after showering and dressing and making a vain attempt to wake Elvis, I returned to the living room and called for Sonny.

That bear of a man, his long, shaggy crop of hair dripping water and showing signs of having only recently been put into some semblance of order, just shook his head when I expressed a slight concern over having gotten no response, even when I tried shaking his boss.

"Nah, don't wake him," the big bodyguard advised, closing the door to his room behind him and walking into the living room with me. "He always sleeps late. Nothin' to worry 'bout. He'll probably get up soon. How about you? Feel like some breakfast?"

"I *am* a little hungry. Think we could get some coffee and Danish sent up?"

Just as it had been with my sister the night before, in almost no time at all we were sitting around talking like old friends while we ate breakfast together. Sonny was the kind of guy a girl—especially a girl who had no brother at all and a mostly absentee father—wished she could have had around during those formative years when you need someone to lean on and stand up for you. Sonny was easy to talk to and, watching him move his brawny body around the room while keeping up a steady stream of humor and pleasant small talk, I couldn't help but be struck by how innately decent and likable he was. I sensed a bred-in-the-bone consideration for others in this man who, as I was also keenly aware, often had to earn his daily bread by intimidating or even physically assaulting people. There would be no shortage of extravagant paradox in my years with Elvis (who raised the term to a higher level all by himself) but no nicer one than Delbert "Sonny" West, the man Elvis felt would lay down his life for him at the crack of a pistol.

When Elvis did finally saunter into the living room that afternoon, the first thing he said after, "Good mornin', honey," was, "How come you're up?" It was my first indication that Elvis wanted my body next to his in bed—even when he was unconscious.

"Had to call my office," I explained. "To let them know I wasn't coming in."

That seemed to satisfy him. "Good girl. Want some breakfast?" he asked, leaning down to kiss me.

"We already had a little something, but I could order you

something from room service. Or would you rather we went out and got something?"

"I think we better order from room service," he said, chuckling. "I don't think I should go walkin' around here. Me, you, and Sonny might cause some commotion."

"Jon Burrows, suite 506 . . ."

I could hear Sonny placing the order over the phone.

"Elvis, who's Jon Burrows?" I asked.

"That's me, honey. You don't think I can register under my real name, do you?"

"No . . . I guess I just didn't stop to think about it."

"Most people wouldn't. They take for granted the fact that they can go shopping anytime or anyplace, and not have to worry about what'll happen if they go out to a restaurant or . . . shoot, maybe I *should* go out. Incognito or something. Maybe put on a mask to look like Sonny here. Then nobody'll recognize me!"

Sonny laughed and I joined in. "Yeah," I said, "I guess being famous does have its drawbacks."

"Hell," he went on, seeming to enjoy a rare opportunity to expand on the disadvantages fame and adulation can bring, "I can't do anything so simple as go to a movie or take a walk in the park. I've never even *seen* the inside of a bank. Most of the time I feel like an animal on display in the the zoo."

"Poor baby," I commiserated. "What a price to pay for fame and fortune."

"It can be *un*fortunate," Elvis responded, choosing not to notice that my tongue had been planted firmly in my cheek.

"The only *un*fortunate thing about your life, Elvis, is that you can get anything you want."

That took him back for a second but then he answered in the same bantering tone. "Then how come it was so hard getting a certain cute little Italian girl?"

"Which reminds me . . . How did Chick single me out to meet you that first time in Vegas?"

"Silly girl, you know the answer to that," Elvis said flippantly. "I get only guys with the best taste to—" He saw my eyebrows go up and hastily changed course. "I mean, it's not what you think, the way it sounds. But when the guys see somebody that . . . Oh, hell, now you've got me on the spot. I don't mean the ones that throw themselves at me . . . But I do need a woman to relate to. . . ." He blushed so adorably, I leaned closer and put my fingertip to his lips.

"You're like a little boy sometimes," I whispered.

"And you're my little girl. As soon as I saw you that first night, I knew right away. And ever since, gettin' to know you, I've never stopped feelin' you're special. You know what I mean? I need more from a woman. I need someone to share things with her."

His eyes had strayed past me on these last words and almost involuntarily, I glanced around. But we were alone. Sonny, discreet as always, had brought in the tray from room service and then made himself scarce while Elvis was talking.

It was the middle distance into which Elvis was staring. Staring and not seeing. At least, not seeing what he was searching for. A mysterious stillness seemed to have invaded him, and though a part of me hated to break into it, another, stronger need made me speak.

"You're telling me you need me, Elvis, do you know that?" I whispered.

"Figured I'd already showed you that." He smiled.

"It's the loneliness," I said after a moment. "I hadn't realized about the loneliness until now, really."

"What d'ya mean?"

"Just that there is a lonely man inside the star, a lonely man searching for something."

"We're all doing that," he said simply, "even when we don't know we are."

"But *you* know, and when you said you needed someone to share things with, that's what revealed it to me."

"And do you know what it is I'm searching for?"

"Not yet," I said.

But I thought he might be searching for what he had lost, or never had, with Priscilla.

"For now it's enough for me to know that the man I care about has opened his heart and admitted he needs me."

He took me in his arms then and we spent the rest of the afternoon like that, huddled and cuddling in each other's arms on the sofa, watching TV and listening to the radio, with Elvis murmuring all those sweet endearing words into my ear that a woman wants to hear at such a time, until . . .

Until, as always with us, as it always would be with us, one or the other had to leave.

This time, of course, it was Elvis and Sonny who were catching a plane.

The limo took us all out to the airport where Elvis took me in his arms and kissed me goodbye.

"I really loved being with you, Joyce, and I don't want to go now, but I have to, y'know. This is only the beginning though, baby, I'll be back in a few days. I'll call to let you know."

Despite everything that had happened between us, despite the passion, the exhilaration, the love, in spite of everything that had meant so much, no matter how hard I tried I could not stop myself from examining the small, narrow reality of it once I was left without him. It seemed I had no choice during the limo ride back from the airport to my place but to face reality, reality in this case being the cold, hard gnawing fact that Elvis was headed for Graceland, headed home for Christmas.

It was a deadening thought and it enhanced the "Alice Through the Looking Glass" mood I felt when I walked into my cozy little apartment, so ordinary and familiar to me. I felt as though I were stepping back from the Fantastic into the Mundane. But weren't Elvis and I "real," I asked myself, slowly changing my clothes.

Because of all the fantasy elements that were built into his life, I knew how vital it was for me, if I was going to keep a grip on anything, including my sanity, to deal with my relationship with Elvis realistically.

Unfortunately, I react to things emotionally, not analytically, and by the time I heard my sister opening the door, I had gotten no further than to comfort myself with the observation that as far back as when we lived in caves, men and women had begun carving out a reality for themselves by making love to each other—and that at least Elvis and I had made a damned good start in that direction.

"Joyce," Janice began before she had even gotten out of her coat, "how was it? Your eyes say it all, but tell me anyway."

Sometimes that ESP thing we twins have between us can be a pain in the butt. That was one of those times.

"All right, but let's take it slowly. I'm still trying to digest it all myself," I said. Janice followed me into the kitchen where I got us a couple of sodas from the refrigerator. We sat down across from each other at the table.

"First, practical matters," I said, sliding her drink across to her. "He wants me to have another phone put in here."

"Another phone?"

"It would be just for him, so he can get through to me without ever getting a busy signal."

"Uh-hunh, I get it. He wants total control, even over the lines of communication. An Elvis Hotline."

"Janice, easy on the sarcasm, please. I really am very happy. Please don't spoil it."

"I'm sorry, honey." Janice got up and put a pot of water on the stove to boil. "You're right. If you're happy, that's what really matters. Speaking of being so happy, what did you two do all day? And, more importantly, what did you do all last *night*?

"Well . . ." I watched her measure out the pasta. "You know, we *are* lucky to have each other to share all this with, Janice. I'd go crazy if I didn't have you to talk to."

"I agree," she said. "But now I'd like to know what comes after the 'Well . . .'"

"Well, *first* of all, Elvis is a true romantic," I said. "This time he wasn't at all arrogant or off-hand like that last night in Vegas."

"No throwing pajama tops?" She slid the thin noodles into the bubbling pot.

"Janice, he was so tender and romantic. I mean, he wasn't macho or overly aggressive or anything." I got up and got the sauce out of the refrigerator and started to set the table. "I just know that what he needs is somebody to care about *him.*"

"I'd have thought from everything you told me that's just what he has too *much* of."

"He's got plenty of people at his beck and call, all right, but that's not what I'm talking about. I mean, Sonny is really devoted to Elvis, naturally. In fact, to tell you the truth, sometimes I don't know how he can stand being at Elvis's command every second of the day. Of course, they all are. It reminds me a little of the Hill, the way so many of the people up there are ready to jump through hoops at a congressman's whim. But at least those people have ambition. They're doing it to climb up the bureaucratic ladder. But the boys in Elvis's entourage, well, sometimes they just seem like slaves almost, afraid and nervous they might say the wrong thing or answer Elvis in the wrong tone of voice, or . . . I don't know, maybe I don't really understand enough about it and it isn't as bad as it looks to me."

Janice looked carefully at me. "You think it might be a bad sign," she said, "like he's got a hidden mean streak or something? The reason I ask," she added, bringing the colander out to drain the pasta, "is because of that remark you made: 'that what he needs is somebody to care about *him.*' I got the distinct impression from your tone that you were applying for the position."

"Well, I do think that's what's missing in his life; I felt that's what he's searching for."

"Still searching, or does *he* think he's found it in you, too?"

"He told me he loved me. Maybe I'm being naive, but I believed him. It's love he wants, Janice, intimacy on a one-to-one basis. That's what he needs."

"As much as he wants and needs the applause and adulation of his fans?"

Janice set the steaming pasta down on the table.

"There's no doubt he's got plenty of that, all right. He *is* Mr. Superstar. I know I can't get away from that fact, but no matter who you are, real love is not an easy thing to find. What more can I say?"

"Nothing. You make it sound wonderful. You make *him* sound wonderful. I just hope it stays that way. And God," she said, digging out a forkful of the hot, slippery strands, "I hope he's for real."

The sudden sadness in my sister's voice settled like a dark cloud over the meal. Janice was worried about me, when the truth was, *she* was the one who was suffering, who truly needed to be comforted. She was going through hell, knowing that she really had no alternative but to end her marriage to a man she loved but dared not live with, and yet, like so many of us, hating to give up, to admit failure. I ached for her, watching day by day as her complexion turned sallow from lack of sleep, the fine, delicate lines of her face drawing taut with worry.

Even if life with Elvis should turn into a fun-filled romp from morning to night, I could never be completely happy unless my twin was, too. I felt she had enough on her mind without my concerns adding to her burden and I changed the subject so that for the rest of the evening we made small talk—about work and clothes and plans for the coming holidays.

It wasn't until I was getting ready for bed that Elvis came up again. I had just come out of the bathroom when Janice looked up from where she was watching television.

"So, what happens next?" she asked.

"Well, he did admit that it was probably going to be tough for me, arranging the time to see him and all." I walked on into my bedroom. "But he said for me not to worry, that everything will work out."

Those last words seemed to echo in my darkened room and I turned right around and walked out and over toward Janice. I waited until she looked up again.

"Do you think it will?" I asked.

"I don't know," she admitted. "I only know I'll do anything to help you. I love you and want you to be happy, no matter what. Just don't worry about it now."

"Yeah, you're right." I headed back to bed. "No point in worrying now."

Christmas has always been my favorite time of year and even though Elvis and I would be apart, the joy and excitement of the season was heightened, anyway. It's almost impossible for it to be otherwise when your heart is bursting with the dawn of a special love. That Christmas Eve, my apartment crammed full of family and friends, I was bubbling over with yuletide spirit to the point where I was sure everyone present could read my private thoughts just by glancing at my face.

Although Elvis had never asked me to, I had already made the decision to be discreet about our relationship. AnnMarie and Karen, having been with me in Las Vegas, had some idea, of course, but there was nothing to gain by flaunting the relationship except a certain dubious notoriety since, in the eyes of the world, Elvis was still a happily married man. Casting myself in the role of "other woman" in a show-business triangle would not go down very well with my congressional superiors in a town where the outward *appearance* of probity counts more than true morality, and the gossip and rumor mills cater unceasingly to the most sordid—and voracious—appetites.

I had broken this self-imposed rule only once and that occasion came to mind the day after Christmas when, family and friends having long since departed, I was sitting alone with just a touch of postholiday depression setting in. And missing Elvis, missing him all the more because I couldn't talk to anyone about him. Janice was trying to resolve her own relationship with her husband and really needed much more to talk about her problems than to hear about mine.

It was in this mood, then, feeling a little bit lonely, a little bit down, that I recalled that slight indiscretion, probably because now, with Elvis so deeply ingrained in my life, it seemed rather comical and lightened my mood temporarily.

It was near the end of the first week in October (and therefore a month or so after Elvis had flung his pajama top at me in Las Vegas) when Murray Kaufman had called my office to ask if I would like to see a young comic who was, "really knocking them dead; the hippest, grooviest stand-up to come along since Lenny."

I felt I could use some cheering up, but arranged to meet Murray at the club itself as a way of emphasizing that I was not his date.

The Cellar Door was in Georgetown, and the young comic who did monologues of black street life, acting out in turn a gallery of pimps and winos, poor souls, and would-be hustlers, then flashing back and forth between them and his own adolescent years, was Richard Pryor.

After the show we were having a sandwich in some little place nearby when Murray said out of the blue:

"You know, sugar, you are definitely not your usual perky self tonight. Matter of fact, you sounded like you were on a down trip the last couple of times we talked on the phone. Something bugging you?"

"What do you mean? What makes you say that?" I asked defensively. Nothing gets me uptight more quickly than somebody I'm not close to trying to get even the slightest peek at my inner thoughts.

"Hey, lighten up," he said, signaling the waitress for the check. "I say that to you because you're a terrific br-uh . . . terrificly bright young person. I mean, what is Murray Kauffman all about, if he isn't about dealing with young people. My whole life has . . ."

"Murray," I said, cutting him off while I could, "I appreciate it, but it's nothing, really. It'll sound stupid even to hear myself say it out loud."

He spread his hands, palms up. "What are friends for if you can't tell them the stupid stuff, too?"

I shook my head and finished my soda. "I don't know, Murray; I've kept it to myself all this time and, to tell you the truth, there really isn't anything to say anymore. It's really over."

"Except that it's not *so* far over that it hasn't turned into a real bummer for you."

He waited until the waitress had brought the check and departed before going on: "That could be a big part of what's bugging you—keeping whatever it is bottled up inside for too long. Let it out. I mean, what have you got to lose? I might even be able to help. You know, this ain't my first rodeo."

What the hell, I told myself; the man obviously *has* been around. I ought at least to show him the courtesy of listening to what he has to say. He only wants to help and maybe he *will* have some decent advice, some words of wisdom, something that will help me finally come to terms with whatever the hell it was I thought I was doing with Elvis Presley.

"Do you remember that I told you I had met Elvis Presley in Las Vegas?" I began. "Well, I didn't tell you the entire story . . ."

He waited until I had finished with a complete account, ending with my walking out of the bedroom in the International. Then, he shook his head.

"What is the matter with you, baby? Do you have any idea how many women in this world would have wanted to be in your shoes?"

"In them, or *out* of them?" I inquired dryly.

"Whatever. Do you know how many women would give their right arm for the chance to go to bed with Elvis Presley?"

"Murray," I interrupted. "None of those statistics are available to me, so you can stop asking."

My sarcasm rolled off him like water off the proverbial duck's back.

"I'm just trying to point out that you made too big a deal out of it, that's all."

"I thought you were pointing out that it *was* a big deal; or at least *would* be to all those one-armed, barefoot women."

"Joyce, cast your mind back to the time I took you to see Engelbert. Don't you realize that's what I was trying to get across to you? In a subtle way, naturally. If you'd played it right, you could have had the same chance that night."

"Wonderful, Murray, just wonderful," I said. "That's the sum total of your advice? Play my cards right and men will take me to bed? Somehow, the wisdom of that is lost on me."

On that note my brief acquaintance with the old Rock 'n' Roll disc jockey came to an abrupt end. As did my *tristesse* on that 26th of December when the telephone in my apartment rang.

"Hi. It's Elvis. Presley, that is."

"Oh! It *is* you!" I cried. "I'm so glad to hear your voice. How are you? Where are you? You're not here, are you?" I asked in a rush.

"No, but I miss you, honey, and I wanted to wish you a Merry Christmas."

"Yeah, it is Christmas . . . and I miss you, too, Elvis."

"I hope you're bein' a good girl. And what about your sister? How's she doin'?"

"Not great," I admitted. "Her husband won't let her go. He keeps trying to get her to forgive him, showing up with tons of Christmas presents . . . I feel sorry for him, I really do. But the bottom line is that he's putting her through hell."

"That's terrible, Joyce. I feel bad for her . . . and for you, too."

It was nice of Elvis to be sympathetic. I was always uncomfortable bringing up anything unpleasant with him. Sometimes I wondered if it was because of his celebrity status. Did I have a subconscious stake in preserving the illusion that Elvis dwelt in a special, untroubled universe? Whatever the reason, I quickly changed the subject.

"Hey, I think you should sing me a Christmas song."

"This is gettin' to be a regular coast-to-coast feature of our phone calls." Elvis laughed. "Okay, here goes."

Elvis began to sing.

> *I'll be home for Christmas, you can count on me*
> *Mistletoe and eyes aglow and candles on the tree*
> *Christmas Eve you'll find me, where the lovelight beams*
> *I'll be home for Christmas, if only in my dreams.*

"That was beautiful," I said when he'd finished.

"Just for you, darlin'. Did you have a nice Christmas?"

"I have now."

"Well, now . . ."

I refrained from asking about his Christmas. I didn't want to know. I wanted him with me.

"By the way," I said, as cheerfully as I could, "I have a present for you. They're installing my Elvis Phone tomorrow."

" 'Elvis Phone', hunh?" He chuckled. "What's the number?"

I told him.

"Good girl. I'll call you soon. I promise."

A few minutes later, we ended the conversation and hung up. I was happy. As happy as I'd ever been.

"Soon" turned out to be only a few days later.

My newly installed Elvis Phone rang and I picked it up to hear, not Elvis, but a man named Gee Gee Gambill. I'd met him at dinner in Elvis's Las Vegas suite.

"I'm relaying a message from Elvis," he said. "Elvis and Sonny will be in Washington, D.C., tomorrow afternoon."

"What time? I need to know because I have to figure out what to do about my office."

"They'll call you tomorrow," he said, and hung up.

At five o'clock the following morning, my Elvis Phone jarred me into consciousness.

"Hello?"

"This is James," a strange voice informed me. "Elvis and Sonny will be at the Hotel Washington later this morning, and Elvis wants you to meet him there in the same suite at eight o'clock."

I knew it would be impossible for me to go back to sleep, so I got out of bed and padded into the kitchen for a cup of coffee. Janice heard me and joined me.

"What's up?" she asked, yawning.

"I'm going to meet Elvis around eight at the hotel. Help me pick out something to wear, will you?"

"At this hour?!? You might as well go in your nightgown!" she teased.

"Janice, stop."

"Okay, okay. How about what I got you for Christmas?"

"Mmm. Those black wool pants with that adorable black and pink, bulky knit sweater? Fabulous."

But by the time I finished my shower, I had remembered with some misgivings all the work that I knew was piled on top of my desk.

Janice was turning on the television to catch the early-morning news when I emerged from the bathroom.

"Something wrong?" she asked immediately. Twins just have *no* secrets from each other.

"Well, I'll tell you . . . To begin with, I have reports of hearings that haven't been edited yet, and the cases that have been investigated still need to be updated. Then there are also a bunch of classified documents that have to be 'sanitized,' not to mention a couple of missing files I ought to go in and find."

I began to put on my makeup, still figuring out loud, partly for my sister's benefit as well as to ease my own guilty conscience. "Maybe, just maybe, I could be a little late for Elvis and stop by the office and make about a half-dozen of the phone calls that should be made today . . . while I searched for those files and . . ." I looked up to find Janice standing there.

"They just gave the weather report." She shrugged and gave me a wan little smile. "Heavy snows are being predicted."

I stared at myself in the mirror. "The hell with it," I said. I put the final touches on my makeup. "I don't care if we're buried in a blizzard and the entire government grinds to a halt without me. Nothing is going to keep me from him."

Chapter Ten

It was exactly eight o'clock on the morning of December 30th when I arrived at the Hotel Washington and found Elvis and Sonny already waiting in Suite 506/507.

I noticed almost immediately upon entering that Elvis was not himself. He had none of his usual vibrancy and vitality and after the three of us made conversation for a while, I had to ask him.

"Elvis, is something the matter? You seem so listless."

"Nothing. I was up all night, that's all, honey. I just need some sleep and I need you beside me." Taking my hand, he led me into the bedroom and once again we were alone together.

Elvis sat me down on the bed. He stood over me and said, "I missed you." Then he leaned down and kissed my mouth.

I kissed back, fervently. Then I reached up and wrapped my arms around his neck and pulled him down onto me. I felt the long, strong length of him pressing into my body and the heat flooded through me, rising from my core to meet and envelop him.

And then there was only his weight on me.

A dead weight.

I opened my eyes. I saw that his were shut, the lids very dark.

After a second they fluttered open. "Honey, let's get some sleep," he mumbled.

In mute, instinctive protest, I began caressing his back when abruptly, he brought his closed hand up, first to his own mouth and then, extending his open palm, toward mine.

There was a tiny, round, purple capsule nestled in it.

"What's that?"

"Joyce, take this."

"What do you mean, 'take this'? What is it?"

"It's called Placidyl . . . just a little something to relax you."

"I don't want to relax . . . I'm relaxed enough now." "It's the start of the day for me, Elvis. I've been up only four hours. I'm not tired."

"That's just it, honey," he insisted. "I need to sleep and I need to know you're sleeping beside me. Anyway, if you take this, you'll feel a lot better when you wake up. Then we'll have the rest of the day and all night together. Believe me," he went on, "it's not gonna hurt you. I wouldn't do anything to hurt you. You're my little girl and I love you."

I was still reluctant, but Elvis was very persuasive. And he knew it. He reached over to the pitcher on the night table and poured me a glass of water. I took it, placed the capsule on my tongue, and swallowed.

It took effect with unbelievable swiftness. Within minutes, I was experiencing a sensation I had never felt before: my body felt absolutely weightless, suspended in space; at times it seemed to be spinning in midair. At the same time, another part of my brain knew that I was lying there like a corpse, unable to move a muscle. Even my eyelids felt frozen in place.

"I want to give you uh . . ." Elvis, stretched out alongside me, began to murmur.

"What?" I managed to mumble.

". . . uh . . . Christmas present. What kinda car'd ya like?"

His slurred words seemed to echo in the room—probably

because my head seemed hollow. "You want to give me a Christmas card?"

"No. A *car*."

"Don't want a car." I started to shake my head but quickly realized that was a major error. "Don't want anything. Just want you . . . not . . . things." I tried to tell him that I loved him for himself—not for his wealth and fame—but the words came out in a voice that didn't belong to me.

And that's all I remember until Elvis woke me that evening and I realized he had been right about how I'd feel—great, absolutely invigorated.

As for Elvis, he was a new man, bursting with even greater energy than usual. At dinner, his eyes seemed to sparkle as he announced his plans.

"Some of the guys are comin' up from Memphis, Joyce, and we're all goin' over to meet Hoover tomorrow."

"Hoover?"

"Yeah, the FBI Director. J. Edgar Hoover is a real live hero, man. I got a lot to tell him. I want him to know that I feel the same way he does about Commies. We need guys like him."

He was deadly serious even as he joked with Sonny about the stir he would cause marching into the Justice Department with his own "agents." They acted out their entrance into the government building as if doing a scene from "The Untouchables." I knew the performance was for me and laughed along with them.

"But for tonight," he went on, "why don't you call Janice and ask her to come over?"

"Sure, that's a great idea."

"Good. Tell her we'll pick her up about eight."

My sister answered the door looking better than she had in days. Elvis answered her welcoming smile with his famous curled-lip smile and a big hug. Up on her tiptoes to receive his embrace, Janice smiled at me over his shoulder, trying to tell me silently how happy she was for me and that she was fine, too.

"You're lookin' beautiful, little sister," Elvis informed her.

After greeting Sonny, Janice turned to me. "Well?" she asked archly. "Did any of the neighbors get a look at you this time?"

" 'Fraid not," I said, "but on the way over I was thinking *we* ought to get a listen . . . to some Elvis music."

"Right. Your portable cassette player. Great idea. C'mon, Elvis, it's only appropriate that you give me a hand." Janice gave me a small wink. She knew what I had in mind.

While the two of them were collecting the eight-track player and Elvis picked out tapes, Sonny remarked on a photo-portrait of Janice and me hanging on the living room wall.

"It's beautiful." He shook his head. "But who is who?"

"Well," I said, "why don't you tell *me.*"

"All right," he said after a moment, "that's you and that's Janice."

I shook my head. "Sorry."

"Okay, but don't say anything. I'm gonna put E to the test."

When Elvis and my twin returned, Sonny was waiting for him. "Hey, E!" Sonny indicated the photograph as Elvis handed him the cassette player. "Look at this. Can you tell which one is Joyce?"

Elvis studied it, glanced at me, then at Janice, and back to the picture. Finally, he put his index finger right on the correct image. "This here is Joyce," he said.

"You're not serious," I bluffed. "How could you be so wrong?"

"I'm not," he said simply.

"All right, all right," I admitted. "But you made a lucky guess."

"A man knows what he knows." Elvis grinned. "Honey, I want a copy of this."

"You really like it that much? Okay, I'll get you one."

It was about nine o'clock when we all got into Ben Guervitz's limousine and started back to the hotel. Janice shook her head. "Damn, wouldn't you know? Not a single neighbor in sight."

We entered the capital on New York Avenue and as we approached the Bladensburg Road intersection, Elvis caught his first glimpse of what would become the site for one of the mythic tales about his life that was always springing up.

Amy Joy's Donut Shop was an all-night drive-in that served as a hangout for the local ghetto youth.

Just seeing Amy Joy's sign seemed to trigger one of those cravings for which Elvis was legendary and, despite Sonny's concern about the neighborhood, he blithely directed Ben into the parking lot, crowded, even at that hour, with young black men. The limo had barely crawled to a halt when about twenty of them bustled over to us, clamoring to know who was inside.

I could hear the first of them to reach the driver's side call out to Ben, "Hey, man, that must be some big shot you got in there."

Whether Elvis heard the guy, I don't really know, but he immediately rolled down his window.

If a chauffeured limousine was rare at Amy Joy's, one carrying you-know-who was unbelievable.

"HEY . . . IT'S ELVIS! . . . THAT'S . . . HEY, IT'S . . . LOOK HERE . . . YOU GUYS . . . IT REALLY IS . . . C'MON, MAN, THAT'S . . . ELVIS . . . ELVIS? . . . HEY, ELVIS . . . ELVIS . . . ELVIS!"

The magic name was shouted and called over and over, not only directly to him in homage, but to late arrivals, not yet able to see who it was, but coming on the run anyway, swelling the crowd to dozens of wildly yelling, pushing, laughing, shoving kids.

Elvis had stuck both his arms out the open window and was doing his best to shake each and every hand that was thrust at him. As soon as he realized that too many people had gathered for all of them to crowd in close enough to that cramped opening, he swung his door wide open and, overriding Sonny's shouted protest, stepped boldly into the now-frenzied mob. In a flash, Sonny followed, forcing his way through the ranks until he was at The King's side.

Elvis was in full Elvis regalia—white shirt with a high, open collar; gold chain around his neck; black jacket with padded shoulders; bell-bottom pants; rings on his fingers and sunglasses (even at night). He was instantly swarmed by scores of kids reaching toward his extravagant "threads."

With cries of: "Man, will you look at the outfit on the dude," and "Heavy, man, that is heav-*y*," or, "Sharp", or "Bad, *real* bad," ringing all around him, Elvis never looked more at ease, completely undaunted and obviously enjoying the hell out of the personal contact with his fans.

"Whatcha doin' *here*, man?" one of them asked.

"Just tryin' to get a few donuts," Elvis answered. "But thanks for remindin' me. Hey, Ben?" He leaned down to the driver's window. "How 'bout goin' in and gettin' us three dozen?"

When he straightened up and turned back to face the crowd, he became aware of how intensely his oversized rings and ostentatious chains were being checked out, and could not resist responding with an impromptu performance.

He held his hands up and took two steps backward to give himself some space, while commanding,

"Okay, guys, keep cool . . . and pay attention, now."

Every awestruck eye riveted to him, he slowly, tantalizingly opened his jacket to reveal the enormous, dazzling, solid gold belt he was wearing. Brilliant with diamonds and precious stones, it blazed like some wayward comet in that drab and dispirited setting.

A tremendous, collective "OOOOOOHHH . . . AAAAAHHHHH" burst from the wide-eyed crowd.

"This here was a gift from the International Hotel in Las Vegas, for breaking their all-time attendance record."

There was an involuntary surge forward by the crowd, necks craning to get a closer look at the gleaming trophy. One got close enough to reach out and actually rub it, mumbling to himself like some latter-day Aladdin wishing for his dreams to come true. Sonny, ready for anything, edged closer to his boss.

Then came the finale. Elvis took one more step back, his right hand inching inside the wide open jacket.

"This belt says I'm the best . . ."

In one lightning swift motion his right hand swooped to the concealed holster under his shoulder.

". . . and *this,*" he said, showing the gleaming, burnished-steel of the automatic pistol in his hand, ". . . says I get to keep it."

That brought a roar of laughter from those tough ghetto kids, along with a chorus of: "It's yours, Elvis . . . Sure, man . . . Okay, take it easy . . ."

Elvis, playing his role to the hilt, flashed them one last curled-lip grin.

"That's it, fellas."

He nodded to Ben, who had reappeared laden with donuts and, reholstering his automatic, climbed back into the car.

We sped away to the cheers of the throng, an exultant Elvis waving with one hand while wolfing donuts down with the other.

By the time we were ensconced back in the suite, he had devoured eight of Amy Joy's best, and seemed ready to party all night, spurred on by the arrival of the entourage he had been expecting from Memphis.

Their arrival triggered a high-spirited session of what we have now come to call "male bonding," with plenty of pranks and earthy, masculine humor.

"Hey," Elvis sang out at one point, "I've got an idea. I'm gonna call Carolyn." He turned to me. "You know Carolyn Jones?"

"If you mean the actress, I know who she is."

"She was in *King Creole* with me."

"I remember."

"She's a good friend. I'd really like you to meet her."

He got her number from one of the guys and went over to the phone. "I'm gonna ask her to come on out here."

"Where is she?" I asked.

"In California, I think."

"Elvis, do you really think she would fly clear across the country on the spur of the moment?"

"She's a good friend and a crazy one, you know. If I can get her on the phone she'll be here. I mean, I *know* it."

But Carolyn Jones wasn't home and, as usual, not being able to bear seeing Elvis disappointed, I immediately suggested inviting my friend, Katharine.

"I think you'll like her, Elvis. She's a pretty savvy girl; she used to book celebrities for interviews on Washington radio shows. We're close friends."

The high-school-football-team-reunion atmosphere was full blast by the time Katharine arrived and after introducing her around, I took her aside, whispered in her ear, and then led her back to Elvis.

"What's this I hear about your causing a near riot at a donut shop?" she piped up.

The King knew a cue when he heard one. His enthusiasm for the event had actually escalated; reenacting the entire episode, playing all the parts himself, he had a great time reliving and embellishing it for a fresh audience. Janice, Sonny, and I loyally corroborated his every outrageous exaggeration and self-aggrandizement.

It was no surprise that the vigor of his playing brought the always unbridled admiration of his guys to new heights, but I could see that even canny Katharine was not unaffected by this more spectacular version in which the crowd grew larger and more threatening, The King more heroic and dashing until, together, they reached epic proportions.

When the curtain fell at last, the cheers in the suite seemed to echo those in the parking lot. Katharine's expression was one of genuine amazement.

"But weren't you afraid at all? I mean, I'd be scared to death to drive through there at night in a *regular* car."

"Well, it had its dangerous aspect," Elvis allowed, "but, y'know, out of the corner of my eye I could always see and feel Sonny right there, lookin' like a big ol' tiger . . . And I caught ya, Sonny, when that one dude kept rubbin' my belt, sayin', 'No shit, goddam; wow, no shit. Man, for me to get somethin' like that I gotta *steal* it.' "

"He was nuts," Sonny observed calmly in his best, "I've seen it all" manner.

"You were ready to pounce, man." Elvis nodded for emphasis and turned back to Katharine and me. "And those guys knew it, too. Joyce, did ya hear that one say: 'Hell, look at that big fucker'? It was a wild scene, hunh?"

I looked up from where I had been putting a tape in my cassette deck.

"You were great, Elvis. But I think the only danger you were in was getting writer's cramp from signing autographs! Those kids loved you—"

"Joyce, listen," Elvis interrupted. "Your tape player. It's off-speed."

"It sounds all right to me."

My objection brought a chorus of concurrence from the Merry Men of the Memphis Mafia, all agreeing that only Elvis, with his exceptionally keen ear, could detect the slightest flaw.

"Well, gee, I'm sorry," I said. "But I'll bet if it were somebody other than *you* singing on that tape, you wouldn't have said a word."

"That's okay." Elvis laughed. "I . . . uh . . . guess I might even sound better that way." He turned to his grinning cohorts. "That's what you guys are *really* thinking. Man, you are all crazy. But I can think of a lot of singers who *would* sound better if they speeded up the sound track."

That brought some knowing laughter from his guys and prompted Katharine to ask, "But who do you *like*, Elvis? Is there any contemporary male singer that you listen to and really dig?"

"Yeah, sure. Tom Jones, for one. I like his style and he's got talent. Y'know, when I first heard him, I thought he was black."

"Didn't a lot of people think *you* were black?" I asked. "When you first started making records, way back when?"

"How can *you* remember, 'way back when'?" Elvis grinned. "Yeah, some of those black people I heard were an inspiration to me. A lot of them were just singin' for themselves . . . in the fields, their houses, church, but their music got to me. Even when I was just a kid. I think most black musicians are more talented than white ones."

"How about, 'In The Ghetto'?" Janice asked. "That was a big hit for you. It sounds like a song a black man should have done, don't you think?"

"Yeah. Sammy Davis, Jr. wanted to record it. But they thought I had a better—better feelin' for the song. Ya know what I mean? And I do. I grew up in a ghetto and they really knew I could do it with more guts, ya know?"

It was about one o'clock in the morning when I walked Katharine and my sister down to the hotel garage. Katharine had offered to drive Janice home and I was grateful not to have to make the round trip in the limo with her.

In the elevator, Katharine shook her head, "I find all this hard to believe, but, my God, he is neat!"

I had to smile at her choice of expression, but, actually, it could have been mine, too. Elvis kind of brought out the adolescent in us, I guess.

"And the thing of it is," she continued, "he really didn't seem to want us to leave."

"Well, I'll tell you," I said, "there's a kind of protocol. Guests are expected to remain in his presence until he leaves or until you are asked to leave. Politely, mind you, but definitely. Undismissed departure is tantamount to walking out on an Elvis show."

Katharine raised her eyebrows and nodded. "Well, all I can say is—it was a hell of a show, I'm really glad you asked me."

"I'm really glad you came. Oh, Janice, I almost forgot," I said. "I've got to give Elvis a copy of that picture of us he asked for, so don't let me forget."

"Here, you can give him the one I carry," she said, opening her wallet.

The suite was empty and silent when I got back. Elvis was in the bathroom. I changed into my nightgown and got into bed and waited.

Elvis emerged from the bathroom resplendent in silk pajamas. When he was settled beside me in the bed, he offered me his cupped hand. "Here, honey, take this. It'll help you sleep."

"No, I don't think I should, Elvis. I have to get up too early."

"But you're probably all wound up, and if you don't take it, you won't be able to sleep. Besides, honey, I've talked to doctors and know as much as they do about this stuff. I know what I'm doing. Now, just trust me. You do, don't you?"

Without another word, I swallowed the pill. What harm, I asked myself, could such a tiny thing do?

We were kissing, long, deep, passionate kisses, pausing only to exchange breathless vows of love, when I found the answer to my question. Gradually, deceptively, my brain numbed until there were no words of love left to say, no deeds of love to perform, no spark of love left to give. I drifted away to a never-never land where, if anything was done, it was done with a body I no longer possessed.

A blistering wind stung my face as I stepped from the hotel onto the street that next morning. It only made me feel more alive. "There's going to be a big snow tonight, miss," the doorman volunteered, holding the cab door for me.

Entering the austere Rayburn House Office Building, the beautiful, sleeping face I had kissed only moments before, lingered in my mind's eye. Once again, Elvis had been right about the pill. I felt great, livelier than I had in days. Approaching the committee suite, I prepared myself to respond with sincerity when asked how I was feeling after having been too sick to come to work the day before.

Since the Ninety-first Congress had adjourned, and the Ninety-second would not convene until the middle of January, there was not much business actually being conducted on the Hill in general, or in my committee in particular. I was able to get through my immediate workload like a veritable buzz saw. By two o'clock that afternoon I was racing down the massive marble corridors, on my way back to the hotel—and him.

I got to the suite just after Elvis and his crew themselves had returned. From a day at the Justice Department.

"We got the special VIP tour of the whole FBI facility, honey," Elvis informed me as an order from room service was being set out.

"And you met J. Edgar Hoover?" I asked while he held my chair.

Elvis shook his head. "Naw, the man was busy, takin' care of business and all. He sent his assistant director, though."

Elvis sat down opposite me, but was too excited to stay put for long—or to do much more than pick at his food, either.

"Man, I can help the bureau with gettin' drugs off the streets," he declared, starting to pace. "I'm somebody the kids'll listen to. I told them I would help them, you know. I mean, the guys here are already deputies. Joyce, honey, drugs are killers. If anybody can get rid of the stuff, Hoover can. He's a great man, Joyce. He knows what he's doin'. Damn, I wish I could've met him. Y'know, just to shake his hand and tell him what a great job he's doin' but, honey, he's a busy man."

He dropped into the chair next to me, looking extremely intense, boiling over with exuberance.

"These federal guys in there fighting every day to keep this country straight and safe from illegal drugs are real heroes, Joyce, real heroes.

"Y'know, this is a great country," he continued fervently, "a great country of opportunity. But there's elements right in show business, in the music industry, that promote the use of illegal drugs. That stuff reaches the kids, it has its effect. Joyce, I told 'em I was willing to do whatever's necessary to eliminate drugs. I can make a difference. I mean, I wouldn't stop at nothin'. Specially in my *own* business, y'know?"

He paused as if waiting for some response, so I asked, "What do you mean? What could you do?"

He shook his head. "I don't know yet. I gotta analyze and weigh. But I can tell you a few things that oughta be done. Those guys, the Smothers Brothers, they should be banned from television. And the goddamn Beatles? They're from England, they're not even Americans. They gotta be made to stop encouraging drugs. And put that Jane Fonda right on her ass in jail . . . and . . ."

By this time his guys were joining in with a chorus of assent, and I decided to try and lighten the mood a little. Reaching into my purse, I took out my wallet and opened it to the photographs inside.

"Here, Elvis, here's a copy of the photo of Janice and me you asked for."

"Thanks. Could I see some of those others you've got in there?"

Of course I handed him the wallet and stood by, smiling appreciatively at his comments as he went through the photos, passing them one by one to Sonny until he got to one of me in a bikini.

"Joyce, could I keep this?"

"Sure, if you really—"

"Hey, what's that? Who is that guy?"

"Oh, just a guy," I answered. "Someone I used to go out with."

"Why's it in here? Why are you carrying it around with you?"

"I don't know." I really didn't know. "Just the remains of a forgotten romance." I shrugged, disconcerted by his switch from sizzling patriotism to sexual possessiveness.

"Come with me," he said and, taking my hand, he led me into the bedroom and shut the door behind us.

"Sit down."

I sat on the edge of the bed while he alternated between standing directly over me and pacing back and forth.

"Joyce," he said sternly, "I think you should understand that you have to be loyal and faithful to me. I gotta be able to trust you completely."

He waited. I knew what he really meant, of course, and since he wouldn't say it, I did.

"What you mean is, if you sleep with Elvis Presley, you don't go to bed with anyone else."

I said what I could to assure him that he didn't have to worry, that I couldn't have more than one man in my life at one time, anyway. Then, indicating the photograph he still held, I said, "Steve doesn't mean a thing to me."

"Are you sure?" he asked. And then all the sternness and masterful posturing just seemed to drain from him and he repeated, "Really sure?" with such a vulnerable expression on his face that I stood up and just kissed him and kissed him, thinking what a head trip it was to have the notorious sexual revolutionary, the fantasy phallus of untold millions of women pleading with me to pledge my fidelity, to save myself for him and him alone.

We broke our fervent embrace. I saw, over his shoulder and through the window, enormous snowflakes beginning to drift down from the sky. "Oh, look," I said and pointed.

"They're beautiful," he said after a moment.

"Aren't they? But now I'm thinking that a part of me should hate them. They remind me that you're leaving tonight, and that with this blizzard coming you might even have to leave earlier than planned."

"Shouldn't. We got our own plane chartered."

"Elvis, maybe the storm will be so bad that you'll get snowed in here," I said hopefully.

"Can't, honey. I've gotta get back to Memphis tonight. But you're comin' with me."

"Oh, Elvis, it's a wonderful thought. But I'm not prepared!" I protested. "I don't have any clothes with me or anything. I left the office early, too, which means there's still unfinished stuff for me to do. And to tell you the truth, honey, I just don't want to leave Janice all by herself right now—"

"Hey, E," Sonny's voice interrupted from the other side of the door.

"The pilot just phoned and said we should leave right away to avoid the storm."

We just had time to exchange a smile and a shrug. Fate seemed to be against us.

Elvis opened the door and his guys piled in to pack the gear he toted around with him. I was just standing there, kind of sad, watching the innumerable philosophical and religious books and the gold-monogrammed EP sunglasses being gathered up, when Elvis pulled me off to the side.

"You know," he said quietly, "you're a little thing, and I've been thinkin' I don't like you drivin' round these streets unprotected. So, I want you to carry this with you."

He reached into one of the bureau drawers and brought out a small pistol and handed it to me. The second thing that surprised me—the first being, of course, just the fact that he wanted me to have a gun—was how light and delicate it seemed in my hand.

"Just in case. You never know. It's a .22 caliber, honey, small enough for you to handle."

"Elvis, I . . ."

"That's not all. I didn't have time to get you what I wanted to for Christmas. There really wasn't time, ya know. But I want you to have somethin' here, to buy whatever you want."

"Elvis, please . . . don't."

"Stop now. I want to. I'm just sorry it's rushed and last-minute . . ."

The brown envelope he handed me had printed on it: American Security and Trust Company. A plain wrapper bound the thick bundle of currency inside. It was signed, "To Joyce, with love." I was touched.

"But, Elvis, I mean it, I don't want this. I want us to be different. You know what I mean?"

"We are, we are. Here." He slipped an enormous ring from his finger. "I want you to have somethin' personal, too."

He placed the heavy chunk of gold with its two bars of onyx (one black, one brown) gently in my hand.

"Elvis, really, it's lovely and sweet of you. But you gave me *this* one when we met." I held up my hand. "I'm never taking it off."

"I hope not. Just wear it for as long as you love me."

"For as long as we love each other."

It was only a ten-minute drive in Ben Guervitz's limousine from the hotel to the airport, but in that time Elvis managed to come up with more rationalizations for my flying back to Memphis with him than an ordinary man might in a week. Finally, after the airport officials gave permission for the limo to drive right onto the field and up to the waiting plane, he played his trump card.

"At least make the flight to Memphis with me if you won't spend the New Year holiday. I uh . . . want you at least to *see* Graceland."

"Elvis, believe me, I wish . . ."

"Oh, come on, I'll have you flown right back afterward. If you insist, I can have the pilot turn around and bring you right back. At least we'll have a couple more hours together on the flight. You can do that, honey, come on."

I shook my head. "Elvis, I have never seen thicker, harder, faster falling snow. And I just *can't* take the chance of being snowed in and leaving Janice alone on New Year's Eve. Not *this* New Year's, not after what she's been through."

With a sigh, Elvis got out of the limo to board the plane. He waved for Charlie Hodge to come over. "Hey, Charlie, write down that number for Joyce."

"You can call this number anytime," Elvis explained while Charlie scribbled away. "They'll be able to get me, no matter what. We're not gonna lose touch again."

I read the number aloud. "Where is this, Elvis?"

"It's Charlie's service in California. Just leave a message for Charlie Hodge and he'll get it and tell me. Okay? And, here is my number in Memphis."

Charlie, Joe, Sonny, and Red each kissed me goodbye on the cheek and then waited dutifully while Elvis took me in his arms.

"Happy New Year, darlin'," he said and we kissed for the last time in 1970.

Then I stood in the falling snow, tears streaming down my face, and watched his plane disappear into the wet, white sky.

Chapter Eleven

Monday, January fourth, broke blustery and bitter cold across the Potomac. "Winds of change"—the phrase was running through my mind even before I threaded the last familiar stretch of parkway and, having made the obligatory right turn off of C Street, eased my big old blue Ford Galaxy into the space reserved for me in the cavernous garage carved deep into the loamy soil beneath the Rayburn Building. When Nell, the cafeteria cashier, greeted me with a friendly word about "business being back in full swing with a new year and a new Congress," I acknowledged her with a smile and a nod. Balancing my breakfast coffee and corn bread, I took a quick glance at my watch and jabbed the elevator button for the third floor. It was definitely not a day to be late to the office. It was a day to be wondering how long I would have an office to come to. The chairman of my committee, L. Mendel Rivers, had died and Armed Services was now to be chaired by F. Edward Hebert, Democrat, of Louisiana. Mr. Hebert would also chair the investigating subcommittee to which I was assigned, and since he had the power to replace any or all of the committee's employees, my immediate concern was whether any such drastic reorganization was actually in the works.

It soon became apparent, as that first week after the holidays wore on, that some of my colleagues in suite 2339 shared the same concern. There was a kind of nervous tension in the air, heightened by a general tendency to avoid long-range planning. That uncertainty was underscored by the number of casually discreet phone calls I became aware of other staffers making to their contacts in the various congressional offices—phone calls made just in case the ax should fall.

As it turned out, those fears proved unwarranted (I told myself, only half jokingly, that somehow the love Elvis and I shared cast a protective shield over everything in my life) when Chairman Hebert decided to retain the present staff.

A week or so later, a week in which Elvis had called with increasing frequency, I was sitting home one night in front of the TV, brooding over how I could be with him as much as he demanded and still fulfill my responsibilities to the committee, when the Elvis phone rang.

I walked over to pick it up, wishing I knew how to be both an independent woman as well as a loved and cherished one. I knew that to be complete, I needed both.

"Joyce."

Elvis started right in, without the usual exchange of greetings.

"I open in Vegas next week and I want you out there with me when I do."

"Oh yes, honey, of course I want to be there; it's just that it's a really bad time."

I was hesitant, hating to keep putting him off, caught in the middle once again.

"My subcommittee has just appointed another special panel besides the one that's finishing up My Lai, to look into the Defense Department's worldwide communications network and—"

"You just tell me who to talk to," he interrupted impatiently as if he wasn't listening. "I'll take care of it. I'll get you the time off."

"Elvis, please," I cut *him* off. "We're talking about an investigation into the central nervous system of the entire United States military. It's going to be a regular inquisition. They're talking about limiting vacation days and the new chairman, Mr. Hebert, has already let us know he will not look kindly upon anyone calling in sick."

There was silence for a moment on the other end, then:

"What if I talk to Nixon?"

Ye gods, I thought to myself. He might actually do it!

"Elvis," I said hastily, "your power may be limitless in *your* world, but not in mine. You can't call the President of the United States about *me*. I'm not a congressman. Everything here is ruled by the seniority system. I only started with this committee a little less than two years ago. I'm still just considered little more than a beginner there."

"Now, don't go worryin' yourself 'bout that, honey, I told you, Nixon's a good guy . . ."

"Please," I begged. "It won't be necessary for you to 'talk to Nixon'." I paused. "Elvis, I miss you terribly and I promise that when you open in Vegas I'll be there, maybe not exactly for the opening, but close."

It was even harder to arrange than I had anticipated, but by the beginning of February, I had worked everything out.

Joe Esposito called a few nights later to confirm things. Later I went to Janice's room to tell her about the arrangements I had made.

"I'm going to meet Elvis in Las Vegas."

She looked up from where she was sitting on the edge of the bed.

"And you're coming with me."

"What? I don't think I can." After a moment she added, "And I don't think I should, Joyce. I'd feel I was intruding."

"You wouldn't be. And I just told Joe Esposito you were joining me."

"Besides, I've got too many problems here to deal with," she argued.

"You mean Vince?"

She nodded. "He's still trying to get me to come back to him. The pressure he puts on me is . . ." Janice shook her head.

"All the more reason why you need some time away."

She opened her mouth to protest again but I knew her heart wasn't really in it. And she knew I knew.

"Not another word," I said firmly. "You're going and that's that. The worst that can happen is you'll enjoy yourself. Besides . . . I really want you to be with me."

Joe called right on schedule the following evening with the information that our prepaid tickets would be waiting for us at the TWA counter and that Elvis's stepbrother, Ricky Stanley, would meet us at the airport when we landed in Las Vegas.

This left one last matter to be attended to before we embarked on our trip together, and Sunday morning found us bound for the quaint old suburb of Ellicott City, Maryland. Janice was still shaking her head as I turned down the familiar street and pulled up in front of our mother's house, the house from which we had in desperation made our escape only a few years before.

"You know it's not that I disagree about Mom needing some attention from us now that she and Dad are separated," I said, "but do we have to drive thirty-five miles one way *every* Sunday to take her to church?"

"I figured of all the things we could do with her, this would make her the happiest."

"I know. That's what you said before. It's also the thing closest to what we had to get away from: Mom's rigid rules . . . and all the fighting between Mom and Dad. If she just didn't make us feel that no matter what we do it's not enough, I could be a little happier about making the effort. Well, I guess we're not kids anymore," I said, sliding the gear shift into park. "Maybe it's not too far to drive once a week to make her happy . . . but don't you think she could let up a little, too?"

Janice had stopped halfway out of the car. "Speaking of our not being kids anymore, you haven't told her about Elvis, have you?"

"Are you out of your mind?"

My twin nodded in silent agreement and climbed out of the car. When she got around to the driver's side, I was already on the sidewalk. "You'll have to someday, though," she said.

"I know."

"God, you'll get the entire morality sermon," she said, taking my arm as we started toward the house. "I can hear her now: 'He's a married man, you're committing adultery . . .' "

"I know."

" 'It's a mortal sin . . .' "

"Believe me, I can hear her already," I said and looked up to find the door being opened and our mother standing there beaming at her two daughters who had come at last to pay her the respect and attention she deserved.

One hour later, however, it was borne home to me in the most dramatic fashion that I was not *feeling* anywhere near so cavalier as it might appear from my outward demeanor.

"Janice," I whispered, "take Mom out to the car and wait for me. I'll be with you in a minute."

"What? Where are you going?"

"Confessimmm," I mumbled under my breath.

"What?"

"Confession," I hissed in a stage whisper that must have carried half a dozen pews.

"What!"

By then I was already on my way to the nearest booth.

"Bless me, Father, for I have sinned. . . ."

Was it my imagination or did my voice revert to the squeak of adolescence? Somehow I got through the first part and cleared my throat, while the shadowy figure on the other side of the screen concluded his part of the ritual and asked me to enumerate those "sins."

"Father, I have slept with a married man . . . a man who is famous. A celebrity." The word sounded even hollower spoken in a confessional.

"And who is this man, my child?"

"I can't tell you that, Father."

"But, my child, you have committed a mortal sin."

"I'm sorry, Father, I just cannot tell you his name."

"I see."

There was a pause.

"But you do understand that you have grieviously offended our Lord and that you must never see this man again, don't you?"

"I don't think I could keep that promise, Father," I answered, surprised by my own honesty.

"You must find the courage in God to turn away from temptation. Otherwise, I cannot grant you absolution for your sin. You do sincerely desire absolution, don't you?"

"That *is* why I'm here, Father, but I also love this man very much."

"My dear child, our Lord is merciful and his understanding great, but you must show that you love Him even more than you love this man by being truly penitent. You must promise."

What was I doing? How could I make such a promise? And yet, I found myself speaking.

"I . . . I . . . promise . . ."

"Then for your penance you will . . ."

"You'll have to find a Catholic church in Las Vegas to take Communion," was Mom's advice on the drive to her house, once she realized I had gone to confession.

"I guess so," I answered lamely. I was burning with shame, not for the sin of adultery, but for the sin of weakness, for having made a sordid, guilty thing of my love.

"Shouldn't be a problem." Janice winked. "Must be plenty of

churches there in Vegas, what with all those bustout gamblers desperate for any edge they can get."

I laughed, but I knew my twin would content herself with wisecracks only for as long as we were with our mother: The moment we were alone, it would be a different story.

"That was a speedy confession." Janice fired her opening salvo one second after I turned the car for home. "I seem to recall that certain sins call for penances like saying an entire Rosary, or even worse."

"I'm afraid the confessional is sacrosanct, my child, and that my penance is a matter between me and my conscience."

"C'mon, Bov," she admonished, trying not to laugh. "Come clean."

"I'm just mad as hell at myself. I actually stooped to lying in there, Janice. I had to want absolution as badly as I wanted to get away."

"And lying got you both? Lying about Elvis?"

I nodded. "Anyway, I really know better than to expect any answers about the rightness of what I'm doing from any place other than my own heart and brain."

"And me."

"And you," I agreed.

It was eight-thirty P.M., almost an hour later than originally scheduled, when our plane finally taxied to a halt after setting down on the long runway in Las Vegas, Nevada, that next Friday. Ricky Stanley was already there, of course, and already frantic. His mop of blond hair falling over his sweating forehead, the features of his baby face contorted with tension, he spotted us immediately and began pleading with us to, "hurry, hurry . . . please."

The more Elvis's poor stepbrother, who must have been all of sixteen, hopped around us, begging and crying that he had strict instructions to get us to the hotel, "right away, so you'll be in time for the early show," the funnier Janice and I found his entreaties.

"The plane was *late,* Ricky," we told him. "It's like an act of God. You can't be blamed for it." We laughed again at his obvious consternation.

Until we discovered that all our luggage had been lost.

"How could this happen on a nonstop flight!" I screamed at the young woman behind the "Claims" desk (Ricky trailing along, dripping sweat and, by now probably tears as well) before she could even open her mouth.

"We've got to have our luggage, right *now!*" I informed her in my most imperious manner.

"We're going to a show, you see," Janice added, opting for logic in her approach. "And we're late. So get our bags for us, *please!*"

"Can't you send someone back to the plane to look again?" was my next request. "I mean, my God, it *was* a nonstop flight after all."

The young woman just stared at us without uttering a word.

"Are you listening?" I asked.

"Don't you want to write this down or something?" Janice suggested.

She opened her mouth at last and we stopped our ranting to get her official response.

"You're twins, aren't you?"

Naturally, that set us off again—only this time into gales of laughter while Ricky merely sighed and mopped his brow.

The early show was almost over by the time Janice and I filled out all the claim paperwork and Ricky got us to the hotel.

"Please don't say anything to Elvis about your luggage being lost," he begged. "It's bad enough you missed the show and I don't need anything else upsettin' the man even more. It'll all be my fault and he'll be mad enough at that."

But by that time we were already up in the mind-boggling

suite on the thirtieth floor and my thoughts had strayed back to the last time I had stood there, staring with nothing but pure loathing at the black and yellow decor.

"Janice, you can't believe how furious I was that last night when he threw his pajamas at me and I stalked out of here."

"Yeah? Well, you apparently did the right thing," my twin replied coolly. "Do you really think you'd be here now if you had taken his crap and stayed?"

"You're such a toughie," I teased.

"Maybe, but I'm also right. And you know it."

I nodded. "I suppose I knew it even then."

"I suppose."

I figured it was time to change the subject and Ricky's glancing at the door every few seconds was beginning to get on my nerves.

"Stop that. You're making it worse and making me nervous. No one is going to blame you for something that was beyond your control."

"He's gonna blame me for your missing the show. I just know it."

"Actually, Ricky," Janice offered, "maybe if we told Elvis and his name was used with the airline, it would get our luggage back quicker than—"

"No! Please, please promise not to say anything about your luggage. It'll make him even madder, and he's liable to want to blow up TWA or me, or somethin'. I mean it."

"All right, all right, as long as you're so adamant." Janice and I shrugged and smiled our best good-natured, understanding smiles at him. Suddenly, the door opened and Elvis strode in, surrounded by a mix of strangers and entourage. His stepbrother vanished into one of the other rooms.

Elvis walked straight to me without breaking stride, his eyes holding mine all the way.

I felt rooted to the spot and made myself stand up to prove

I wasn't. He stopped dead in front of me and I watched his lips move. "I missed you," they said, forming each word slowly and distinctly and drawing closer and closer until at last they met mine.

Then he turned and draped his arm around Janice's shoulder. "Hiya, little sister. How'd y'all like the show?"

It was directed to us both, but I answered. "We missed it. The dumb plane was late. So you better get yourself really geared up for the next one. Because this will be the first time ever that Janice is going to see you perform in person."

"That's right, Elvis," my sister kidded him. "That's the only reason I came out here. I can't take Joyce doing her Elvis impression any longer. I need to experience the real thing."

While Janice was carrying on, it occurred to me that not only was Elvis in an incredibly "up" mood, but that he had taken the news of our missing his show in stride. It seemed obvious that Ricky had overreacted and I made a spur-of-the-moment decision.

"You know, Elvis," I ventured, "the airline lost our luggage, as well. They said it would be here first thing in the morning, but if it isn't, do you think you could get somebody to speed them up a little?"

"Sure, honey," he replied without batting an eye. "Sonny," he said, turning to the entourage, "find out what Joyce and her sister want, any clothes, whatever, and get it for 'em."

"Oh, Elvis, no," I protested. "It's all right. We just need nightgowns. Maybe just a few things from the drugstore."

As Sonny went off, I turned and caught a glimpse of Ricky peeking out at the proceedings from behind a corner. I walked over to him.

"I told Elvis about our luggage," I said.

He stared at me, speechless, the color draining from his face.

"No, listen, Ricky, he wasn't at all upset."

"Really?" he asked and took a tentative step forward.

"Really," I assured him.

"Damn," he said and finally took a step into the living room. "You just never know what that man's gonna say or do."

He shook his head and started to melt into the crowd, only to be suddenly frozen in his tracks as Elvis's voice boomed out:

"Ricky. I want to talk to you later, man."

Chapter Twelve

"I can't believe what I just saw, Joyce. It can't be for real." Janice had reappeared, all agog over her "room." She had been shown the guest accommodations on the floor below by Sonny, on their way back from the drugstore.

"I know. Don't forget that's Elvis's old suite, the one he had when I first met him here."

"Joyce, how am I *possibly* going to be able to fall asleep in that bedroom? You can't shut your eyes—there's just too much going on! The colors and mirrors everywhere you look. It's absolutely the *height* of decadence! I'll probably never see another place like it in my life. I lost count of how many rooms there were, there probably *isn't* another place like it and . . ."

Aware now of Elvis and Sonny both smiling in amusement at her reaction, she concluded by whispering her lament discreetly in my ear: "And I'm going to spend the night there all by myself. There's just no justice in the world."

"Maybe not. But there *is* compensation. You're going to see Elvis perform in person for the first time."

Only a short time later we were approaching the booth reserved for him in the showroom. I could see that although my twin was doing her level best to present a blasé facade to the world, her eyes were excitedly scanning the huge room.

"Joyce," she said, gripping my arm as we sat down. "Do you see all those people looking in our direction? They're wondering who we are, aren't they? I wish I could yell out and tell them!"

"Then you better do it quickly," I kidded her.

"What do you mean?"

The answer came with the deafening orchestration of "Sprach Zarathustra."

"God, you're right!" Janice yelled. "It's like a volcano erupting."

The crowd was up on its feet, a mass of humanity suddenly wrought to fever pitch, shrieking and shouting and pounding their hands together.

Elvis had appeared, brilliant in his white, high-collared jump suit.

He strode out onto center stage and the audience went into a frenzy of adoration. I felt Janice's hand reach out and take hold of mine. We were engulfed in hysteria, the sound of it breaking over us in wave after shattering wave.

Elvis brought the microphone slowly to his mouth and, as the din gradually subsided, the curled-lip grin appeared. With self-effacing mockery he drawled, "Lawd have mercy."

I was seeing him onstage for the first time as my lover. The beat of "That's All Right, Mama" swelled through the room and before my eyes the man became Myth, became the legend who wove his magic into every heart and soul, whipping his worshipers into a delirium, his fist clenched, his hips gyrating, the legs widespread and quivering defiantly until they flashed out in wild karate kicks.

He began to croon "The Wonder of You," his voice deep, sensual, and quavering, his eyes closed, his body swaying gently. I felt Janice turn and look at me.

"Every woman here thinks he's singing only to her," she

whispered, "but *you* know . . ." Her voice trailed off and her hand tightened on mine.

When it ended—when "Love Me Tender" had been sung, scarf after scarf bestowed on the female fans arching their bodies achingly over the edge of the stage, faces uptilted and pleading to be kissed, those tear-streaked faces strangely mirroring their idol's, his own cheeks now glistening with sweat from eyebrow to dripping chin—then and only then, did my twin relax her grip on my hand.

Looking up, I saw Joe standing there. I motioned to Janice and, without a word, we rose and followed him out while the noisy, chattering, still-buzzing throng provided a Greek chorus, underscoring and reflecting upon the spectacle we had witnessed.

"The boy's still got it . . ."

"He's my man . . ."

"Better than anybody ever—and a real hunk, too!"

This last was uttered with heartfelt enthusiasm by an elderly, gray-haired woman, but the accolades came from people of all ages, including a bunch of guys in their midtwenties all decked out in Elvis regalia from the fifties—from leather jackets, boots, pegged pants, and shades. Even the fingers with which they ostentatiously patted their long, greasy black hair were bedecked with oversized baubles in imitation of The King.

As we left the cries of adoration behind us, Joe turned and chuckled his distinctive chuckle as if he, too, would never get over the adulation and loyalty his boss commanded, no matter how many times he experienced it. I was struck by the thought that, of all the members of the Memphis Mafia, Joe Esposito was the most relaxed around and *about* the phenomenon that was Elvis. He was always low-key, always gave the impression of being able to "take care of business" as indicated by the pendant Elvis had given him that bore, in gold, the initials "TCB."

Back up in the suite, the atmosphere was only slightly less charged than it had been at the performance. Elvis was the center from which all that energy came. He looked up as we walked in.

"Those lights are bright out there, but could you see me smilin' at ya?" he called.

I walked over to him. "Yes. And didn't you sneak a look at me out of the corner of your eye when all those girls started grabbing and kissing you?"

He delivered a perfect, curled-lip grin in response, then reached out and gently touched the palm of his hand to my cheek before turning to Janice, who hugged him and told him how wonderful he had been. "And, Elvis," she went on, "I can get one of those scarves just by asking you for it, can't I?"

"Sure," he said and kissed her affectionately on the forehead.

"I swear, when you were throwing them out there to the audience tonight, those women looked like sea lions in a zoo fighting for the fish at feeding time!"

He turned back to me. "Joyce, you know your sister is nuts, don't you, honey? But I like her and you can bring her with you, anytime."

"That's good," I said as he made a place for both of us to sit next to him. "Because you know we twins are really uncomfortable when we're far away from each other."

"Unless, of course," Janice interjected mischievously, "it happens to be final exam time."

When I laughed in response, Elvis treated each of us in turn to the seriocomic, exaggerated version of his piercing stare.

"Okay, time out, now. Just what does that mean? And don't either of you two pixies try to put old Elvis on."

"We're not, honest!" Janice protested. "It's just that when we were in school, as soon as we realized our teachers couldn't tell us apart, we figured out that we could divide up the curriculum. You know, we switched subjects so that the one who was best at something took it for the other, as well. That way we could cut our studying time in half."

"We just had to make sure that during finals," I added, *"two* classes one of us was best in didn't hold their exams at the same time."

"Pretty damn clever." Elvis laughed. "Now, long as you two are finally fessin' up, how about guys?" He turned his attention to me. "I'll bet you worked that switch with dates, too, didn't ya?"

I looked at Janice who was smiling her mischievous smile again. "Well . . ." I said, feeling it was a good time to change the subject. "Janice, do you remember the time we both got a chance to model for that fashion show in Baltimore?"

"Oh, right! The people who organized it purposely positioned Joyce to walk down the runway followed by another model who was followed immediately by me. The audience was amazed that Joyce could change clothes so quickly!"

"Then," I concluded, "the mystery was solved in the finale when we appeared together wearing identical chincilla coats."

Elvis looked from me to Janice and back to me again. "But, uh, no switching dates?"

I shrugged with exaggerated innocence and looked at Janice, who did the same.

Elvis nodded. "Unh-hunh," he drawled and winked for the benefit of the group of admirers clustered around him.

He got his usual appreciative laugh and, since his high spirits always proved to be contagious, that was the way the rest of the night went, Elvis winding down with jokes and stories, until finally the mob was dismissed and we were left alone together at last.

"Hungry, darlin'?"

"Starving."

"How bout some burgers and ice cream?"

"You know, somehow I thought that's what you might have in mind."

"You're gettin' to know me awful good. Must be gettin' in a rut," he said, shaking his head in mock despair while he gave the appropriate orders.

Later, we were just settling under the covers in the dimly lit bedroom, when I whispered in his ear that I was too keyed up to sleep.

"It was seeing you tonight, onstage. You excited me, Elvis. I'm still excited thinking about it now. Your performance . . . all that energy. It was great, the way you move . . . But you know all that, don't you?"

A modest, half-embarrassed look came over his face.

"The only thing I know is it pleased you, and that makes me happy. But my energy was so high up on that stage tonight, honey, that getting back to normal is tough. Man, it's not easy to calm down, ya know what I mean . . ." His voice trailed off and he reached across to the nightstand for the vial of pills. He downed his, dumped some into his palm and handed me the glass from which he had just drunk.

"Here, honey. I'm still so wound up I really need these . . . and you do, too."

I wanted to say, "What's going on here!" But I didn't. I just swallowed the pills, along with my disappointment. It was hard not to dwell on his incredible sensuality, on the tremendous display of sexual energy I had seen him put out on that stage only a few hours earlier. I mean, there I was, not only in bed with Elvis Presley, but in bed with Elvis Presley for the first time after experiencing what he did to an audience. Wasn't it only natural to want some of that power for myself, only natural to expect the power I'd seen arouse and inflame a thousand strangers to fever pitch do the same for me, the woman lying dutifully alongside him?

I don't know if Elvis read my mind, or my downcast expression, or whether he never really intended to deny the special excitement that the aftermath of his performance might inspire, but the next thing I knew, his hand was tilting my chin so that his eyes could hold mine.

"Yeah," he said softly as he reached over and took back the glass. "I need these, but I need you more." He smiled dreamily. "I really played that audience tonight and . . ." The intense expression came back. "I think now it's time to play Joyce Bova."

"And I do want you to play me," I whispered, reaching up and touching my finger to his lips.

"That's real good, ma'am, 'cause I won't take no for an answer." He smiled.

He was being playful—and I was aching for him.

"I love your mouth," I said, still whispering. "And you."

"And I love you." He was stroking my hair.

"I want to please you, Elvis."

I could feel his desire as he lightly traced the outline of my face with his fingertips. His hands were smooth and soft. Pampered.

"That's it," I breathed. "I want to please you . . . and pamper you."

"You already do, baby." The sensual drawl was almost a playful chuckle. "But I want to *spoil* you, like a little doll."

"Elvis," I said, "I don't know how, but you make me feel like such a little girl—and like a grown woman, at the same time."

"Because you're both, silly. But it's the little girl I love best. D'ya know what I mean? It's just that . . . I mean, any female can be a 'woman' if she's over the age of . . . of twelve, I guess. But to keep that little-girl quality, that's special. That's what I saw in you from the beginning."

I shivered. His hands were traveling slowly down my neck.

"It's okay, baby." He paused a moment while he reassured me. "It's just me . . . just Elvis."

I shivered again. I've got to be honest and admit it wasn't only his caress that was heightening my desire at that moment. It was also his murmuring, "just Elvis" in my ear. *Just* Elvis? How many women all over the world would have given anything to be there in my place, hearing those words? It was a head trip, and a hot one. I recalled a quote I'd once heard: "Fame is a great aphrodisiac." I'd never believed it until now.

While all that was racing through my mind, Elvis had sat up, pulled back the covers and begun taking off his pajamas. He was moving quickly, much more quickly than usual; maybe he feared the pills would take effect and prevent us from making love. Wanting to keep pace, I sat up and started to pull my nightgown over my head when suddenly I found I was struggling, my arms heavy as lead. The pills . . . Twisting and turning, I had just managed to get free of the nightgown when I felt Elvis's hands. He had reached around and cupped both my breasts.

Elvis had said he was going to play me and I wanted him to—but I also knew I would have to fight the pills to fully enjoy it. My body stiffened to his touch at first, but soon warmed to the light, tantalizing dance of his fingertips, pulsing with each smooth circle they traced over my breasts. His mouth moved down my spine almost to the tip, and then back up again to the nape of my neck. My temperature rose with each beat of my heart, yet at the same time I shivered with goose bumps. I was the instrument and Elvis was the maestro, playing a melody only he could hear and only the two of us could feel. When he paused, I feared it was the pills taking hold of him. I could feel them, too. Fighting their potency somehow elicited an even more powerful response from deep within, somehow made me want *his* potency even more. Holding back as he caressed me was pure agony. I had to wait, had to remain submissive, I told myself, had to hold back and yet hold on. Elvis must lead and I must follow . . . and yet . . .

"Oh . . . Elvis, I want to . . ."

"I know, baby, I know." Gently he pulled me backward down onto the bed, laying my head in the palm of his left hand. He rolled over on top of me, rearing up on the knees that he thrust between mine. His right hand traveled tenderly down to my thighs, then up my tingling body. He gazed deeply into my eyes before leaning down to meet them with his lips and shut them with soft kisses.

"My sweet, beautiful Joyce," he whispered as his mouth

moved to meet mine. I loved hearing his voice; it intensified the pleasure of his touch.

I was afraid to open my eyes, the room must be whirling around my head. He placed my hands on his chest and guided them down the length of his long torso. I felt his passion grow harder and stronger. He sighed—or was it more like a moan?

"I love the touch of your hands, baby," he murmured.

He covered me with his body, enveloped me, and I felt and loved the weight of him pressing down on me now. All my nerve endings seemed to leap through my skin and I knew by the weight of him that he was feeling the same and I had to have him . . .

At last his body fused with mine and my thighs were squeezing his hips . . . wanting all of him . . . squeezing with every ounce of strength.

The vision of him on stage flashed into my mind and it was as if he was physically infusing me with the rhythms of his music. Absorbing them, I began to match them, began to match the famous Elvis gyrations with my own as my chest began to heave and my heart to pound faster and faster.

It was the first time we had made love in a time of his performing and the sense of this added to the intoxication. His private nature was to be soft and tender, playful and cuddly rather than boldly erotic, but making love this night my soul could not help being seared in the fire that forged his art. As if the energy that had been generated in the screaming, pounding, writhing, orgiastic frenzy of the audience still lingered. I felt it on a visceral rather than a rational level, something between the spark of genius and the scent of fame, something as charged as an electric current and as explosive as nitroglycerine.

I flashed back and forth between the Elvis onstage in my mind's eye and the Elvis wrapped around me in reality.

"Joyce," he breathed, "I love your body."

I forced my eyes open and looked up at him.

"Never stop, Elvis . . ."

The words had just slipped out in a gasp.

"Promise . . ." he mumbled, barely lifting his mouth from mine. I closed my eyes again, my hands exploring his body, searching, fondling, caressing . . .

He sighed a deeper sigh and stepped up the tempo of the song he was singing within me. My body answered in beautiful harmony with his. I was in perfect sync with his furious beat, the Elvis beat. We raced together in a crescendo of passion until we reached that point—the one that transports you together to a time and place where the music never ends.

In a short while, I felt the little pills take effect. In a matter of moments I was enjoying the familiar sensation they induced, a feeling of floating free of my mind, stripped of all conscious control. Elvis rolled over and put his hand on my face, but I could not open my eyes to see, could hardly force my brain to think.

Many hours later, finally coming out of that deep, drugged sleep, I kept blinking my eyes at the clock, expecting with each blink to see it do the decent thing and rearrange itself into a more reasonable hour. Finally, I faced the fact that we had slept away almost the entire afternoon. I crawled out of bed, leaving Elvis to sleep peacefully on. We had vowed at one point over our hamburgers to get up early and take advantage of the desert sun to get "a healthy tan," but there wasn't enough sun time left to justify disturbing the slumbering monarch.

By the time I finished showering and dressing (our luggage had arrived) and returned to the bedroom, Elvis was nowhere in sight. Hearing the water running in his bathroom, I called in to him that I would be in the main suite.

It was almost evening by then and I had put on one of my nicest outfits, taking great pains that my makeup and hair looked just right. "Just right" meant the look that *Elvis* felt was just right: a heavy sensuality trip with plenty of eyeshadow and my hair coiled and piled high to top off the effect.

There were about a half dozen of Elvis's guys sitting around the living room when I entered, but it was Janice who greeted me first. She grabbed my arm and demanded, "Where the heck have you been? Do you know what time it is?"

"I've been getting ready. I got up only a little while ago. I guess those sleeping pills really worked. Elvis just got up himself. We were knocked out."

"Sleeping pills! What sleeping pills? What do you mean . . . he gave you sleeping pills? You've never needed sleeping pills."

Just then Elvis made his appearance. We both did a double take watching him traipse briskly into the room outfitted in his gold-initialed sunglasses and black silk pajamas. This time with a holstered revolver belted around them. As usual, Elvis was in no danger of being upstaged.

He plopped himself down at the dining-room table, already set for breakfast, awaiting only his presence. The guys stayed where they were, spread out around the room, but Janice and I took the chairs on either side of him and looked on in amazement as he stacked up a half-dozen plate-size griddle cakes and then smothered them in syrup and applesauce.

"Elvis?" I pointed to a pint-size container next to his plate. It was filled to the brim with pills in a variety of shapes, sizes, and colors.

"They're vitamins, honey. I oughta get you started on takin' 'em, too."

"Don't think I could ever get that many down, Elvis." I smiled.

"We'll see. Anyway, I need 'em, and you will, too," he observed, serenely taking them until the huge container was empty.

"Everybody needs 'em," he said, noticing our discomfort.

"You sure will," I remarked pointedly as he stuck his fork into the sticky mess in front of him and sent applesauce and syrup oozing over the sides of the plate and onto the table.

"If you think this is somethin'," he said, "you shoulda seen the chow they served in them army mess halls!"

This remark was shouted, obviously for the benefit of his merry men. For once, however, instead of being riveted to his every word and gesture, they began to cut up among themselves.

"Watch this," he murmured, nudging my arm. "I'll get their attention."

With that he bolted to his feet, his hand snaking like lightning, in one simultaneous movement slapping leather and reappearing with the revolver out, leveled, and cocked.

Everything stopped. Every eye fastened on Elvis as he raised the revolver and sighted down the barrel at the ornate chandelier over our heads. It was like a movie. I could actually see, as if we were in slow motion, his finger tighten on the trigger. I held my breath . . .

Click! The hammer came down on an empty chamber.

There was a moment of stunned silence. Elvis looked around and then doubled over in hysterical laughter. It took only a second for his guys to join in, laughing just as loud as Elvis. Not louder, but just as loud.

"Honey," he said, finally getting control of himself and noticing the expression of disbelief on my face, "you gotta do some crazy things around here to stay sane. Just hope I didn't scare you. How 'bout you, Janice? You're okay, aren't you?"

My twin smiled a little crookedly, but nodded gamely. "Here . . ." She reached across and neatly sliced off a dripping hunk of griddle cake and fed it to him. He accepted it regally, winking at me so that I felt obliged to follow suit. The absurdity of two grown women feeding a grown millionaire moved Janice to whisper, "The boy in the gold-plated bubble." But it didn't move either of us to stop doing it. There was something about him that made the most incongruous things seem natural.

Later in the day, Elvis dragged us along while he gave an audience (my somewhat uncharitable phrase, not his) to three young "friends of the guys." They were three young girls who not surprisingly, could not take their worshipful eyes off Elvis from the moment he began displaying some of his collection of guns and badges. Joe, Red, Sonny, Lamar, and Charlie gathered around as well.

"You don't mind, do ya?" Elvis inquired under his breath. "I kinda promised the guys I'd play the role for 'em, y'know?"

Well, the simple truth of it is, I always enjoyed watching Elvis showing off. I know I've said it before, but there was something contagious about his enthusiasms. And his enthusiasms always seemed to bring out his spontaneity, a quality vital to a man who spent so much of his life in rehearsal. I also sympathized with his need sometimes to simulate being "just plain folks." Making an impromptu run for donuts or exhibiting his various collections brought him as close as he could get to the taken-for-granted experiences of regular people. In this instance, he wasn't so far removed from any average guy showing off a hobby of which he was proud.

At one point, we were all sitting on the floor scrunched up in front of the closet from which Elvis produced gun after expertly crafted gun, each one, he took pains to inform us, unique either because of its design or its history.

The girls were so starry-eyed that when one interrupted his monologue to ask, "Do you really know how to shoot a gun, Elvis?" I couldn't resist quipping, "Are you kidding? He took lessons from Wild Bill Hickock."

"Really?" She turned to me. "You mean you know *him,* too?"

Elvis caught my eye and laughed. But you couldn't help feeling sympathetic toward them. They really were young and quite attractive in their own way, all dolled up for their big evening in almost matching knits of different colors, their bouffant bubble coiffures sprayed stiff as boards.

It all seemed so harmless, bland almost to the point of boring, that when it happened, it caught me completely off guard.

Sonny beckoned me over to him. "He hates us to interrupt

him, but I figure Elvis won't mind if you tell him it's time for him to start getting ready for his show."

"Be glad to," I said and went over and knelt down beside Elvis.

"Excuse me, honey," I said gently, tapping him on the shoulder. "But it's late and you should be getting ready for your show."

He spun around and those blue eyes seemed to bore clear through me. "Leave me alone!" he snarled. "Can't you see I'm busy?"

I was stunned. And not a little humiliated. I took a step backward as he almost shouted, "And I don't need to be reminded about the time."

I felt like crawling into a hole. Without another word I walked out and back into the living room. Only seconds passed before I felt his hands on each of my shoulders. He turned me around to face him. From the expression on his face I knew I had tears in my eyes before I felt them myself.

"Elvis, why? You embarrassed me," I said, struggling to express my outrage.

"Honey, I'm so sorry."

I could see that his remorse was genuine and my anger softened. "Elvis, is there something wrong? Is there anything you need to tell me?"

"No, honey, really. I guess I'm just gettin' jittery before the show and all. You know I wouldn't hurt you for anything; you're my cute little girl now, aren't you? Come here," he said, taking me in his arms and holding me tight against him. "I do love you, you know," he murmured and kissed me and held the kiss and me for a long, long time.

Well, of course that was a pretty persuasive move on his part and since I certainly wanted to be persuaded, I just blocked out the whole damn incident as some kind of aberration. It wasn't long, anyway, before another troubling incident provided me with something to think about in its place.

It was later that night while Janice and I were in the booth waiting for Elvis to make his entrance onstage that my twin first noticed the three women.

"I'm serious, Joyce, they really are staring at us. Look." She nudged my arm. "They're getting up and they're coming this way."

They were good looking and not more than twenty years old. While two of them whispered to each other, the first one, a really striking brunette who let her hair fall down over her red and white midriff top and almost all the way to her red bell-bottom pants, leaned in and, very quietly and discreetly, asked me for my autograph.

"I'm sorry," I said, "but you must have me confused with someone else."

"Aw, come on," one of the others said. "Don't be like that, Priscilla."

"What?"

"Aw, come on," the blonde one whined, holding out a pencil and a menu with a likeness of Elvis on it. "All we want is your autograph."

"I told you, I'm sorry, but I really am not who you think I am."

Before they could say anything more, the whole place erupted, the musical intro for Elvis setting off a tumultuous response from the audience.

With the show about to begin, the three mistaken young women were forced to back off by the people behind us demanding they sit down and stop blocking the view of the stage. They turned sullen then, retreating to their seats with nasty words that were drowned out by the crowd noise.

And the sound of Elvis.

Which, as usual, drowned out everything else for me, even worries.

———

By the time we were finally alone that night, when the last guest had departed, it was time for bed and I was much more interested in being snuggled, kissed, and caressed than in relating any incidents that could possibly bring Elvis down.

I still brooded over the incident, and after the last show of our last night together in Vegas, as soon as he closed the bedroom door behind us, Elvis asked abruptly, "Somethin' bothering you, honey?"

"Actually, there is," I mumbled. I launched into the story of my being asked for an autograph.

When I finished, he grinned: "Well, did you give her one?"

"Very funny, Elvis. You know it's only because they think I'm Priscilla."

"What *did* ya do?"

"I told you, I said, 'I am not who you think I am.' "

"Hmmm. Does it really bother ya that much?"

"The thing is, they don't believe me. I don't like to be told I'm lying."

"I'm really sorry, honey," Elvis said. "But actually, I meant bein' mistook for Priscilla and all?"

"Of course! I know she's beautiful, but it makes me uneasy. How do you feel, Elvis? Do you think we look alike?"

"I guess I can see how people who didn't know could confuse you. But you're both really different, ya know," he said. "You have different . . . uh . . . personalities. But don't worry, Joyce, it doesn't bother me and you shouldn't let what happens bother you. Just remember that you're my girl. You're so sensitive and sweet and I'm so proud of you. Everybody likes ya, y'know, all the guys. You're fun and smart, too, workin' in Congress and all. So don't you worry, honey, everything's gonna be fine."

"Elvis, there was something else strange about it," I continued. "We couldn't figure out why they singled *me* out. Why would they think *I* was Priscilla and not Janice?"

Elvis shook his head slowly from side to side and murmured, "Hmmm."

"But on the other hand," I concluded hastily, seeing him get a faraway look in his eye and afraid I was losing his attention, "it's obvious Janice and I are identical twins, so how could *any* fan who knew anything about Priscilla think *either* of us was she?"

"What's your twin think? She got any ideas?"

"She's baffled, too."

"It *is* kinda baffling," he said. "But it's kinda interesting, too, the whole thing of how people . . . uh . . . mistake appearances and all."

"I guess," I said. I didn't see what he was driving at. "I don't mean to make too much of it, but I did want to mention it before I went home in the morning."

"You shouldn't leave me, Joyce," he said and reached out for me. I moved closer to him and he put his arm around me.

"There was something you said before, Joyce."

"When? What did I say?"

"You said: 'I am not who you think I am.' "

"Oh, to that woman who wanted the autograph."

Elvis nodded, his arm around my shoulders tightening as he reached for the pills. "It's something I'm going to have to say, Joyce, soon."

He handed me my Placidyl and I took them automatically.

"I am not who people think I am. I'm not just 'good old boy' Elvis, old good-time Elvis, the hillbilly cat with his wild bunch of Memphis Mafia. I'm a serious man. And I have a serious message for the world." He picked up one of the books stacked near his bed but put it down unopened. After what seemed a long time, he went on. "I have powers, Joyce, that I don't go bragging about. I could announce them to the world."

"Why don't you?" I asked, even though I didn't really understand what he was talking about.

"No. People aren't ready for me to announce that yet . . .

Joyce, at least stay another day?" His tone was so tender, he seemed so vulnerable, that my eyes filled with tears. He brought his other arm around and held me tight.

It was the last thing I remembered until the phone went off the next morning. "Joyce." It was Janice. "Get moving or we'll miss our plane."

Still groggy, I crawled over Elvis and out of bed. He had asked me to wake him before I left so that he could say goodbye, but he looked so serenely beautiful lying there that I couldn't bear to disturb him. I just pressed my lips to his cheek and tiptoed from the room.

Chapter Thirteen

It was a Friday afternoon, March the nineteenth, and I was gathering my papers together after a staff meeting when Diane came in and said there was a man named "Charlie" on the phone. The meeting had been in the small hearing room adjacent to our suite and, practically flinging my stuff back onto the witness table, I scooted past the rostrum and through the Members Door located next to the dais. I knew only one "Charlie" and that "Charlie" meant Elvis. An Elvis call could not have come at a more fortuitous moment. I had had a bitch of a week, culminating in a blowup with Janice.

We had gone shopping in Georgetown and I was looking at a couple of outfits in this little boutique when suddenly, in the middle of the bland stuff they usually played, Elvis's voice came bursting out of their sound system.

"Can you believe that?"

I looked up to find the young salesgirl waiting on me shaking her head.

"Can you believe there are still people who like that kind of singing?"

"Exactly what kind of singing is that?" I asked bitingly.

156

"Uh, well, you know . . ."

"Janice!" I hurled the merchandise into the poor girl's face. "I won't buy anything in here. This girl has no taste—in music *or* in clothes."

Out I stormed, leaving the startled salesgirl with clothes draped all over her. Janice caught up with me about three blocks away, where I'd parked the car.

"Joyce—"

"How dare . . . Did you hear what she said? How dare she!"

"Stop it." Janice grabbed my arm. "Stop it this second."

"Okay, okay, just let go."

I got in and slammed the door shut while Janice walked around to the passenger side. She waited until I started the engine and pulled out to head for home before saying, in a tone that obviously must have cost her some effort to keep as calm as she did:

"You know you can't go around acting like an ass, don't you? I know how you feel about him, but Elvis is a big boy. He doesn't need you to defend him. So not everyone loves his singing. Who cares? I've never seen you act like this. It must be those damn pills."

"Now *you're* the one being an ass!" I cried. "So I take a sleeping pill once in a while. Big deal."

"It is the pills, then." She pounced. "You *are* still taking them?"

"What does that have to do with anything?"

"Maybe everything, Joyce. And what do you mean by 'once in a while'? I mean, the point is, where does it stop?"

"Don't be ridiculous. I'm not stupid; I know what I'm doing."

We drove the rest of the way home in utter silence.

But now, hurrying to my office for Charlie's call, those worrisome thoughts were the furthest thing from my mind. All I could think of were Elvis's last words to me, spoken over the phone only a few days before and still running through my mind: "I want ya t'come to Graceland," he had said. "Mainly cause I want to show you my home, where I live. I'm happiest here, Joyce, and you'll love it, too."

"Hello?"

"Joyce?"

"Charlie, what's wrong?" I asked, immediately sensing something was not right from the way his voice sounded.

"Well, I don't want to alarm you, but E's in the hospital."

"What?"

"It's all right. Take it easy. He's gonna be okay, but he wants you to come out here."

"Where? When? What's the matter with him?"

"He's in the hospital in Nashville. I'll tell you all about it when you get here. Can you come?"

"I'll call the airlines right now. But first tell me what's wrong with him. *Please.*"

"Not over the phone. Call me as soon as you know the time you'll be getting in." He gave me the name and phone number of the hotel in Nashville.

I raced back to the hearing room and finished what I had been doing, making a mental note for another, less pressing time, that we were running out of space in our safes for all the classified documents that had to be secured. Luckily, there was no hearing scheduled for that day, which would make it easier to get away.

"God, please let him be okay," I prayed as my plane took off from Washington National.

Faithful Charlie was at the gate waiting for me when I landed at the Nashville airport.

"C'mon, Joyce, we've got to hurry."

"All right, all right, Charlie. But what is it? Please tell me."

"They released Elvis from the hospital and he's waiting for us out on the airfield here."

"But, Charlie, tell me, I have to know . . ."

"Not now, Joyce." He put his arm around my waist and half

dragged me along. "There's a private plane waiting for us. We're going to Graceland. We gotta hurry. This way."

My mind was racing, imagining the worst as Charlie Hodge steered me out of the American Airlines terminal and onto the airfield itself toward the limousine I could now make out, pulled up close alongside a plane with idling engines. As soon as we were near enough, I saw that Elvis was seated in the back of the car between Sonny and Red West. He looked ashen and strangely helpless. I opened the door and his bodyguards helped him out and onto the plane. It didn't look as if he could have made it without them. I followed, and sat down alongside him, frightened and depressed that I was powerless to help the man I loved. I looked closely at him. He was dressed in one of his usual high-collared outfits, his head back, propped against the headrest. His dark glasses prevented me from seeing his eyes and I reached out and put my hand to his cheek.

"Elvis, it's me, Joyce. Honey, how are you?"

"I'm uh, okay, I guess. I'm real glad you're here, though . . ." He lifted his head slightly. ". . . cause I don't feel real well. So excuse me if I . . ."

He reached out for my hand then and I placed it in his. He held it tightly in his lap.

"That's all right, honey," I said. "Just rest now."

He put his head back on the headrest again and seemed to fall asleep.

Charlie was seated across the aisle from us and I turned to him. "What's wrong? Why is Elvis so weak? He doesn't look okay to me. You said he was okay."

"He is. He is. The doctors say he has something called secondary glaucoma. It's like a real bad eye infection. Right now he's on a lot of medication. That's why he's so weak. But he'll be okay, otherwise they wouldn't have sent him home. Don't worry, he'll be alert soon."

Elvis's dad, Vernon, was waiting behind the wheel of a Mercedes pulled right up to the plane when we landed at the Memphis airport. I got into the back first with Elvis being helped in beside me.

"Thank you for coming for my boy, Joyce." Vernon tried to smile, but his face was almost as pallid as his son's. He started the engine and I saw the concern in his face reflected by the rear-view mirror. "How do ya feel, son?" he asked, but Elvis managed only to nod in response.

There had been very little conversation during the short flight and just about none at all on the drive to Graceland, so different from the other times I had been with Elvis. I was still holding his hand, but now it was limp and lifeless.

As we drove down Elvis Presley Boulevard and I approached the famed Music Gates for the very first time, I couldn't help thinking this was not the way either of us had envisioned my coming to Graceland.

There was a group of fans clustered there and, probably to avoid them, Vernon drove past and turned down a narrow side road to the left of the house. Once inside the grounds, however, we drove directly to the main entrance.

I watched while Red and Vernon helped Elvis up the steps to the pillared entrance, Vernon holding tightly onto his son. An anxious-looking black lady had the door open before we even reached it, her face and voice filled with concern for "Mr. Elvis."

I stepped into Graceland.

But I barely remember it from that first glimpse. It was Elvis I was watching and caring about. A glance revealed the living room off to my right, furnished mostly in white, with a piano that seemed speckled in gold, and a formal dining room to the left with an ornate chandelier.

"Joyce, c'mon with me," Elvis called and I followed him up a staircase that led to the second floor. Except that for one second I was frozen by the sight of Priscilla. A portrait hung at the foot of the stairs. Priscilla was shown in semiprofile with Elvis beside her. She looked so beautiful that I almost said out loud how lovely she was. It also struck me that they had been captured looking almost like brother and sister, both in facial structure and expression. I wondered why it was still there if she and Elvis weren't . . .

"Joyce!" A voice called from above. "Elvis is waiting for you."

I hurried up the stairs and past a room that was set up as an office with a big console desk that had a television set built into it along with other electronic gadgetry.

And into Elvis's bedroom.

It was huge, that was my first impression, and the only one I had time for. Joe Esposito immediately took me aside and introduced me to a rather tall man, probably in his early forties, and dressed in a business suit.

"Joyce, this is Elvis's doctor."

I shook his hand and listened intently as, guarding his words, he reiterated pretty much the same diagnosis Charlie had conveyed on the flight to Memphis: "Elvis is suffering from secondary glaucoma and inflamed eyes, but he'll be fine with some rest and care and as long as certain precautions are taken."

I found the doctor's genteel manner and soft voice comforting. And then some of the guys brought an oxygen tank into the room and the doctor began to give me a crash course in its use. "Just in case," he stated blithely, "although it's unlikely it will be necessary."

I couldn't help but wonder if they weren't keeping something from me. Why an oxygen tank for an eye problem?

"Please have Elvis take these through the night at the intervals indicated on the label," the doctor concluded, handing me a vial of pills.

As soon as they had all left, I sat down on the bed next to where Elvis was stretched out.

He looked at me and tried to smile. "I knew you would come, Joyce. I knew you wouldn't let me down."

"Of course, Elvis. I love you."

I kissed his moist cheek. He sighed and took my hand and managed to squeeze it hard, the first time he'd been able to make even that effort. After a little while he dozed off and I got up and walked around the room.

Heavy velvet, haremlike drapes covered the windows and the dark wood furniture was bulky and masculine. The room's heavy feel was accentuated by a red and black color scheme that, in the dim light, made me feel hemmed in. The bed was big enough to sleep a family, nine feet by nine feet. It had a black leather, rolling pleated headboard constructed so that if you wanted to sit up, you could pull out two of the pleats to use as armrests, while, simultaneously, a backrest would protrude, the combination offering you enough support to make you think you were in a comfortable easy chair. There was a large console TV at the foot of the bed, but the Elvis Touch was supplied by the two additional sets that were recessed in the ceiling directly overhead for more relaxed viewing pleasure. The entire setup was outrageous, but pure Elvis.

I sat down in the oversized chair by the console at the foot of the bed. I couldn't keep my eyes from straying to the oxygen tank. It made me nervous and I got up again and walked over to the closed-circuit television across from Elvis's side of the bed (the one he used to keep track of everything going on throughout the house and grounds) and turned it off; it made things too spooky. Then I checked the door to the adjoining office, found it ajar, and shut it.

I walked around to "my side" of the bed and stared down at Elvis. He was sound asleep and my thoughts drifted back to those days when I would eagerly plunk down my hard-earned teenage savings to see him on the silver screen. Did I ever let my fantasies run riot to the extent that I dreamed that someday I would be. . . . ? Probably. The romantic yearnings of a teenage American girl know few bounds.

On the other hand, these were hardly the circumstances my overheated imagination would have conjured for my triumphant arrival at my Lord and Liege's manor. Difficult and worrisome as the situation was, in a way it was also a revelation. Elvis had chosen me to be the woman at his side during his crisis, and we all know that when we're really ill, we want only the one we love and trust the most with us. The realization coming so abruptly in Graceland, very nearly overwhelmed me. Could I still have any question as to Elvis's commitment to me . . . to *us?*

Only one. The same old one. What about Priscilla? It wasn't just seeing the portrait. Her presence was everywhere in that house. Like a poltergeist, it disapproved of me. She had lived at Graceland since she was fifteen years old. It was almost as much her home as it was Elvis's. She was still his wife, the wife whose bed this had been. Graceland had never known another mistress . . . unless . . . No, not yet, anyway. God, the whole thing was like a gothic romance. Anyway, the jury in my head was still out as to whether I was the one and only love, or simply the conveniently exciting, but definitely intruding, "Other Woman."

It must have been after two in the morning when Sonny knocked.

"I'm gonna have to take E to another room so the doc can look at him," he explained.

Together, we helped Elvis out of bed and then Joe, who had been waiting outside the door, assisted in getting him down the hall.

"Honey?" Elvis twisted around in their arms and reached out to me, looking even more pathetic being shuffled along like that in his black silk pajamas. "You come with me," he mumbled.

The room we brought Elvis to, though darkened and set up with medical equipment, had obviously been his daughter, Lisa Marie's, bedroom. Vernon was already there waiting with the doctor, and though the doctor himself had assumed his most professionally confident air, I saw that the elder Presley's face was tense and strained.

After they sat Elvis down in front of a strange-looking contraption for the purpose of examining his eyes, I leaned down to tell him that I probably should wait outside.

"No, Joyce. I want you to stay with me."

tually, I wanted to stay, but I had to be sure that Elvis really
d me to. I also wanted to give the doctor, who had by then
d into his basic whites, an opportunity to raise any objection he might have to my presence on medical grounds. But,
calm and genteel as ever, he merely looked at me and nodded
his approval.

Elvis began to show signs of becoming more alert as the
examination wore on. This turned out to be a decidedly mixed
blessing when the doctor, having looked into each eye in turn,
announced in a voice totally devoid of emotion, "I'm going to
have to give him an injection." His next words made my blood
run cold. "Directly into the eyeball . . . and, I'm afraid, no anesthetic is possible here." I looked around. All eyes were on Elvis.
I realized my teeth were clenched so hard that my jaw was
numb. No one uttered a sound, then Elvis gestured with his hand
as if to say, Go on, I can handle it.

The doctor moved in close with his needle. Elvis sat straight
up and braced himself. I held my right hand over my mouth as
if it could hold back the pain for him; with my other, I clasped
his hand and held it as tightly as I could.

"Now, just-don't-move . . ."

Elvis didn't. Only the slight pain I felt as his much bigger
hand tightened on mine gave evidence of his excruciating
agony.

With a sigh of relief, the doctor withdrew the needle. "That's
it," he said. "Let him rest now."

We walked slowly out of Lisa Marie's room and across the
hall to a rear door that led into Elvis's dressing room, then
through the bathroom and back into his bedroom. He settled
into bed and I got in beside him. The temperature in there now
seemed cold enough to keep meat. I turned up my side of the
dual-controlled electric blanket and said a silent prayer that he
would be all right.

Elvis slept through until the next afternoon except for those
times I woke him to give him his medicine. The doctor's progno-

sis proved correct and he seemed to grow stronger each day—days I spent almost entirely in that room with him. Actually, I wasn't bothered by the isolation. Elvis needed me, and I wanted to be there for him, to provide aid and comfort in every way I could.

The lifestyle at Graceland was such that there was almost no need for Elvis to leave his quarters. We were waited on hand and foot. The meals, plain but substantial, of course, were served by various maids and I soon discovered that it was fortunate I had no problem with the cuisine to which Elvis was accustomed.

When, for our first meal, the maid inquired if I wanted a steak, as that was what "Mr. Elvis" was having, I requested mine to be "well done"; she informed me that well done was the way it would be, "because that's the way Mr. Elvis eats it."

After a while, in those intervals when he wasn't sleeping, Elvis became quite talkative. And philosophical, especially my last night there when, after dinner had been cleared, he began to dip into some of the dozens of books on philosophy and religion that, I began to realize, made up the bulk of his reading.

The choice of material was surprisingly heavy and brought out an intensity in him. I remembered the cryptic remarks Elvis made about himself on my last night with him in Las Vegas, when he had talked about his powers and the serious message he had for the world. But I had dismissed them at the time, deciding that people who never hear the word, "no" (like high officials in Washington, for instance) are prone to pontificating when the mood is on them.

"I was raised attending a 'Holy Roller' type church, y'know," he began, turning to me and marking the place in the book he was holding with his finger. "That's where I got to love gospel music. It gave me a special feelin' for it."

He reached over and got a Placidyl for himself. I hadn't taken any since I'd been at Graceland because I couldn't chance its effects on my performance in case of an emergency. But I wanted one then. And got it.

le turned his attention back to me, he extended the hand
; the book. "Would you read to me, please, Joyce?"

)dded, reaching out to take it and reading the title. " 'The
Impersonal Life'?"

He nodded. "I marked a passage . . . Y'know, Joyce, entertaining is really just a stepping-stone."

A little startled, I looked up.

"I feel I was put here on earth to serve a special purpose."

I waited, but when he didn't continue I went back to the
book until I came to the part he'd chosen. Something struck me
just then, however, and I looked up at him again. "Elvis, don't
you think that maybe those thoughts are just a natural reaction
to feeling . . . well, a sense of your own mortality? I mean,
because of being sick and everything?"

He mulled it over for a minute before saying, "Them old
prophets got The Word, got their message out wanderin' in
deserts and all, lost, weak, half crazy from thirst and hunger.
Sometimes it takes special conditions—craziness and pain—for
a man to become truly sane. To see the light. Could ya read that
to me now, honey? I'm getting kinduv drowsy again."

I read. " 'You have no ideas of your own and could not
possibly have a desire that came from other than ME, for I AM all
there is. Therefore, *all* desires are GOOD, and when thus understood unfailingly come into speedy and complete fulfillment.' "

There his marker indicated to skip to the next page and I
did. " 'So it is that every thing, every condition, every event
that ever transpired, was first an idea in the mind. It was by
desiring . . .' "

By then Elvis was fast asleep and I closed the book and
joined him.

The next day, before leaving, I phoned Janice.

"Why haven't you called before this, Joyce? Never mind, tell
me about Elvis—and how the two of you are doing? I've been
waiting on pins and needles, worrying . . . How is he?"

All right, I thought, you asked for it, so I told her, sparing no gory details. Especially when it came to the needle.

"Wow. He didn't feel it? That's impossible. What was he, unconscious?"

"Just a little out of it, from the medication."

"I'll bet. And you, what about you? Don't they know you get weak at the knees when you break a nail? I can't believe you didn't keel over. Oh, well, as long as everything's all right. But in the future, try to keep me informed."

Elvis still looked frail when I was leaving, but even in that weakened condition he mustered his usual protest that I stay. One look at my suitcase waiting by the door was enough, however, to remind me that my time had run out.

"Elvis?"

"Changed your mind?"

"No, you know I would if I could . . . but, could I have a few sleeping pills to take with me?"

Without a word he handed me a full vial.

Downstairs, he took me in his arms. "Honey, thanks for being here when I needed you."

"Elvis, you don't have to thank me."

"Did Charlie take care of your flight?"

"Yes, he made my reservation and he's taking me to the airport. Everything is taken care of for me, Elvis. Just you worry about taking care of yourself. I'm sorry to leave, but happy that you're feeling better."

"Yeah, I'm better, but not perfect. Maybe if you stayed one more night."

"Elvis, you need rest, not me."

"Never say that, baby, you were wonderful."

"Yeah, too bad you don't remember."

"Oh, I remember more than you think. And I do need you. Don't ever forget that."

Then he kissed me again and again.

When Charlie and I reached the airport I turned to him and

for the umpteenth time, "Do you really think he'll be

on't worry, Joyce. He has the best of care. The doctor said a few more days will do it."

"You guys are really good to him; he's really lucky for that."

Charlie got my suitcase out of the trunk and carried it inside. At the counter I waited while he bought my ticket.

"Well, Charlie, thanks for everything."

"Joyce," he said, handing me the ticket, "it was nice of you to come. E really wanted you here," he said, and kissed me goodbye on the cheek.

Chapter Fourteen

About a week after my return from Graceland, I was walking through the main suite of our committee's offices, when I overheard a group of coffee-klatching colleagues discussing something that had been on television about Elvis and his eye infection. I could hardly believe my ears. Priscilla was being hailed as the loyal and concerned wife who had stayed by his side through the crisis, nursing him back to health.

I almost freaked. I flashed back and felt his hand gripping mine as the needle went into his eyeball. I turned angrily on them—

And shut my mouth. And swallowed hard. What was I going to do, make a spectacle of myself? Shout, "No, you've got it all wrong, they're wrong, your television is wrong, the tabloids and fan magazines and everybody else in the world is wrong! It wasn't Priscilla . . . it was me! It *is* me! It's *me* who Elvis Presley really loves! Only nobody knows it. No one but us."

Right.

But it galled me for days afterward.

Several mornings later my Elvis Phone woke me at the unusual (for Elvis) hour of six-thirty A.M.

"Elvis?"

"Hi, honey."

"How are you? Are you all recovered now?"

"Actually, I'm not feelin all that well."

"What is it?" I asked. "What's wrong? Is it your eyes? Did that infection come back?"

"No, it's not that, it's . . ."

In the middle of the sentence, his words began to slur.

"What is it, Elvis? I can't understand what you're saying. Elvis? Elvis!"

I raised my voice to the point where I was actually yelling, but still he didn't answer. Then the line went dead. I was frantic. I didn't know what to do. I hung up for a second and then started to dial him back. And stopped. I put the phone back down.

I wasn't going to put myself and Elvis in an awkward position by calling Graceland just then, in case there was some slight particle of truth in what had been reported and Priscilla had put in an appearance after I had gone. I knew he had made the point over and over that I should feel free to call him there anytime, but . . .

Damn! My own timidity made me feel as if I were doing something dishonorable. How could love be so shitty? I was not cut out for the role of Other Woman. In fact, I hated it.

I dialed the number Charlie had given me. As he indicated, his service answered and, as he had also indicated, he called me back in less than ten minutes.

"Joyce, don't worry. He's okay, really. I talked to him as soon as I got your message. It's only that he took a sleeping pill and I guess he just fell asleep. But he knew he was calling you."

"He did . . . Well," I said, laughing, "that's something, anyway."

"Yeah, he wants you to come out to Graceland today."

"Charlie, can't you do something about the pills?"

"Not me. Now, what about getting out here?"

"Today's impossible. I don't dare chance it after being away that last time. Little sarcastic remarks have been dropped at work about how nice it is to have me around now that things are really busy and they need me. And it *is* really busy, so busy that any disappearance on my part would cause a real problem."

"Well, when do you think? 'Cause I gotta tell E something."

"I think I can work things out to be there in a couple of days. How would Thursday be?"

"I'll tell E," he said and we hung up.

Spring had come to Washington, the loveliest of all its seasons, with thousands of pink and white cherry blossoms in full bloom.

As was I, bursting with love and happiness and excitement as I picked up my tickets, prepaid and charged as usual to Charlie's Amex account, at the American Airlines counter in Baltimore's Friendship Airport.

I had picked the Thursday before Good Friday and was delighted with the prospect of a weekend with Elvis (knowing, of course, that I would have to be back to celebrate Easter Sunday with my mother and Janice) as Charlie drove me out of the airport and into Memphis. The first time I was there, it was the dead of night, my mind preoccupied with worry about Elvis, but now it was as picture perfect a day in Tennessee as it had been in the nation's capital.

Memphis: the city of Elvis Presley, I told myself, his hometown. First, I noticed some cornfields, then we drove past gas stations, package-good stores, automobile dealerships, little stands that sold fireworks, and places that displayed in their windows what I imagined were real, down-home country hams. There were motels and scrap metal yards and poolrooms and all the rest of the ordinary, bordering on the tawdry, jerry-built debris of the left-by-the-roadside American Dream.

I drank it all in; it all seemed wonderful to me. It had all shaped Elvis, it was all there in his music and I loved it.

After that came the housing projects and, of course, I knew that Elvis had grown up in one. I had Charlie take us by Beale

Street, that legendary place of the blues, where B.B. King remembered a teenaged Elvis hanging out and listening. But daytime is not the time for Beale Street and we soon moved on, Charlie allowing as how it was "not so wild even at night as it used to be." Soon we were on Elvis Presley Boulevard, passing office buildings and restaurants and shops and approaching once again the Music Gates of Graceland.

There were a dozen or so people standing around outside it as a tall, thin, elderly man opened it for us.

"Joyce," Charlie said, "this is Elvis's uncle Vester Presley."

Vester saluted and waved us through and we cruised smoothly up the long driveway. We parked at the front door, shielded by its four massive columns and, before we had climbed the last step, it was opened by the same black woman who had been so concerned for "Mr. Elvis" on that terrible night. Only now her face was wreathed in a smile.

"It's nice to see you again, Joyce."

I barely had "Thank you," out of my mouth when Joe Esposito appeared, his arms outstretched for a hug.

"How have you been, Joyce?" he asked, kissing me on the cheek and asking after Janice. "E is waiting up in his room for you," he added. "He wanted you to go right up."

I started for the staircase, but my eyes couldn't help searching out—what wasn't there. I hope it doesn't make me sound too insecure or competitive, but I sure was gratified to find that the portrait of Priscilla and Elvis had been taken down.

I reached the landing at the top of the stairs, knocked gently on the door to his bedroom, and walked in. The head of the bed was just to the left as you entered and I could see Elvis lying there asleep on his back. I thought to surprise him by waking him with a kiss, but as I leaned over, I got the surprise instead.

His hand shot out and pulled me down on top of him where he wrapped both arms around me in a bear hug and kissed me good and hard and long on the lips.

"Elvis," I gasped when I got my breath back. "God, you scared me. I thought you were sleeping."

"No. Been lyin' here waitin' to ambush ya. Heard ya come in the house."

"Honey, I am so glad to be here. You look wonderful and . . . you feel even better."

He laughed and loosened his hold slightly so I could sit up a little more comfortably alongside him.

"Yeah, I'm fine now, honey. And you sure look beautiful. But how come you couldn't get here before this?"

"Well, it's not easy for me to get away at the beginning of a week."

"Why?"

"C'mon, you know what my job is like—and that I have people to answer to."

"You shouldn't have to answer to anyone but me. I can take care of it, if you'll let me."

The offer was made with his usual generosity, but there was a distinct undertone of annoyance in those last four words.

"You do too much for me already," I answered, leaving unsaid that something deep within would not allow me to become dependent on any man. Not even Elvis—who, if I cared to face it, could cut me off like a flash. I knew he wouldn't, I knew he loved me, but I still felt there needed to be a basic space where he ended and I began.

"Anyway," I went on, hurrying to change the subject, "you've got so many things you take care of, you don't need another one." I leaned in close and scrutinized his eyes. "Have they cleared up entirely, Elvis?"

"Yeah, they're all better, honey." He slid his arm around me, dropping the inquisitorial stare. "Boy, I was really out of it then, wasn't I? I knew you were here, but, yaknow, I hardly remember anything that happened."

"Well," I said, chuckling, "that's because there wasn't a whole lot *to* remember."

He laughed, too. "Well, then tell me what's new up there in the House of Representatives? What's the inside gossip?"

"Sorry, no inside gossip. Just a lot of talk about the pay raise the Senate and they want to vote for themselves. They want to keep it from becoming a real hard issue—they don't want to appear to be flaunting their greed or something. Afraid to upset their constituents, the ones who pay the taxes that pay their salaries."

I'm afraid I must have sounded a mite cynical because my words immediately set Elvis off on one of his boyishly sincere patriotic sermons.

"Let me tell you something, little one. It wouldn't upset me none if they got more money. And plenty of their salaries come out of my pocket, 'cause I'm one dude who pays every cent to Uncle Sam that he's got comin'. But they deserve it, they have a lot of responsibility running the country and all."

"If they thought everyone felt the way you do, Elvis, they'd vote to *double* their salaries! But don't worry, I'm sure they'll figure a way to sneak that raise through. They'll probably tack it on to some other piece of legislation." I paused. "Oh, I know, I *do* have something to tell you."

"Oh, yeah? What?"

"There's this older guy who works in my building, and he was telling me that although he lives in D.C. now, he's originally from Tennessee. Now, I never told him I knew you, but we got to talking about the Grand Ole Op'ry and all, which of course I've never seen, when he mentioned you."

"Ah-hunh."

"He said that he used to know Senator Estes Kefauver and that the senator volunteered on more than one occasion that he really liked, 'that boy from Memphis.' This guy quoted him as saying: 'that boy sure can sing, and he's a good boy, too. Proud he's from Tennessee.' "

"Knew there had to be *some* guys up there with good taste," Elvis quipped. He got up and walked into the bathroom. I couldn't help but notice how thin he looked from the back, still almost frail after his recent illness.

I slid over to the edge of the bed and sat. My eyes wandered around the room where we had been secluded on my first visit. Everything was the same: the oversized, unmade bed, the closed-circuit television silently monitoring Graceland, the nightstand overflowing with books, pamphlets, and pill bottles. The only thing missing was the oxygen tank.

When he came out of the bathroom Elvis was dressed in a western-style jacket, its padded shoulders adding much needed bulk to his lanky frame and making him look a lot bigger and stronger.

"Elvis, I'd like to freshen up, myself."

He nodded. "I'll be downstairs. Just come on down soon as you're ready."

The bathroom was as masculine as Elvis. Everything was done in slick, sable black and studded with gold fixtures. The shower looked like shiny black marble. It was big enough to have company in and didn't require a shower curtain to keep the spray from splashing out. The sink had a large counter that was covered with an assortment of combs, brushes, lotions, toothbrushes, and three tubes of Colgate toothpaste. Adjoining the bathroom I could see there was a large dressing room filled with a seemingly endless variety of jackets and pants and a kaleidoscopic array of fancy shirts.

When I got downstairs, Elvis was with his father and the guys in the dining room, Elvis seated at the head of the table. He motioned for me to come in and sit beside him on his right.

The first thing I noticed was the console model television set playing at the other end of the room, situated so that the screen was directly in his line of vision. The food was served and Elvis tucked into his usual fare: overdone meat, black-eyed peas, and mashed potatoes, with a vigor that was an obvious testament to his renewed health.

After a while he put his fork down on his plate, sat up straight and, his mouth still full of food, said, "Hey, you guys, I want you to know that I'm thinkin' 'bout goin into politics."

Everyone had been following his lead, laughing when he did, joking for his benefit, and now, since Elvis looked serious and intent, so did they.

"Yeah, Joyce here could give me some pointers. And I think it's about time the State of Tennessee had another crime-fightin' senator like ol' Estes Kefauver."

He finished chewing his food and swallowed. I noticed everyone else had stopped eating. Elvis waited about three beats while looking at the silent faces surrounding him. Then he burst out laughing.

"Damn! I could tell you guys anything and you'd believe it."

The boys laughed (in relief, it seemed to me) while I told him, "Considering some of the people I've seen sent to Congress, I think you could win."

"Well, there's a vote of confidence," he replied, digging into his meal once again.

When dinner was finished he turned to me. "You come with me, Joyce," he said, giving me a hand up from the table. "There's someone I really want ya to meet."

I followed him out into the foyer to a door in the hallway. He knocked and it was opened by a very thin, very old lady.

"Joyce, this is my grandmother, Minnie. Only I call her, 'Dodger,' have since I was a kid."

Minnie smiled from ear to ear and asked me into her room. Elvis made a discreet exit and I sat down on the sofa.

Minnie's favorite subject, I soon discovered, was her famous grandson, which was okay with me. She had a thick drawl that took time to understand. After we had chatted for about half an hour, I thought perhaps I'd better be getting back to Elvis and said as much.

"Sit just awhile longer, child," she said. "There's somethin' I'd like to tell you 'bout. They was somebody, I don't know who, that was makin calls here sayin' that I was old and ugly and that

I was embarrassin' to Elvis, that I shouldn't be let out to be seen in public. Well, when Elvis heard 'bout that he got real mad."

Tears shone in the old lady's eyes as she went on.

"You know what that boy went and did? He insisted on gettin' out one of his fancy cars and drivin' me all over town. Then he took me out and up and down through the whole town, all through Memphis, walking up and down the streets together with his arm around me, just to show 'em how he really felt."

My own eyes weren't any too dry by the time she had finished her lovely story and my heart was aching to be with Elvis, with the man we both adored. I stood up to leave.

"Child?" She looked up at me. "Do you have any children?"

"No, I don't . . . Dodger." I felt close enough to her after what she had told me to use Elvis's term of endearment.

"Don't you wait too long. A woman should have plenty of children. Then maybe you get lucky and one of 'em turns out good. I had five. Three girls and two boys. None of 'em turned out too good, 'cept maybe Vernon . . . cause he made Elvis."

I thanked her for her advice and left to look for Elvis, finally tracking him down in one of the hallways where he was talking to his father.

"How'dya like Dodger?"

"She's amazing. I hope I'm as sharp at her age."

"I'm glad ya feel that way, 'cause I love that old woman."

Elvis took me through the kitchen and then up a narrow staircase that provided an alternate route to the second floor and his quarters. When we were alone at last in his room, I told him about his grandmother's story and he got very modest and blushingly shrugged it off. It was one of the truly sweet things about him, this casual but innate decency.

"I don't mean to embarrass you," I said, "but that was a wonderful thing you did."

"Well, Dodger, y'know, she always loved me," he said. "Even when I was nothin', just a poor kid."

I nodded.

"Just like my momma. I been lucky with the women in my life." He took me in his arms. "Real lucky, Joyce."

"Oh, I don't think it has anything to do with luck, really. I think the thing is that you only get what you give."

"What about giving and not caring about getting?" he asked.

"What do you mean?"

"I mean . . ." He began to pace. "That's the kind of man I mean to be, an unselfish man. The kind of man who gets his satisfaction from giving, not from receiving."

"Well," I said, "I think you're pretty okay the way you are." But I wasn't sure if he was just putting me on or if he really meant what he said.

He stopped pacing and faced me. "Do you know the saying, 'It's better to give than to receive'?"

"Yes, of course," I said.

"Well, if a man could live and love that way, what would that make him?"

"Let's see—a saint?"

"I like that." He chuckled. "Saint Elvis."

Without any warning he reached for my blouse and proceeded, one by one, to deftly undo my buttons.

"What are you doing, Elvis?" I breathed.

"Just going to show you what I mean," he said blithely without missing a beat or a button.

"You don't have to show—" But his warm, soft lips stifled even that mild demur and, as we kissed, he spread open my blouse, reached around to my back and in one dextrous motion unhooked my bra.

"Pretty accomplished fingering for a singer," I murmured.

"Pretty *simple* move for a gee-tar player," he responded with rakish bravado, sweeping my blouse and bra over my arms and dropping them down at my feet while he sent my pulse soaring.

Somehow, impromptu love in the afternoon with Elvis had never occurred to me. Lovemaking had always been a precursor to sleep, something reserved for bedtime when we were sedated for the night. My body began to tingle all over as I contemplated the excitingly unexpected. When his hands moved across my chest, my breasts seemed to reach out to welcome them.

"Joyce," he said, moving his hands slowly, teasingly down to my hips, "I'm gonna show you what I was trying to explain before."

"What do you mean?"

"Just this: In love, giving is more satisfying than getting. Understand?"

"Uh-huh . . ." I nodded, but at that moment all I really wanted to understand was that I was now completely naked, Elvis having smoothly unzipped my skirt and quickly drawn it and the bikini panties underneath, down to my ankles. I stepped completely out of my clothes and pushed them aside with one foot. Despite a surge of desire that ran through me like a fever, I heard my voice say calmly, "Let me help you take your shirt off, Elvis."

That composed facade cracked though, as he intercepted my hand, stretched my arm out by taking a step backward, and looked me over from top to bottom while he smiled his crooked-lipped smile. "Damn," he said, slowly shaking his head from side to side. "I sure am lucky to have a woman who looks this good naked. I mean . . ."

"Elvis . . ." I pulled my hand free of his grasp. "You're embarrassing me."

His "I am?" was overly innocent, but he did shift his gaze to my face and when he spoke, seemed genuinely contrite. "I'm sorry, baby. I'm not trying to . . . and, anyway, you shouldn't be embarrassed. Not in front of me."

"But Elvis . . ."

"No, honey, listen, it's just, you know, you're really beautiful and your . . . uh . . . body . . . well, I just wanted . . ."

He was stammering, even blushing slightly, and otherwise behaving like a shamefaced schoolboy. But whenever that shy, almost adolescent side of him would emerge to betray his public image, its effect was always the same. It was always so endearing, I just could not resist him. My embarrassment seemed to dissolve in the warmth of it and I smiled and placed my hand on his cheek.

"It's okay, Elvis. Really. Sometimes, you're like a little boy."

I took hold of his hand with both of mine for balance and stepped out of my shoes. Drawing him to me, I pressed my body tight against his. I could feel his passion rising as he whispered, "Joyce, the truth is I love you, and your body, and I want you to know how much."

"Take off your clothes then, Elvis, and let me see *your* beautiful body . . . the one *I* love."

Still holding me close, he went on, "I missed you, Joyce, and having you here like this makes me realize how much."

"Doesn't it also make you want to be . . ." I tried again. "You know, undressed?"

"No." He grinned. "It makes me want to dance."

"Elvis, you know the one thing you really cannot do is dance," I kidded.

"We'll see about that," he said and laughed wildly as he seized me in a dancer's grip and, in an erotic parody of "The Tennessee Waltz," danced me to the edge of the bed. Scooping me up off my feet as gracefully as if he were Fred and I were Ginger, he laid me gently across it. I looked up into those profoundly blue and seductive eyes.

"Elvis, take off your clothes, please."

But his hands and mouth had already begun a slow and shameless journey over my entire body. I closed my eyes. His lips began to tease every part of me, exploring and lingering over the most sensitive areas while his hands discovered erogenous zones I didn't know I had. He stoked the flames that licked deep inside my belly, kindling and rekindling a smoldering inferno of desire.

"I want to make love to *you,* too," I gasped.

"You are, little one, you are. I can feel it."

I looked down the fervid length of me, past the perspiration-flecked flesh of my abdomen, seeing and feeling his endless, tender touch permeating my body until it reached the core of me. My back arched and my hips thrust without conscious effort. I was overwhelmed, my head falling back onto the bed. I sighed and moaned and purred, until at last I welled up and there was nothing more left to give.

I lay there for a few moments in his arms, staring past him at the gates of Graceland on the motionless, relentlessly staring screen of the closed-circuit TV. I had just begun to bask in the warmth of my knowledge that it was me those gates enclosed, me they protected and made secure, when I was startled by Elvis's voice.

"Guess I'm not ready for sainthood after all," he said, and proved it by shedding his clothes and getting on top of me almost before I knew it, his voice whispering urgently, "Kiss me there, honey."

I hesitated, a little shocked, a little surprised; after all, he had always seemed to want to anoint *me* for sainthood.

"Elvis, I . . ."

"Please, honey. I know you haven't done this before, but it's okay, really. Go ahead. I want you to."

And I did. Did as he wanted, wanting to do anything for him . . . to him. His response pleased me more than I could have imagined. He savored the pleasure I gave him, savored my complying with his wishes.

My thoughts, my feelings, the immeasurable joy of the moment all blended then into one reality—us.

Later, relaxing next to him once again, a different reality pervaded my thoughts. My sister's admonition. "Control yourself," she had said before I left for Graceland. "Don't be fooled into believing this can last forever. It may be only a fleeting, magical moment."

No, I said to myself. It is exactly those fleeting, magical moments of true closeness with another human being that really do matter, even if the end result is heartbreak.

I snuggled tight up against Elvis and cooed into his ear.
"That was wonderful."

"Shhhh . . . little one." He put his finger to my lips. "You are a sweet little girl. That's why I love you. Believe me, sometimes giving pleasure is the best pleasure."

There seemed no point in questioning that and I didn't. I just lay there alongside him in his big, comfortable bed. The more profound point, I realized, was that the passion we had shared meant something beyond physical pleasure. This was made manifest by what the closed circuit monitor so vividly projected: we were in Graceland, in *his* room, in *his* bed. That was where it was all happening and it was overwhelming. Graceland was sacred ground to Elvis and he had consecrated it for me, too, as if in his own way he was proving to me that I belonged there by making me feel like a cherished treasure in the palace of his realm.

Afterward, I was in the bathroom, staring at my image in the mirror, just as I had that first time with him in Washington. He told me I was beautiful. But what I saw was mussed hair and a face that needed help from Revlon.

"Joyce," he called, "I'll wait for you in the office."

I hastily repaired my makeup and brushed my hair until a cool confidence, almost an aloofness, stared back from the mirror. Love can do that to you. Please, God, I said almost out loud, don't let me be punished for being so happy . . .

"Here, honey." He motioned to me as I came out. "I want you to give me some advice."

I walked into his office and joined him beside the stereo.

"There's somethin' I want you to hear, and tell me whatya think."

He put a record on the stereo and sat back down in a chair alongside his desk. I cuddled next to him on the arm of the chair.

"The First Time Ever I Saw Your Face." A voice I didn't recognize sang a haunting ballad that was new to me.

"It's just lovely," I said when it ended.

"It's a demo. They sent it to me hopin' I'll record it."

"It was so poignant. I really felt touched, moved. Like when you see the first brightly lit Christmas tree of the season."

"That's real poetic. Have to get you writin' some lyrics for me."

"Elvis, I want to hear you sing it."

"Oh, noooo."

"Yes, I have to. Pleeease?"

"Okay, okay, but I don't really know it yet."

He reset the needle and lowered the volume. Then he raised an eyebrow and grinned at me as he cleared his throat.

He was into it only a few bars when I think he realized how much the melody was enhanced by the beautiful richness of his voice.

"You look mighty pleased with yourself, Mr. Elvis."

He shrugged.

"It's made for you. Please sing it again."

This time he didn't need any coaxing. He put even greater feeling into it as he grew more and more comfortable with the material.

"Elvis, you must record it. It's a wonderful song and you sing it magnificently."

"I think you're right. Maybe I will."

He sang it one more time for me and then switched off the turntable. "Joyce," he said, kissing me on the forehead, "I think your taste in music is matched only by your taste in men."

He switched on the television that was in the desk's console unit. I was surprised and delighted to see an old Elvis movie, *G.I. Blues,* fade in. And then astonished when he reached across to turn it off.

"No." I grabbed his hand. "I want to watch it."

"If you want to see a movie," he said, switching the set off anyway, "we can go downstairs. "I've got *Cool Hand Luke* with Paul Newman. I like that film and I like Paul Newman."

I dutifully followed him downstairs to the screening room. Four or five of the guys joined us and it soon became apparent that *Cool Hand Luke* was one of Elvis's favorites. He could mouth most of Paul Newman's dialogue in perfect sync with the sound track.

After the movie ended, we walked back up the stairs to his bedroom.

"Do you really like my movies?" he asked abruptly.

"Of course."

"No, really. What do you think of them?"

"Why? What do you mean?"

"Because they're no good. Just second rate. The stories are dumb and the dialogue is worse than dumb. Do you think Paul Newman would make movies like that?"

I was a little taken aback by his vehemence. I didn't know what to say. Not that it mattered; he wasn't waiting for any response.

We entered the bedroom and he sat down on the bed facing me.

"When I made, *Love Me Tender,* I didn't know anything about movie-making or acting and it was a thrill for me just being there and doing it. But, damn it, by the time I made my tenth picture, I knew I could do better. I hated those rotten stories. I wanted something better. But the Colonel would just say, 'Elvis, don't mess with success.' "

"I'm sure you'll get the chance you want, Elvis," I said lamely.

"I watch guys like Newman," he said, shaking his head in exasperation. "I've seen all his pictures and he's great. But you see some of his early stuff like *The Silver Chalice* and the writing's no good and neither is he. I've learned that I can act, Joyce. And, damn it, I'd love to get a chance in a real good movie. I made thirty pictures and hate 'em all. There's something wrong with that, don't you think?"

It was a strange Elvis I was seeing that night or, if not strange, different. And more intense than I had ever imagined. "Do you know," I said finally, "this is the first time I have ever heard you admit that something you wanted might not be obtainable."

He merely shrugged for an answer, his thoughts apparently now somewhere else. I stood up. "I'm going to change for bed," I said and started for the bathroom. I was almost to the door when I heard his voice.

"Wait . . ."

I turned.

"Honey, I want you to use the other bathroom."

"What other bathroom?"

"There's one by my office. I think you should start using that one." He pointed to a door I'd never even noticed before.

"Okay. I won't be long."

Two steps into it I froze; I had intruded on someone's most private space. The bright, fluffy, pink room exuded the scent, the musk, the spoor, if you will, of my rival. Elvis had sent me into what had been Priscilla's bathroom. Of her prior tenancy there was no doubt: a pink shag carpet covered the entire floor and even crept up one of the walls. The dressing table was filled with perfumes and lotions and a partly opened drawer even revealed family photos.

I took off my clothes, sat down on the ledge inside the huge pink tub and turned on the overhead shower to let steaming hot water cascade over a body that inside was feeling as cold and hard as the porcelain sending chills up the tip of my spine.

He was sitting up in bed reading one of his religious books when I returned. I got in beside him without a word. He waited, stealing an occasional glance at me, but when I wouldn't give him the satisfaction he finally spoke. "Yeah, I did it on purpose, to see how you'd react."

"You did? It was a rotten thing to do, Elvis. I love you and you play games with me. I think you've been honest with me about Priscilla, but maybe you can't be honest with *yourself* about *me*. After what we had together today . . . maybe you're afraid you're getting in too deep, with someone who is *too* different." I indicated the bathroom. "Maybe you put me in her place as a way of putting me in *my* place."

"No," Elvis replied. "Just the opposite. I'm sorry, honey, I just wanted you to get used to this bein' home; I do really love you, Joyce. I need you and I want you here with me. I have a lot left to accomplish in my life and I need you to share it with me."

He picked up one of his religious pamphlets, at the same time handing me two Placidyl. "Here, honey, take these and let's get some sleep."

And that was it. That's all there was to it. I was left to drift off beside him, bits and pieces of phrases filtering through my rapidly numbing brain—"I need you . . . really love you . . . want you . . . things left in my life to share with you . . ."—and into my disquieting dreams.

Some of my uneasiness remained the next afternoon and, needing an understanding shoulder, the *most* understanding, I telephoned Janice. But the tone of her answering "Hello" immediately turned my thoughts from my own problems to hers.

"Janice, it's me. What's wrong?"

"Oh, Joyce, I'm so glad you called. How is everything?"

"Everything's wonderful with me. But something's bothering you. What is it?"

"I'm seeing Vince tonight. Joyce, I think I'm going crazy or something. I love him . . . I hate him . . . I love him . . . I hate him . . ."

"I understand."

"I don't. I don't know what to do. But I can't stay away from him."

"Do whatever your heart tells you for now," was all Miss Bromide of 1971 could muster off the top of her head. "The answers will fall into place later." How true, I thought to myself, if not particularly cheering.

Janice hung up crying, which was probably a testament to my efficacy as a marriage counselor.

"Come on in here, honey, I want your help on this." I looked up to see Elvis motioning me to join him in the family room.

I walked in to find a stranger kneeling in front of the sofa where Elvis was seated. Dozens of pairs of shoes and boots were strewn all over the floor.

"You see anything you like especially," The King inquired of me.

"Well, I don't know, Elvis." I giggled. "Something's missing, isn't it? I don't see any blue suede shoes here."

Actually, it seemed Elvis had pretty much settled on two pair of boots, one white and the other black.

"Well, as long as you *did* ask my opinion," I ventured, "what about this tan pair over here? They'd look a lot better with the brown pants and a beige leather jacket you're wearing.

"Aw, I don't know. That color's for creeps, man."

"No, no, they're pretty. Come on, try them on. There, they look great. And I'll bet they fit perfectly, don't they?"

Elvis rolled his eyes at me and grinned. "Okay, I'll take 'em."

"I know you're only getting them to shut me up, but don't think I won't be watching to see that you wear them."

"Well, you're in a fun mood, I see," he acknowledged, laughing along with me. "How 'bout a game of pool? Wanna see if you have a good eye and a steady arm."

I laughed and said, "My father should be here."

"Oh, yeah?" Elvis asked as we picked out cues, along with Sonny who had come to join us at our game. "Your daddy some kind of ol' pool shark?"

"He's a legend at Klein's pool hall in Baltimore," I said proudly. "He used to take Janice and me with him when we were little. He'd sit us up on those tall chairs they have in pool halls and we'd spend hours in that dark, dingy place, alternating between watching the layer of cigar smoke that hovered over the table like a volcanic cloud, which fascinated us, and watching Daddy play, which we loved."

"And I'll bet he taught you all the tricks, hunh?" Elvis was sighting down one of the cues as if it were a rifle.

"I wish! We begged him and begged him, but he would never so much as teach us how to hold a stick. He'd just shake his head and say, 'I want my girls to meet a better class of man than the busted valises that hang out in these joints.' "

"Busted valises? I never heard that one before. It's pretty good. Sonny, you ever hear that?"

"Can't say I ever did, E," Sonny responded, handing Elvis the cue he had chalked for him.

"There was only one other stipulation he laid down for Janice and me. We had to be absolutely quiet—until his opponent was shooting."

Elvis laughed appreciatively. "I'd like to meet that old man of yours. He sounds all right. C'mon now, honey, I wanna sharpen up my game. You never know, they may want to remake *The Hustler* and I can play the Newman role. There might even be a part in it for your daddy!"

Elvis and Sonny humored me as I pretended to know what I was doing, snickering and winking at each other whenever one of them would roll the ball into the appropriate pocket after my stroke. At least I was able to hit the damn things, which surprised even me. Elvis won every game, but an impartial investigation might have uncovered some point shaving by Sonny.

"Elvis, I hope you don't mind my saying this, but you wouldn't stand much of a chance against my dad."

"That's it." He laughed. "Game's over. Okay, Joyce, c'mon, we're goin' out to a movie tonight."

"At midnight? What theater's open this late?"

The Memphian, in downtown Memphis, if you're Elvis Presley. So, by twelve-thirty it had an audience consisting of Elvis, myself, and a dozen or so of his friends and entourage. The rest of the place, except for the projectionist, was empty. That was how Elvis went "out to a movie." He had rented the whole shebang, lock, stock, and refreshment counter. Our row had even been set up with trays of bottled soda and bags of popcorn and assorted chips.

"I forgot to ask what we're seeing," I said once we had settled in.

"Patton."

"Great, I never saw it."

"I've seen it five times. I love it. Wait'll you see George C. Scott as Patton, he's fantastic. And watch this opening scene," he added, his eyes riveted to the screen as the lights dimmed. "Man, that's the way to make movies," he said fervently.

The mood inspired by this depiction of the controversial general's career stayed with Elvis long after the picture had ended and we were lying in bed in Graceland. He talked about his stint in the army, declaring that he was glad to have had the opportunity to serve his country.

"Suppose Vietnam was going on then? Would you have felt the same way?"

A look of astonishment came over his face. "How can you even ask such a question? I would have jumped at the chance to repay my country for all it's done for me, Joyce. The trouble with kids today is they don't respect anything. God, country, nothin'. It's the Commie influence. If we're not careful it'll take us over. How 'bout those kids wouldn't serve their country and went runnin' to Canada to avoid the draft? It was the Commie influence. Kids without belief in God, runnin' when their country needed 'em most."

"Then I guess, Elvis, you agree with my old chairman, Mendel Rivers, who said to a witness once that either you believe in God or you're a Communist."

"Right. He was right. That's it. God against communism. You're either on one side or the other . . ." His words began to slur as his pills kicked in.

Though I woke, as usual, before he did the next day, I did not wake in time for my scheduled flight back home. Showering, I got in my daily quota of fretting about my work versus Elvis, followed, after dressing, by a totally unnecessary stint of tiptoe-ing around the pitch-black, freezing bedroom so as not to dis-turb him while in actuality I damn well knew that the explosion of an atom bomb would not so much as budge him. Not even a Communist atom bomb.

When Elvis came bounding down the stairs a bit later looking absolutely stunning in black pants and a brilliantly red, high-collared shirt, I couldn't help but speculate how he managed the incredible exuberance and energy he invariably displayed when finally he did make his initial appearance of the day. I was well aware how much more slowly I moved those times and I also knew that the number and combination of pills Elvis took far exceeded what he parceled out to me. Whatever he was doing, I had to admit it seemed to work.

After breakfast I sat with him on the sofa while he restlessly switched channels, finally pausing to ask: "Why don't you stay another day? You don't have to go to work tomorrow."

"No, but it's Easter Sunday and if you remember, Janice and I promised to take our mother to church and then to a family get-together for dinner. I'm sorry, honey, but you do understand, don't you?"

"Yeah, religion is good for ya, keeps you humble. Know what I mean? You get to thinkin' how great you are and then you think about God and that big universe out there and you realize you really aren't much at all compared to that. You a good Catholic, Joyce?"

The question startled me. He'd never before referred to my religious upbringing. "I don't know. I'm not sure anymore. I don't go to mass every Sunday, so, I guess according to the Church's standards I'm not in very good standing. Why do you ask, Elvis? What are you trying to say?"

He reached over and took both my hands in his. Those in-tense blue eyes stared into my brown ones and I felt that now familiar warm glow come over me.

"The point is," he said gravely, "it's not important that a

person is a good Catholic or whatever, or even that you go to church. What *is* important is that you reach out to God and open up and let him in. Y'know, I was brought up in the First Assembly of God Church . . .''

"You told me." I nodded. "Holy Rollers, you said . . ."

"Right, honey. But the thing is, uh, I don't know if *they* have any answers either. That's why I want to study about all religions. I know the answers are there somewhere."

He let go of my hands and turned abruptly back to the television.

A news broadcast was presenting something I was a lot more comfortable dealing with than questions of the Deity: the My Lai Massacre convictions and Richard Nixon's intention of involving himself in the appeal process. The newsman had just quoted the army's prosecutor to the effect that it was a blatantly political act since there had been fifty previous murder convictions for killing civilians and never a murmur from the White House.

Elvis, however, was one hundred percent behind the man he had met. "Nixon's right. That guy Calley was only doin' his duty as a soldier."

"Even if that's so, Elvis, and it's debatable, what about the soldiers who convicted him? They were doing their duty, too, weren't they?"

"I'm talkin' about soldiers in the field, Little One. *Their* duty is defendin' this country."

"Maybe the court's duty was even higher—defending the *laws* of this country. That's what they teach us in school, isn't it, that we're a nation of laws? That's what makes it all . . ."

"Joyce," he interrupted, "you spend too much time around them lawmakers." Then he changed the channel. It struck me that his "kidding on the level" tone was nothing more than a by-product of the good old male ego. In public, he always doted on and proudly promoted my "Washington Woman" image. This was my first real inkling that, one on one . . .

He had spoken. "What Elvis? I'm sorry, I was lost in my own thoughts for a second."

"I just said maybe you should move into Graceland."

If he had planned to render me speechless, he couldn't have chosen a more effective way. I just sat there and stared at him.

Keeping his eyes fixed firmly on the television, he put his left arm around me until it reached to where his hand could play with the big rings on his right hand, which now rested casually in my lap.

The entire scene was like that, misleadingly casual—except for telltale things like the spasmodic twitching of his leg and the perspiration I felt sure had broken out on my upper lip as if in direct imitation of the President he admired.

He squeezed my arm. "Just think about it," he said in the most matter-of-fact, devoid of emotion tone, as if he were afraid to hear my answer.

Which was just as well, I had to tell myself during the flight back to Washington. Because I didn't have one for him.

Chapter Fifteen

I landed in Nashville on the twenty-first of May 1971, on a spring evening beautiful enough to take your breath away.

I would be seeing Elvis for the first time since he asked me to move into Graceland. In the intervening weeks he hadn't pressed for an answer when he telephoned, only reiterated his parting adjuration that I "Just think about it."

He need have no fear in that quarter. Except for my work, I had thought about little else. The problem was, those thoughts invariably took the form of questions. The same questions, over and over. Was he serious? And assuming, as I must, that he was, what would it actually mean, in practical, day-to-day terms, to "move into Graceland"?

Did it mean he was about to divorce Priscilla? Was he truly suggesting we raise the level of our commitment to each other? It had been me, not him, who was vigilant about keeping our relationship secret. That was for my own protection, of course. Congressmen have enough transgressions of their own to cover up. They take a dim view of subordinates getting involved in messy (and public) adultery scandals.

Or, was the whole issue merely a testing of the waters? The

Priscilla's bathroom incident lingered in my mind as evidence that "testing" me was not entirely beyond the realm of possibility. But wasn't that an unduly harsh judgment considering how sincere he seemed about needing me, and wanting to share with me the things he still needed to accomplish in his life?

They were questions for which I, alone, could not find the answers. Only *we* could.

His call had come while I was getting ready to go to work. Hearing the phone ring at that early hour, my initial reaction was one of anxiety. I picked up the receiver with a silent prayer that it not be Charlie or someone informing me of another medical crisis. It was a trepidation that evaporated instantly when I heard Elvis's healthy, cheerful voice.

"Good mornin', beautiful."

"Elvis, what are you doing up so . . . What am I saying? I mean, why haven't you gone to sleep yet?"

"Not ready for sleep. I've been thinkin' about things.

"Like what?"

"First, to remind you about reading some of these books I have so you'll have a better understandin' of what I was talkin' about when you were here."

"Of course; you know I mean to, but—"

"And second," he interrupted. "I got a job for you."

"Oh, you fired the Colonel, huh?"

That broke him up.

"Not yet, not yet. But I want you in Nashville on Friday."

"Nashville? Friday? But . . . oh, Elvis, *this* Friday? I can't keep taking . . ."

"Now, let me finish. I'm workin' on a new album and I need somebody with a good ear and an honest opinion."

" 'Honest opinion,' hunh?" I chuckled. "You mean somebody who thinks every note you hit sounds like a choir of angels?"

"Exactly!" He chuckled back. "Seriously now, Joyce, I want you there."

"Well, let's see," I said, dragging out my response as if actually weighing his incredible offer. "I suppose I can somehow make the time to see Elvis Presley record an album. It'll mean a great personal sacrifice on my part, of course, so we'd better discuss terms right now. What's the going rate for a good ear and an honest opinion, anyway?"

"Weelll, let's see. Would ya settle for an evening of love and affection?"

"You got a deal."

"Good. Charlie will call you later to work out the flights. See ya Friday."

"You," said Janice, as she turned the car off Interstate 395 and onto the exit for Washington National Airport, "need a keeper. This is really nuts, you know that, don't you?"

"Janice, just hurry up, please, or I'm going to miss that plane."

"How many times do you think you can get away with calling in sick on Fridays and Mondays? They're not stupid, you know."

"I know, I know. But pleeease hurry!"

There were only moments to spare when I finally jumped out and ran for the American Airlines terminal. "Coming home tomorrow, right?" I heard my sister call. "Right!" I yelled back over my shoulder.

I had never been to *any* recording studio, so witnessing a session at RCA's historic one in Nashville, famous not only for the part it had played in the rise of Elvis but for its role in modern American music, was really exciting.

I was surprised how small the rooms appeared, possibly because they were jammed with all kinds of paraphernalia (the console alone, with its zillion buttons and knobs, looked like it was capable of launching a rocket at Cape Kennedy) and every conceivable type of recording equipment. All that was missing, in fact, were musicians; the music had been prerecorded and Elvis was there to lay his voice over the soundtrack.

The album was to be called, *Elvis Sings the Wonderful World of Christmas,* and I soon discovered that my sweet Elvis was a tyrant, every inch the perfectionist, at work. He would do a song over and over until satisfied. As I watched and listened, it was obvious that despite all the high-priced technical talent RCA had taken pains to surround him with, Elvis was the man in charge.

I sat spellbound on the uncomfortable chair some well-meaning soul had brought as Elvis exhibited his uncanny ear, detecting from each playback whether or not it was precisely on key. A towel draped around his neck like a boxer, beads of sweat streaking his face, he knew exactly what he wanted and his smile would light up the room when something like Kathy Westmoreland's backup truly moved him. "That Kathy, man, she has a voice like an angel. Don't ya love it?"

Even then he could find a way to improve it: "Hey, man, we need a little more bass at this point here . . . and the horn section is too loud over there."

With everything else he had on his mind, Elvis was still thoughtful enough to try and involve me wherever he could in the behind-the-scenes mechanics of producing the album.

"Joyce," he'd ask after a song was played back, "what do ya think of this number?"

As he knew, my objectivity was extremely questionable; he could have sung the Mickey Mouse Club theme and it would have been a classic for me. "Gee, I don't know, Elvis," I'd say, playing my role to the hilt. "I think I should hear it again."

"Come on, guys," he would chuckle, "let's have it again."

At one point, he had trouble remembering a lyric and came right over to me. "Joyce, honey, can you write down the words to 'On A Snowy Christmas Night' for me so I can read 'em?"

Before I could move a muscle, three pens and two pads were being offered. Elvis's guys always had to anticipate.

After the session had gone on for hours, I asked, "Elvis, do you think we can get something to eat? I'm getting pretty hungry and I know the guys have to be starving. And you must be hungry yourself."

"I'm, uh, okay, honey. Maybe a little hungry. Hey, get some burgers or somethin' . . . and french fries! Don't forget the french fries," he yelled to no one in particular.

When the orders came, everyone tore greedily into their food. Everyone but Elvis. He barely nibbled at his. I tried to get him to eat some more, but he just pushed it away.

"I'm not hungry, really. I'm really not. I'm too keyed up, got too much nervous energy. Let's get back to work."

It was after midnight when he finally finished and we left the studio.

"Thank you, honey," Elvis said as we were getting in the car. "You were a big help, writin' down those words . . . and just being here with me."

I took his hand. "Thank you, for making me a part of your world."

"Well," he went on, slipping me a little of that self-deprecating charm that worked so well on his fans, "I know you must have been bored and all . . ."

"Sure," I said, catching him off guard for a second. "Who wouldn't have been bored . . ."

He was staring at me.

". . . by the privilege of being around all that incredible talent and energy, watching Elvis Presley do what he does better than anyone in the world! What I'm saying is that I enjoyed *every second* of it—as you know full well."

He beamed. The car started up and we headed for the hotel.

It took me only a few minutes in bed with Elvis to realize that he was totally spent. The demands of his performance at the studio had drained the last drop of even his usually boundless energy.

"Here, honey," he said, divvying up the nightly ration of Placidyl. "I think I'll just read for a few minutes."

"Actually, I'm pretty exhausted myself," I admitted, offering my lips for him to kiss good night.

I couldn't have been asleep for more than an hour when I suddenly woke to find myself being shoved off the bed.

It was Elvis. He was moaning and kicking and his thrashing around had nearly knocked me over the edge.

"What is it, Elvis! What . . . ?"

"Get Sonny . . ." he moaned. "Get Red . . ."

I ran to the little parlor and called Sonny's room.

I ran back into the bedroom. Elvis looked worse, lying on his back, holding his stomach, his moaning and groaning even louder. I was scared. I put my palm to his forehead. It was cold and clammy.

"What's wrong? What is it?"

"Don't know," he moaned. "Terrible pain . . ."

He was groggy from the pills and slurring his words.

Sonny's bulk burst into the room.

"Get a doctor," I shouted at him.

"No, get a plane." Elvis's voice was close to a shriek. "Take me to Memphis . . . right now!"

Sonny barreled out to phone. His cousin Red, whom I hadn't even seen come in, helped Elvis up and into his clothes and I got myself packed and ready in about five minutes even though I was also still half in a fog from the Placidyl.

Half an hour later we were on board a chartered plane roaring through the night toward Memphis. I asked one of the guys whether the hospital had been notified or any other arrangements made to get Elvis there as quickly as possible.

"Not going to a hospital," was the tight-lipped response.

"Where are we going?"

"Dr. Nick."

"Who?"

"Doctor Nichopoulos," explained Sonny. "He's E's personal physician."

"And friend," Red added. Which seemed, at least in their eyes, to close the case.

Once again it was Elvis's dad, Vernon, who was waiting for us at the airport in his Mercedes.

We drove to a fairly ordinary, but comfortable-looking house with only one light showing through a window. We pulled in and Vernon shut off the engine and got out from behind the wheel. I noticed Red West say something to Charlie and Charlie nodded.

"Joyce, would you mind please staying in the car while we take E in to see Dr. Nick?"

I said I would and sat in the dark and watched Charlie and the two Wests help Vernon take his son into the doctor's house.

After a while the darkness—there didn't seem to be another sign of life anywhere—began to get to me. The complete and utter silence was also eerie. I began to feel spooked, sitting there alone in that silent, pitch-black night.

I responded the way any normal, hopelessly vain young woman would. I pulled out the mirror, turned on the car's interior lights, and checked my hair and makeup.

In about two seconds, Red came racing out of the house on the run.

"Are you crazy!" he hissed, ripping open the door. "What do you think you're doing?"

I was so shocked by his tone and manner that I just stared at him without answering.

"What's wrong with you! Turn those lights off."

He reached in and turned them off himself.

"What's wrong with *you?*" Now I was mad. You all told me to wait out here, where it's pitch black. And *scary* being alone."

I put the mirror back and moved to the door.

"What's going on here, anyway? And how is Elvis? I want to be inside with him."

"I'm sorry, Joyce." Red held the door for me. "Let's go in."

Elvis spotted me as soon as we walked into the doctor's office and a big smile lit up his face. "I'm fine now, little girl."

"Thank God! What was the matter?"

"Just some bad cramps, that's all."

Elvis introduced me to the gray, curly-haired man sitting behind the desk. He stood up and I was surprised to see how short he was. He gave me a kind of half smile, as if to indicate there was no problem now that Elvis was in his hands. I thought he was quite proud and pleased with himself.

We were about to leave when I asked Elvis if his doctor would write me a prescription for Placidyl to take home with me. All it took was a word from him and it was done, no questions asked.

Though it was dawn by the time we were settled in his bed at Graceland, Elvis was now more wide awake than ever. He read for a while from one of his religious pamphlets, but it was obvious that he was really geared up to talk.

"You're loyal to me, aren't you, Joyce? You wouldn't do anything I didn't like, would you?"

"What are you talking about?"

"I told you I'd know if you were dating another man; you believe that I'd be able to know that, don't you?"

"You mean that you're clairvoyant or something? I don't know. But what I can't believe is that you think I could do that. You should know me better than that by now."

"Yeah, but you go to all those parties and things there at the Congress and . . ."

"They're just people I work with, just friends. I thought you were proud of where I worked. You always seem to enjoy my stories about what goes on up on the Hill. You know, whenever other people are around, my anecdotes about Washington amuse you but when we're alone . . . Anyway, why are you even questioning me like this?"

"Joyce, I *am* proud of the work you do. But you're young and beautiful . . ."

"Thank you. But, so what?"

"So, I'm sure the guys up there . . . uh . . ."

"What, Elvis?"

"I'm sure plenty of 'em are after you. You know what I mean."

Actually, I was wondering if he wasn't acting jealous because he was feeling guilty over conking out instead of making love our last couple of nights together. That was a difficult area to confront him in, so instead I told him not to worry, and that I was flattered he wanted me all to himself.

"But what about you?" I countered. "Girls and women throw themselves at you, literally. I mean, they practically take their clothes off for you in public! What am I supposed to think about that? And lately, you seem more interested in those books than you are in me," I added.

"Hey, you know I don't go for those kind of girls. You know, Joyce, I, uh, never even made love to Priscilla . . . not really . . . you know what I mean . . . until we were married."

"What are you trying to say, Elvis?"

"What I mean is, it'll be better when we can be together all the time. When you really care for someone you should be patient. And I do love you. You understand what I'm saying, don't you, baby? I need you."

"I know and I do understand, but it's what you need me *for* . . . that's what I'm—"

"I need you to understand me and . . . ."

He was no longer really listening and his sentences had begun to drag. Of course, Elvis always took more pills than I did, and it didn't surprise me when they took effect on him first.

". . . and care about me."

I felt I had to hear more, that I had to get some answers, while *I* was still coherent.

"I *do* feel you love and need me, Elvis, it isn't that so much. But why did you tell me that about Priscilla? Do you see Priscilla in me? Or, more importantly, do you *want* to see her in me? Am

I a replacement for something that you've lost? And there's something else that's been bothering me. Why haven't I met any of the guys' wives? Or even your daddy's? I mean, I've seen some of the guys' dates, but where are the wives?"

I had been staring straight ahead, digging these things out of myself and when he didn't say anything I looked over at him. He was sound asleep.

It was unfortunate. I was going to ask him next what it was Dr. Nick had given him that had worked a miracle cure. Elvis had made a point of telling me that he knew as much about prescription drugs as any doctor; he even had a copy of the *Physician's Desk Reference* on his nightstand. "Hell," he had said, "if they can read a book and learn about 'em, well, so can I."

I believed him to a large degree; of course, short of walking on water, there was very little I didn't believe he could do. I was vaguely aware there was a tinge of hypocrisy in my taking him to task about drugs. Not only was I allowing Elvis to sedate me, but, upon encountering his Dr. Nick, about whom I instinctively had reservations, I had lost no time in making sure he became my supplier, as well.

I didn't get up until seven o'clock that evening. Originally, my flight back had been scheduled for that afternoon and, after showering and dressing, I telephoned Janice.

"Joyce, where are you? What happened?"

"I'm at Graceland."

"What are you doing there? I was getting worried. Why didn't you call me?"

"Something happened with Elvis. Let me tell you."

"Please."

Even after I had explained about his suddenly taking sick, Janice was only slightly mollified. "You still could have called before this."

"I couldn't. I just got up."

"Just got up! Are you aware it's seven-thirty at night?"

"Very much aware."

"Well, when are you coming home?"

"I'm not sure, exactly. I'm waiting for Elvis to get up. He was supposed to leave for California today, but obviously that's been changed, too. But don't worry. I'll be home tomorrow no matter what. I have to be at work on Monday.

Elvis came gamboling downstairs, frisky as a colt, about an hour later and, after kissing me, announced he was starving. "You must be, too," he added. "Let's have breakfast."

"Breakfast?" I couldn't help glancing at my watch. "Sure, breakfast it is," I said. "Just let me go punch out."

He stared at me. "Punch what?"

"As long as I'm living the schedule of a night watchman, I figure I should have a time clock to punch out on."

Breaking up, he put his arm around me and hustled me off to the dining room. "Should've had you around to write my lines for those corny movies I did; at least there would've been some things for the audience to laugh *intentionally* at."

Over a big, southern-style breakfast with plenty of bacon and ham as well as biscuits, eggs, griddle cakes, and potatoes, he announced, "I'm gonna put off goin' to California so we can spend more time together here in Graceland."

"Oh, that'd be . . . great."

"Yeah, I thought you'd—"

"No, Elvis," I interrupted, shaking my head. "It *would* be great, if I could stay. I love being with you more than anything, and what we've shared here together in Graceland means everything to me, but I can't think only of my own pleasure. I have a commitment, too, and I just don't dare take any more days off from work. Maybe if we'd known sooner that you were going to change your plans . . ."

"Well, honey, I'm not leaving till six-thirty, so make sure you don't leave before. If necessary, I'll charter a plane for you."

"Oh, Elvis, that's a waste of money."

He laughed. "You're worth it."

That night we were lying in bed watching the late news on

the ceiling TVs when footage appeared of rioting at a rock concert in Chattanooga, precipitated by the failure of three of the groups to show up. This set Elvis off on one of his favorite diatribes—the lack of professionalism among "drug-taking rockers." That soon paled, however, before the next item. "The presence of President and Mrs. Richard Nixon at the dedication of the Lyndon Johnson Memorial Library in Austin, Texas, brought out more than two thousand anti-Vietnam war protestors who booed the Chief Executive . . ."

"That's what I was talking about that time, Joyce. No respect, that's what kids have today. No respect, not even for the President. Man, today they even burn the flag. Those dudes who do that should be shot."

"I don't know, Elvis," I protested. "I think what makes this the greatest country in the world is that you *can* boo the President and burn the flag. And that no secret police come at four o'clock in the morning and drag you away. Maybe what the flag really stands for is the freedom to burn it—and to not lose your right to life, liberty, and the pursuit of happiness. You know?"

I knew he was looking at me and I took my time before turning and smiling coyly at him.

He seemed to be mulling over my statement. "Damn," he said finally, "you been doin' some heavy thinking."

He was right there. After his last patriotic outburst, I had decided I would be prepared and checked out the thoughts of some of the more liberal members of our committee.

"Well, I gotta admit you do have a point or two there," he conceded and leaned back to watch more of the newscast.

"You're just too mellowed out to fight tonight," I joked.

"Oh, damn," he said and reached for his phone.

"What is it?"

"I'll get somebody up here to fix it."

"What? Fix what?"

He raised one arm and pointed. It was the picture on his TV screen. It had gone fuzzy and out of focus.

"It probably just needs a little fine tuning," I said.

He hung up. "Somebody'll be up real soon."

"We could probably fix it just by fiddling with the knob," I offered.

He didn't pay any attention, just leaned back and picked up one of his books.

"Elvis," I persisted, "don't you think between the two of us we can figure it out? I'm sure . . ."

He still wasn't paying any attention and only moments later there was a knock at the door.

Elvis got up and opened it.

"Hi, Daddy. The darn TV isn't working."

"It probably needs just a little adjustment, Elvis. Here, let me just . . . excuse me, Joyce . . ."

More than a little disconcerted, I picked up my negligee from where it was laying on the blanket, put it on and got up so that Elvis's father could climb up and stand on the bed to reach the TV. He fiddled with the knob and in a few seconds the picture was clear again.

"That's all it was, Elvis," he explained. "Just needed to work that knob right there. It's okay now, son."

He stepped down and headed for the door.

"Thanks, Daddy. Hope it'll be okay for the night. But you sure took care of it. Thanks again."

"See ya now, good night," Vernon said, his eyes avoiding mine. He closed the door behind him.

He was embarrassed as hell—and so was I. Maybe even more so. Partly for myself, but mostly for this old man who had obviously been wakened in the middle of the night and come running to perform a simple task that Elvis—or even I—was perfectly capable of performing.

The next day I was in the bedroom packing my suitcase when Elvis came up and put his arms around me.

"I'm glad you came back here to Graceland with me. You know I don't want to go to California, but I got business to take care of out there. I'll be back soon, probably in a couple of weeks."

I closed the suitcase and turned to kiss him goodbye. I thought to myself . . . now. This is the time to say something. If my love for him was real and not a sham it had to give me the strength to do this. If I never did anything else for him. For him—and for me. Because my having asked Dr. Nick for that prescription was beginning to scare me. I was worried about the level of my own dependence.

Our lips parted. "Elvis," I began, and took a deep breath. "Because I love you, I want you to promise me something. I know I've gone along with it up to now, but . . ."

"What is it?"

"Well, this isn't easy for me. And please don't take it the wrong way . . . but do we need to take so many pills?"

"Joyce, now . . ."

"Something to put you to sleep, something to get you going again when you wake up—" I had the bit in my teeth and couldn't stop. "I can understand when you're performing, but—"

"That's enough." Elvis's expression was stern. "I told you I know what I'm doin'. I know as much about drugs as any doctor—and certainly more than you. I don't need advice from you or anyone else, so drop it!"

"I'm not trying to give you any advice," I cried. "I'm trying to tell you I'm scared. You think I'm too naive to figure out why Red went crazy just because I put a car light on while you were getting your miracle cure? That cure must have been something pretty potent. But maybe you ought to think about—"

"I don't need you to tell me how to think, either. I *know* how to think!" He stormed into the bathroom.

I sat down on the edge of the bed. Well, Bova, you blew that one. And what did I expect? This isn't something that can be dealt with on the spur of the moment, with one foot out the door.

It would take a concerted effort with some thought and planning behind it. Because I wasn't going to let this stop me.

In a few minutes, he came out of the bathroom. He flashed me the curled-lip grin. As always, it made me smile back. He sauntered over and sat down next to me. Draping one arm over my shoulders he put his lips close to my ear.

"Let's not part this way."

I turned to him.

"We'll be back together in a couple of weeks," he said and moved his lips to my mouth, murmuring, "Don't worry, Joyce. About me or anything. Everything is okay. Trust me."

Chapter Sixteen

Only a short time later, on a particularly hectic day at the committee, I came back to the office after wolfing down a hurried lunch to find my phone already ringing.

"Joyce?"

There was no mistaking that voice, and not because of any particular drawl—it was the distinctive, adorable way in which he said my name.

"Elvis! What a nice surprise in the middle of the day!"

"I miss you."

"Where are you?"

"At Graceland."

"Is everything okay?" I asked. "You sound funny."

" 'Funny'? No. Uh, what about you? You workin' hard right now?"

"Of course; you know we don't waste you taxpayers' money around here!"

He laughed appreciatively. "What exactly you workin' so hard on?"

"Well, the committee's planning hearings to receive testimony from at least twenty witnesses on an inquiry into Marine Corps procurement prac—"

"Actually, Joyce, I'm not feeling good," he interrupted abruptly. "I need you to come here to Graceland. Today."

"What do you mean? What's—"

"I don't know what it is, but I mean it, I need you."

I sighed. We'd been through this so many times before. "Elvis, I can't walk out like that. I mean, we're also fighting a deadline trying to get out the report on that Department of Defense communications thing I told you about and . . ."

"I know, I know, but I need you *now.*"

"Elvis, you know I want to be with you, and especially if you're not well. But I just took a couple days off for my parents' divorce— Oh God, it isn't your eyes again, is it? Did your infection come back?"

"I'm not sure exactly. I just know something's wrong. I'm feelin' bad, honey, and I got to have you here with me."

"All right." I gave in. "I'll be there. How can I not . . ."

I guess I knew from the first I couldn't refuse him. Besides, I could tell he wasn't going to take no for an answer. And I would never forgive myself if it were something serious and I wasn't there to help.

"But *tomorrow,* Elvis," I insisted. "There's no way I can make it today. And I can only stay one night. I've *got* to be back here the following day."

Asserting myself with that ultimatum did not, however, prevent me from spending a restless night worrying about it all— and worrying about what was wrong with Elvis.

The next day proved to be even more unsettling. It was while I was in the middle of packing to go that my mother phoned. She was upset and wasted no time coming to the point.

"Why can't you pick me up and bring me over there so I can stay with you for a few days? Unless you could stay here instead? I need help with this big house. I can't stand being here alone."

"Ma, I know you're going through a tough time right now, but . . . I can't. That is . . . I mean . . . I'm in the middle of packing."

"Packing? Where are you going?"

The second I said it, I knew I had made a mistake. I should never have mentioned packing. But it was too late now. "To . . . uh . . . Memphis, Tennessee."

"Memphis! Why Memphis?"

Mistake number two. I should have lied, should have stated some safe, simple destination she wouldn't question, like, "I'm going to Vietnam to check out armed services morale, Mom."

Deep, deep, breath. "Well, Mom, you see, I have kind of been dating Elvis Presley and Memphis is where he lives."

"Elvis Presley? Are you telling me you're having an affair with him?"

I was silent.

"What are you doing, *running* to a man? To his *house?* Well, I don't think it's right. What do you do when you're there with him?"

"Ma," I said, ignoring that loaded question, "just don't worry. I'll be gone only one night. Then I'll come and get you."

"I don't know what to say to my own daughter. If you're going to date him, why can't he come here and take you out like a normal person?"

"Because he's not a normal person, Mom, he's *Elvis Presley.*"

"I know who he is. The one with the hips and the greasy hair . . ."

"Maybe fifteen years ago—"

"And I also know he's a married man, and that's *not* fifteen years ago."

"Ma, think about it. If he's so married, how come he invites me to his home?"

"I don't know and I don't care. I just don't approve, that's all. "You're committing a mortal sin and—"

"That's it. Stop right there. I'm sorry if you're going to be upset with me, but I'm going and that's all there is to it."

Janice had come out of her bedroom in time to catch this last part and she quietly took the phone from me.

"Hello, Mom? Now calm down, Mom, Joyce is over twenty-one; she knows what she's doing. Uh-hunh . . . uh-hunh . . . Now, you know that's not true . . . We both love you. All right, I'll come over after work . . . Right. Goodbye."

"What did she say?" I asked, when Janice had hung up.

"The usual. That I always take your side, the two of us always stick together no matter what, we think alike, act alike and never, ever agree with her, that's why she can't get either of us to do what's right."

"Thanks, honey," I said and resumed getting ready.

Janice pitched in, helping me fold and pack. "You just don't worry, Joyce. I'll take care of Mommy."

"I know I can count on you."

"But I probably won't stop worrying about you myself."

"Remember what you just told Ma. I'm a big girl now. I know what I'm doing."

"Yeah, I used to think that. I mean, it's okay if he's really worth it. But, let's be realistic, how sensible are we when our hearts are in control? The main thing is that I don't want to see you hurt."

"I know, I know. Believe me, neither do I."

"Call me. And be careful . . ."

As always, Janice's woman-to-woman advice was excellent, I thought to myself as my plane began to go into its landing pattern over Memphis. Too bad that with the man we love, careful is usually the last thing we are.

"Elvis!" I exclaimed, seeing him stride toward me, arms outstretched, across the foyer of Graceland. "You look great! What exactly *is* wrong with you?"

"Well . . . I . . . ah . . ." he stammered. "I felt terrible, terrible without you, and I just wanted to be with you."

"Damn right that's what you wanted! And you got your way, didn't you, like always. Look at you, standing there, the picture of health." I tried hard to be furious at him, but he was so charming—

And he knew it! He grinned and said, "Now, Joyce, you can't be angry at a man who wants his little girl with him." He took me in his arms and began to kiss me. All I could do was murmur, "But I was worried about you, and frightened something really *was* the matter. You know it isn't fair for you to . . ."

"To ask you to come because I was sick? When the truth is that I just really missed you and needed you here."

"You're incorrigible. You know I should be angry." I sighed, punctuating each word with a kiss. "And I am, a little . . . a very . . . very . . . very . . . little."

He had made me feel so wanted that any resentment I might have felt simply evaporated before the intensity of that need. The tone now seemed set for a warm, cozy evening of romantic reunion, followed by our usual late dinner and then a sweet and ultimate consummation. Which was exactly how it went—until we came to the sweet and amorous part.

I hadn't only anticipated, I'd also prepared, putting on a brand new nightgown and negligee before I snuggled into bed. Once there, I began to nuzzle Elvis's chest and whispering how glad, how really glad I was that he wanted me so badly. Suddenly, without any of the charming and romantic preliminaries that had always characterized his lovemaking, Elvis grabbed me and pulled me hard up against him. He covered my mouth with kisses, also hard, and completely devoid of warmth and tenderness. Not since he threw the black silk nightwear at me in Vegas had he acted so foreign to his true nature. There was not even a hint of the endearing shyness, none of the tender foreplay. Instead we were making love like machines . . . no, not making love at all . . . we were having sex . . . no . . . *he* was having sex. I was merely the means of his sexual gratification. I pushed him off me gasping that I had stomach cramps. I pulled down my nightgown from where it had ridden up around my neck and ran into the bathroom. Turning to shut the door, I saw he hadn't even bothered to take off his pajamas.

By the time I finished wiping the tears from my eyes and

came out of the bathroom, Elvis passed me on his way into it, without a word, without a single question as to how I felt. Well, I felt *used*. I wasn't just resentful, I was furious. I sat down on top of the blankets.

He sauntered into the bedroom then, buttoning his pajama top and announced, in a tone of voice that made it seem more like an order, "I want you in Tahoe when I play there next month. I'll call you when I'm there and tell you when's the best time for you to come."

"Best time for who? You or me?"

That got him, all right. He stopped short at his side of the bed and looked at me.

"What did you say?"

"Do you mean best for you, like maybe when whoever else is with you is gone—" I admit that was a low blow; he'd given me no cause to be jealous. "—or best for me, based on your infinite knowledge of the workload of the Armed Services Committee?"

He just stared at me.

"Aren't you going to say anything?" I prodded.

"What I say is *you* best shut up." He sat down on his side of the bed, propping himself up with the pillow.

I pushed myself up to a sitting position and, softening my voice, tried a different approach. "Elvis, let me explain. Sometimes you act like my life and responsibilities are unimportant and that I should always defer to *your* wishes and *your* whims."

He folded his arms across his chest, leaned back and listened.

"Look, I realize that overall your lifestyle is more demanding than mine," I continued. "That you have pressures that I . . ."

"There's the first sensible thing you've said," he said, cutting me short. "That's why you should be available when I am. I made the decision to get you here because it was a time I could be with you."

He looked at me as if trying to gauge my reaction. Then,

adopting a conciliatory tone, he asked, "Don't you want me to make *some* decisions in your life?"

"No. I mean yes, yes . . . God knows I could use some help in that area. But I want the decisions to be made with *my* best interests in mind, too."

"And I don't do that, huh?"

"Well, how about today? Because of your—for lack of a better term—childish ploy, I left a pile of important work on my desk. If I don't get back and finish it tomorrow I could be in for a lot of grief. I have to take responsibility for my job, for myself, for *my* actions. I need to . . ."

"What about what *I* need you for?"

"And what exactly *is* that, Elvis?" I argued. "I'm not big enough to be a bodyguard and since you have a full coterie of managers, servants, and gofers . . . there doesn't seem to be a position open for—"

"That's enough!" He turned his back on me, grabbed one of his books from the night table and proceeded to read to himself.

Sliding under the covers and facing away toward the heavy drapes, I reflected that just possibly, sarcasm had not really been my best move. It didn't take long for the old female insecurity to begin seeping through the shell of self-rightous anger I was glowering behind. Had I really screwed up and actually jeopardized our relationship? This should have been the lovely, intimate finale to my visit. Instead . . . Maybe I had overreacted from the start. Just because he wanted to be with me—after all, isn't that what I wanted, him to *want* me? I loved him, I was sure of that. And wasn't that all that really mattered?

Damn you, Elvis, why can't you understand! I had turned my head to peer over the wall of tension I was now ready to blame myself for. He was lying on top of the covers, still apparently engrossed in his book. I felt I had to make up with him or I would never be able to tear myself away from him in the morning.

"Elvis . . ." He laid the book down and faced me.

Janice and me (I'm on the left), in a formal portrait taken on August 2, 1948. We were three and a half years old.

Janice, me, and our mother on the day of our First Holy Communion in June 1951, standing outside of St. Edward's church in Baltimore.

Janice and me, in a photo taken across the street from our grandmother's house on June 24, 1951. Who's who? Neither Janice nor I can remember!

This is just me, without the make-up and hair pieces.

This is the photo of Janice and me (I'm on the right) that Elvis first saw in my apartment and requested a copy for himself.

Me, in the early 1970s, while on vacation with Janice. When Elvis saw this picture, he wanted a copy.

Amy Joy's Donut Shop, the site of Elvis's wonderful scene with a mob of kids from the Washington, D. C. ghetto.

Here I am on the platform bed that bore witness to Elvis's throwing the pajama top in my face and my walking out on him.

This was taken in Las Vegas, August of 1971. That's me on the right, but I don't think the guy on the left needs any introduction.

Me, in the living room of the Elvis suite at the International Hotel in Las Vegas.

The bedroom suite at the International, with the damned exercycle that Elvis made me climb up on when I was so sick.

The dining room of Elvis's suite at the International. The table had been set for Elvis.

We called this one, Guess Who?

This is the Library of Congress' most requested photograph, but until now, Elvis Presley's biographers have been puzzled by what brought him to Washington in the first place.

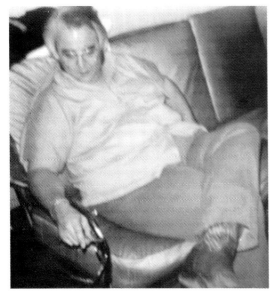

Lamar Fike, who figured prominently (and unhappily, for him) in that last terrible time Elvis and I were together.

Sonny West, who, happily for me, figured even more prominently, risking his job to save my health (and possibly my life) at the terrible end of it all.

Charlie Hodge, another friend to me.

Marty Lacker, one of Elvis's main men.

Elvis captured as he asked me to return to the tour with him on the night he sang, " The First Time Ever I Saw Your Face" to me at the Baltimore Civic Center, on November 9, 1971.

My sister and me with Elvis on that fabulous night.

A kiss of gratitude for Jerry Schilling who came all the way from Los
Angeles with Elvis to track me down in D. C. after the pajama fight.

Jerry Schilling seems amused by my mom posing with Elvis's dad, Vernon.

This picture was taken by Janice in Elvis's dressing room. Mom, Jerry, and Vernon I've identified previously. The gray-haired man (next to Mom) is the notorious "Dr. Nick." The man second from the right is George Klein, who escorted me on Colonel Parker's plane when I was in possession of Elvis's needle, the morning after that scary night in Philadelphia.

Mom getting into the act again, this time with me and a certain well-known
rock n' roll singer.

Here I am in 1970. You can understand why I often was mistaken for Priscilla.

Me, in 1992, with Francois, the beloved pet I share with Janice.

That's me on the right, in black. This is the outfit and hairstyle I was wearing the last time Elvis and I were together — the time I decided to look like *myself*.

"Elvis, please, don't . . ." I moved closer.

"I thought you missed me as much as I missed you," he said. "Guess I'm not important enough to you," he added, his eyes now fixed on the ceiling.

"You're wrong, you're the most important person in my life."

"I try to show you how much you mean to me and all I get is hostility. That crack about me bein' with other women and all . . . that hurt."

"I'm sorry. I didn't mean it, I was just upset."

"I want to have you here with me, to get closer. Now I just don't know anymore."

His voice had sunk almost to a whisper and, despite the anger and disappointment he was venting on me, all I could see was how vulnerable he looked and sounded.

"Elvis," I pleaded. "Hold me. Make love to me. I can't let our night together end this way."

I knelt and pressed myself against him, taking his face between my hands, my eyes beseeching him to relent. I whispered, "I love you, please, I want everything to be all right again."

There was no response, no return of my embrace when I kissed his lips. Still, I was not going to be denied.

God, I wanted him then. No, it was more than "wanting." I had to have him, to make things right between us.

I stroked his hair and my lips moved from his mouth to his eyes to his nose and slowly down his neck. I heard his book thump to the floor as I unbuttoned his pajama top and began to nibble at his chest. I sat up and pulled my nightgown over my head so the glow of his reading lamp painted my bare flesh.

"Elvis, do you want me?" I leaned over him and caught just the barest smile on his lips, a smile that immediately faded when he realized it had been detected. It dawned on me that Elvis was playing a little head game, feigning indifference to my advances. Then I knew—tonight he wanted it this way, wanted me to lead, to be the aggressor. This would be my ultimate apology, a way of saying I was sorry that meant more than mere words. I would show him I loved him in a way I never had before.

I leaned across him, pressing my breasts against his chest and sliding my hand down his body until it slipped inside his pajamas. Without a sound he raised his hips and I tugged and pulled the bottoms down to his knees. There he was, no longer able to feign indifference, exposed in a way he couldn't make fade away like the little smile.

My hair came undone, as unbridled as my passion, and cascaded across his gently heaving chest. His warm, smooth skin became moist and taut and I could feel it fairly scream for more . . . more . . . as it stretched to its limit over the firm, rigid flesh that belied his stoical silence. Quickly I raised myself up and over him, straddling his hips. I hesitated once, looking down into his eyes.

"I want you too, Joyce." The words came out in a little gasp.

Gently, teasingly, little by little, I lowered my body. I heard a soft moan as I descended until, slowly, slowly, I had encased all of him. We looked into each other's eyes. My hips began to move, a slow, circular motion dictated without conscious thought or effort by the undulating, rhythmic waves of passion that were stirring deep inside, stirring me to the brim. I could feel him throbbing with pleasure . . . my thighs squeezed tighter . . . tighter . . . until at last he responded in the way I needed . . . the way we both needed.

When, a little while later, we were lying side by side, a loving atmosphere having been restored, Elvis took my hand. "Sorry if I worried ya," he said. " 'Bout anything."

"It's all right now," I said. "I guess worrying about you is probably dumb, anyway."

"Probably is." He laughed. "Doesn't mean I don't want you to, though." He took his hand away and I felt his weight shift in the bed and heard him rummaging around.

"Here." His hand was back.

"Oh, Elvis, no pills—not tonight. If I oversleep and miss that early-morning flight, there'll be real hell to pay at work."

"Honey, please . . . for me. I can't rest easy unless I know you're sleepin' beside me. It's important to me, 'specially after us arguin' like we did before."

He knew how to play to my weaknesses, just as he played to his audiences. I mean, what are great entertainers but master manipulators? He knew how to hit those responsive chords, all right. But, in all fairness, as long as I'm coming up with some insight here, I should face the fact that nobody can play me unless I let myself be played.

I knew it was ultimately my responsibility. It was just that I couldn't bear to say "No" to him, not tonight. So, I dutifully swallowed the pills—and my sense of self-preservation, both in one gulp.

My flight had left long before I opened my eyes that next day. My first reaction, naturally, was to be angry with Elvis for insisting I take the pills.

After I thought about it for a while, my second reaction was to be furious.

With myself, as well, though, because I *did* know better. And, to be perfectly honest, I probably would not have been able to sleep a wink if I hadn't taken them. Standing there, barefoot and shivering in his freezing, dark cave of a bedroom, I still felt all keyed up.

Unfortunately, however, the quivering, sensual turbulence of the night before had moved upward and into the pit of my stomach. I was faced with a sudden realization: I was terrified of losing my job.

My usual act while Elvis lay conked out and I got ready to leave, was to be stealthy as a cat burglar. That morning, a combination of anxiety and anger turned me into a clumsy klutz. Frantically hurrying to be in time for the next plane and show my face before lunch, at least, I stubbed my toe, dropped a few things, and then managed to slam full force into the bed.

"What's going on?"

I heard the slurry voice that I almost never heard in the morning. Well, that was something, anyway—my *body* stirring him in his deepest stupor, even if it was just by banging into his bed.

"I just got up, Elvis, that's what's going on. How did this happen? How did I *let* it happen?" As usual I turned some of my anger inward, away from him, to avoid a real confrontation. He looked too groggy to comprehend much of what I was saying, anyway.

"I am going to be inexcusably late for work, if I get there at *all*. Why the hell did you insist I take those pills?"

"I want you here . . ." he mumbled. "You stay, Joyce. Come on, you don't have to go. . . ."

"Yes, I do. Why can't you understand that? And those damn pills! I can't do without them anymore and I don't like it."

"That's enough, now . . . hear!"

He was doing his best to be forceful, but having a tough time just enunciating his words.

"You should be trustin' me. If I tell you they're okay to take, you should believe me and listen, and if I tell you to stay, you should do that, too."

"Why? Because everyone else in your life does? But I'm not Joe, or Charlie or Sonny . . . or even Priscilla!"

He tried to mumble something in response, but I was already closing the door behind me.

The entire flight back I alternated between self-pity for having put myself in such a position of impotence, and self-flagellation for having lashed out and tried to hurt him as I had. The irony of the situation was also not lost on me. He was used to showing his mood swings and temper and I had probably astonished us *both* with a sample of my own. So now I was on my way home, feeling guilty and terrible.

I thought of Janice, who by now would have impatiently phoned my office and discovered I had blown it again. Ominously, prophetically, her parting admonition came back to me: "Be Careful."

Perhaps, on some intuitive, subconscious, instinctively female level, I already knew. Because I had been many things on this trip: I had been a loyal woman racing to her man's side; I had been a fiercely outspoken woman stating my case when I felt he had taken advantage of me; and I had been sensual and provocative when lovemaking was called for. But there was one thing I had not been. I had not been careful.

Chapter Seventeen

As soon as I got back to Washington, my life started caving in on me, piece by piece, and from every direction. It began the moment I walked into my apartment.

By the time the plane had landed it was too late to put in an appearance at work. I was in such a state of depression anyway that all I could think of was to grab a taxi straight home and get into my bed and pull the covers up over my head. I needed my own space, to be alone and shut off from the world and all fears, doubts, and questions for a little while. I craved the lonely bliss of solitude.

What I got was my mother.

"Joyce, is that you? Why aren't you at work?"

Of course, Janice had brought her to the apartment to stay those "few days" she had requested. Perfect, just what I needed.

"Mom, I'm really tired, so if you don't mind . . ."

"Joyce, I want you to know, I am extremely disappointed in you."

"Please, Mom, not now. I have a splitting headache."

"I don't wonder. It's probably a guilty conscience. You're living a life of sin, you know."

"I'm sorry if that's the way you feel," I said tightly. "It isn't the way *I* feel."

I went into my bedroom to unpack, but my mother, never one to honor anyone's privacy, followed right after me.

"Why couldn't he have come here to see you?"

"I don't know, Mom." The best course with her was to try to blunt the interrogation with short, terse answers. Not that it would do any *real* good, but it might save me some aggravation.

"I talked about it to your sister, you know. She's worried about you, also."

"Good. Everybody's worried about me. Keep it up. Pretty soon you'll have me worried, too."

I slammed my drawers shut and walked back into the living room, plopped on the couch, and kicked off my shoes.

"I don't understand why he can't take you out like a normal boyfriend."

I leaned back and covered my eyes with my forearm.

"You know something, that's actually a very funny image when you think about it. Elvis Presley coming to call in his limo, maybe bringing me flowers or candy, and all of us, his bodyguards included, going to dinner or out dancing. Of course, he'd never get to eat or get in a dance what with the crowds that would form, but at least he'd be *normal*. And then afterward, since neither of us drink, we could go to a malt shop and play his records on the jukebox while the bodyguards called for reinforcements to contain the mob that would have formed outside by then."

I sat up straight and looked at her.

"The problem is, he *isn't* 'normal.' He's Elvis Presley, the most popular entertainer in the world. And"—I lay back down again and shut my eyes—"I'm his girlfriend."

"And he's a married man."

"That's right," I said. "And I'm an adultress. There's a good, old-fashioned term for you."

"Don't you try to be smart and sophisticated with me, young lady. I'm your mother and I raised you to be a—"

I started feeling bad. I knew I was hurting her. "I know you're my mother," I interrupted gently, "but that also makes me *your daughter* and I think you ought to try and show your own flesh and blood some compassion and understanding instead of coming on like I was on trial and you were the judge."

"You were always such a good girl, both of you were such beautiful girls. You always reminded me of myself when I was young . . ."

"Mom, it doesn't mean I'm not a good girl because I make love to someone I love, no matter—"

Nothing I said could stop her now. "When I think of how people used to stop me on the street when I would be pushing the two of you in your strollers and say, 'Mary, only you could have had *two* such beautiful girls who look just like you' . . ."

I couldn't take much more of this, especially since I knew she was near tears. Luckily, Janice arrived home just in the nick of time. It took some doing on her part, but she calmed our mother down and got her home, before returning to give me hell herself.

But by that time I was in bed and (with the aid of my dependable Placidyl) in no state to care any longer what anyone—including me—said or thought about what I was doing with my life.

The morning after, however, was, as it almost always proves to be, a different story entirely. It began when Jack Reddan, the subcommittee counsel, and therefore my immediate superior, sent for me first thing on my arriving at the office. That skyrocketed my anxiety level back up into the stratosphere to which it was now getting accustomed.

"Joyce, if you're having personal problems . . ." he began after asking me to sit down.

" 'Personal problems'?" Oh yeah, I might just be able to conjure up a personal problem for your listening delectation, I thought, as I looked around his office for an ashtray. In Jack

Reddan's case, the surroundings reflected the man. All business: big, wide desk with everything in perfect order; no pictures of his family or signs of a personal life of any kind. The consummate bureaucrat.

"Well, unh . . . my mother and father are going through a very difficult divorce right now," I muttered.

"But nothing in your own life, something that is affecting you more directly?"

He was showing more concern than I expected. He was a bright man, very articulate and almost as wide in girth as he was tall. I wished I could have confided in him. "No, nothing like that. Not really," I said.

"If there is," he went on kindly, "we should talk about it right now, because I've gotten to know your work well, and you're too valuable to this office for us to lose if it can be avoided."

"Thank you." He waited, but I had said all I could. It was difficult meeting his eyes and not telling him the truth and I found myself looking past him at his bookcase with its complete and bound set of the *United States Legal Code*.

He delivered his ultimatum. "But I also know you well enough to know you couldn't have been sick on all those Fridays and Mondays. You must understand, Joyce, that has got to stop. As of now."

"I know," I said. I thanked him for being understanding and got up and went back to my office.

I felt hemmed in on all sides by people judging me or telling me what to do—no, judging me *and* telling me what to do.

Even Janice ricocheted back and forth. She provided a much-needed buffer between me and my mother, insisting on my freedom to see Elvis, but seemed to devote the rest of the time to freeing me *from* him.

"For once Mom isn't entirely in the wrong on something," she declared one evening while we were sitting at the table doing our nails. "You really did look awful when you came back that last time from Graceland." She got up and went to the stereo and put on a record. Not an Elvis one, either. As she sat back down, she shook her head. "I mean, you're always getting these calls about his health, but *you're* the one who looks and acts like your sick. What was wrong with him this last time, anyway? You never did tell me."

"Nothing."

"Nothing?"

"No. He just missed me and wanted me there."

"And you think that was all right? You think that's the way to treat someone you're supposed to love? Whatever happened to being honest and up front?"

"But you don't know how great he can be, so sweet and loving!" I protested. "Janice, I really *believe* he needs me and loves me."

"Well," Janice smiled wanly, "you should know."

That's right, I thought to myself, I do. And hugged that tiny, secret knowledge to myself like I had my favorite doll when I was a child.

Until the days went by and turned into weeks and there had been the opening in Lake Tahoe and still he hadn't called.

I knew that he was punishing me for asserting my independence the morning I left him in bed. At the time, and for a short while immediately after, I wasn't positive he'd even remember my leaving, considering he'd been barely conscious. Once I determined he actually was trying to get back at me, though, I derived a certain perverse satisfaction. It proved I carried some weight with him, that when I hit home, he bled.

Then, one Saturday afternoon, following an especially bad morning (mornings were always the worst), my hand shot out for the phone as if it had a will of its own. I had almost completed dialing before I put the receiver back down.

I looked up and saw Janice staring at me. "Should I call him or what?"

"No. He'll call. He always has."

"The truth is, as much as a part of me wants to see him, I've been feeling so putrid lately, I don't think I can."

"What do you mean. Are you getting sick?"

"I don't know," I admitted.

"It's him. It's his fault. He's got you upset all the time. It's a wonder you don't have an ulcer. The way he acts about your job . . . I don't know how you keep it together. And those damned pills are going to kill you. If you don't feel better by Monday, you are going to the doctor and find out if anything—"

"I don't want a doctor. I want him."

Janice came over and sat next to me on the couch. "I know you do." She put her arm around me. "Don't think I don't understand. It's just that you're in such limbo with him, his still being married and everything. Did he say anything this last time about getting a divorce?"

"Janice, think about it: I'm invited to Graceland all the time; when I go there I sleep with him in his bed. His grandmother, his father, everybody, they're all there. They all know me. He makes a point of my being part of things. Even with the servants, for God's sake. Does that sound like I'm some kind of casual affair—with a man who was brought up to respect family above all else? Are those the actions of a man who still considers himself married?"

Janice took a deep breath. "We always come down to the same thing, don't we? You believe he loves and needs you." She stood up. "There's really nothing for me to say anymore. Only *you* can know what to do."

She started to walk away.

"Janice! Maybe I really don't know. Maybe I'm just trying to convince myself about his feelings. Maybe I'm all wrong. Maybe he doesn't care about me at all. Maybe I should just put myself out of this misery and call him. No . . . no, I won't do that. Oh, God, I can't stand this. It's just that . . . What you said before, about going to the doctor?"

"I still think it might be a good idea."

"I think I know what he would tell me."

"What do you mean?"

"That I'm pregnant."

"Oh, Joyce, no!" Janice came back and took my hand. "Are you sure?"

"No, not *sure* like I've been to a doctor, but I . . . I just know it."

"What do you mean?"

"I just know, that's all. I can feel it."

"Honey, what are you going to do?"

"For now? There's nothing I can *do*. We've *done* it, really. What I need is to think, to think things through."

I didn't see Elvis in Tahoe, so I don't know for sure, but I doubt his performance could have been any better than the one I gave over the grueling days that followed my revelation to Janice. Days in which I sat perkily through the testimony of 21 witnesses in one hearing after another, and prepared the documents and organized the statements for committee members and counsels while managing to hide from everyone the fact that my stomach was sliding queasily into my bowels.

On the evening that particular ordeal had ended, Janice and I were standing on the balcony eating ice cream and staring out at the trees being rustled by a rare August breeze when the Elvis Phone rang.

Of course, I wasn't ready yet to tell him, and I panicked.

"Oh, no! Not now. God, what should I do?"

Janice carefully put down her dish alongside my untouched one.

"Answer the phone."

"What will I say?"

"Just answer it. You'll know what to say when you hear him."

By the time I got to my bedroom, Janice hard on my heels, it was on its fifth ring.

"Hello."

"Hey, little girl."

"Elvis. Hi."

"I've missed you, baby."

"Missed me? It's been over a month since I saw you," I answered, my voice shaky. "You couldn't be missing me *too* much."

"But I am. I just had a lot of things to take care of with Tahoe and all . . . and now Vegas. That's why I'm calling. I need you to be there."

"And I want to be with you, too, Elvis. I just don't know. There's a lot to do at the office." That was a lie. Congress would be in recess, but I didn't know if I could face him. Not telling the truth must be getting easier, I thought, remembering my talk with Jack Reddan. Still, that was the first time I'd ever lied to Elvis and it left me with a strange, unpleasant feeling.

"Oh, come on, baby. You can get away a couple of days."

He was so adorable, I couldn't stand it. We talked a little longer and before we said goodbye, I told him I'd work out something to be in Vegas and promised to let him know the next day. I hung up and turned to Janice.

"He wants me to come to Vegas."

"You have to talk to him."

I walked slowly back into the living room. I sat down on the sofa with my legs crossed under me. In a moment my sister followed, stopping to stand in front of me.

Janice reached out and took my hand. "I'll go to Vegas with you."

"I wouldn't be able to do it any other way."

"You know, Joyce, you've got to come to some decisions in advance. First of all, are you absolutely determined to have a baby? No matter what?"

"I'm not sure," I admitted. "I'm really not sure of anything right now, but I think I would need for my baby to have its father."

"Well, Elvis should certainly be able to help with that decision, don't you think?"

Janice was trying to put me in a lighter mood, and I appreciated it, even if I didn't exactly respond. "I wonder what Mom would say? Not that it matters. She'll never know."

"But *he* has to, right?" Janice sat down beside me.

"Don't worry," I said. "I'm enough of a romantic, or idealist, or whatever—to believe in love. As a force, as something that is basically positive. I think if there truly is love between two people, something good deserves to happen out of it."

"Honey, I'm not sure I know what you're saying, or even if you do. But trying to be logical here, don't you think it could be possible that he might want to get a divorce so that the two of you could get mar—"

"What!? My God, Janice, I *am* trying to be logical, but it's so hard to think straight." I sighed. "I'm just too confused and . . . humiliated and . . . and . . . upset and sick over how this could affect not just me but . . ." Tears came to my eyes. "Everyone I love."

Janice reached out to me and I cried myself into exhaustion in her arms.

I handled the plane ride to Vegas well, considering flying's effect on morning sickness. The experience persuaded me that I could get away with revealing none of the weakness I felt inside. I even managed to kid Janice when she began to carry on about the turbulence we were encountering.

"Lighten up. The plane's not about to crash. Besides, you're the one who's supposed to be calming *me* down, remember?"

The heat was drier in Las Vegas, as was laconic Joe Esposito, who met us at the airport. He kissed us affectionately and asked if we'd had a good flight.

We were already driving down the Vegas Strip when I asked, "How's Elvis?"

"He's okay. Anxious to see you."

"And the shows?"

"Good . . . good. You know how he gets, a little uptight before he goes on. But he always manages to blow 'em away."

We had barely enough time to change our clothes and still make the dinner show. The comic was halfway through his act by the time we were escorted through the International's huge showroom and seated in Elvis's booth.

It was during his performance, perhaps even because of seeing him standing up there, so in command, that I made the decision not to beat around the bush or try to feel him out or go into any of the preparatory speeches that had been running through my head.

"Janice," I whispered and nudged her.

"What?"

"I'm just going to flat out tell him."

"That's right." She squeezed my arm. "I'm sure it's the right thing."

For the rest of the show, I thought about how exactly I would "just flat out tell him." At the same time, knowing Elvis would expect me to comment on every nuance of his performance, I tried to concentrate on the show. It was impossible, and by the time he got to his favorite gospel song, "How Great Thou Art," I was worn to a frazzle.

You could hear the ice melting in the glasses when, in the middle of the number, the arrangement called for a dramatic pause in the music and vocals.

"Hey!" A voice bellowed out of the darkness. "We're not here to listen to church music!"

Elvis turned and pointed in the direction of the drunken, raucous voice. "You shut up right now or you get the hell out!"

A chorus of cheers went up from his audience and he finished the song without further incident.

When Elvis sang "Teddy Bear," a number that traditionally called for him to toss little stuffed bears at random into the sea of hopeful female faces, one sailed over the forest of outstretched arms and headed directly toward us. Janice and I reached out and each of us managed to clutch a chubby little leg. I yanked the bear from her and spun sharply at the sound of laughter behind me. It was Joe, appearing early for some reason, grinning and nodding his head in amusement.

Later, in the suite, after a word with the bodyguards just as he entered, Elvis headed straight for us.

"Great show," Janice said as soon as he was close enough.

"Yeah, uh-hunh, thanks, little sister. Glad you liked it. How've you been?"

He was leaning over and kissing my twin on the cheek, but his eyes were on me.

"Well, Joyce," he said, straightening up. "Did you like it?"

"Of course, Elvis." My voice was even and controlled, without even the slightest trace of gush. The ritual of telling him how great he was after every single performance paled beside the importance of what I had to tell him later that night.

"You were great, as usual," I said. He put his arms around me.

"I really missed you, baby," he said and looked deep into my eyes. "Come on, sit with me."

We moved together to the little yellow sofa, four or five of the guests drawn in his wake, as filings to a magnet.

"You winked at Joyce, didn't you?" Janice asked. "Right in the beginning of the show?"

Elvis nodded and laughed.

"But that was nothing," my sister went on, "compared to the teddy bear sailing right to us."

"Well, now, that wasn't so tough," he exclaimed with false modesty. "I just zeroed in on Joyce with my special radar, aimed, and let fly! It knew where to go from there."

"Yeah, Elvis can talk to the animals, man," Lamar Fike piped up from where he'd been listening on the outskirts of the group.

"Shut up, Lamar." Elvis obviously wasn't in the mood for the huge retainer's brand of sycophantry. "You're one big ol' ugly animal yourself, man. And how 'bout that animal in the audience? Sonny? Red? Did you guys take care of him?"

"You mean the wiseass who yelled at ya, E? Yeah, we took care of him. He didn't want to leave, but we persuaded him it was the thing to do."

"Jerks like that shouldn't be let loose, y'know what I mean? I wanted to take care of him myself, man."

At three in the morning it was still going strong, that unending magic carpet of unabashed admiration and calculated flattery that Elvis seemed to need after each performance. I still sat next to him, but by then the tapestry being woven out of anecdotes and exaggeration no longer needed my simple seamstress skills. I had long since tuned out and was rehearsing what I had to tell him after everyone left. And wishing the time would come soon.

Janice caught my eye. A few minutes before, I had noticed her talking to a couple of girls at the bar, and now she motioned for me to join them.

Carol and Judy, both blonde, both very tall and thin, and both dressed in hot pants and white boots, had proposed an excursion to the hotel lounge to listen to some music.

"Sorry, but I don't think I should."

"Oh," Judy said, immediately diffident. "I never thought *you* would. We really meant only Janice."

"Oh, come on, Joyce. Elvis is so engrossed," my sister pointed out, "he'll never even notice you're gone till you're back sitting next to him."

I followed her eyes back to the sofa. It was clear The King was still holding his courtiers spellbound and was a long way from dismissing them. "Well . . . all right," I said. "Just for a little while, though."

The lounge was filled with dancing couples and blaring music. I enjoyed the change of pace for a few minutes, but to tell the truth, I was already longing to get back to Elvis when I saw Sonny and James heading straight for us.

"Hey, Joyce," Sonny called. "Why did you leave? Elvis wants you back . . . right now."

"I didn't think he'd even notice I was gone. He certainly seemed preoccupied."

"You know he doesn't miss a thing."

We all trooped dutifully back to the suite.

"Come here, honey." Elvis waved me over as soon as I entered. "Tell everybody what happened at the donut shop when we were in D.C."

About an hour later I was changing the LP on the stereo when Janice came over to me. "I'm really tired, Joyce. Do you mind if I go to my room? Call me tomorrow as soon as you can and tell me what he said."

I walked her to the door. "I can't stand this waiting. I've got to get him alone and talk to him. Soon."

"Where are you going now?"

Sonny had appeared behind us.

"I'm just going to get some sleep," Janice told him. "I'm really tired."

"You can't go yet." Sonny seemed almost indignant. "Elvis isn't ready for anybody to leave."

"What? You're kidding."

"At least go over and ask him."

"Don't be ridiculous. He's surrounded by all those people. I don't want to interrupt."

"Go ahead, Janice, you're exhausted," I said. It seemed time to introduce a note of common sense into all these royal prerogatives. "Don't worry about it, Sonny. If Elvis asks, I'll tell him where Janice went."

I walked back to the sofa and sat down.

Elvis's voice came, under his breath and in my ear. "It's time to go to bed."

Whew . . . finally!

I followed him into his private quarters within the suite as his guys did their thing of gently but firmly dismissing the gathering.

232

Elvis went immediately into the bathroom. I sat down on the bed. My stomach was nervous, but at least not nauseous. Mercifully, the nausea had ceased a while before.

I needed a little something to bolster my courage. I went back to the living room and got a bottle of vodka from behind the bar. I had to hand it to Elvis's guys. Not more than ninety seconds had passed since he'd decided the party was over, and the room was empty. I poured a couple of fingers of the vodka into a glass of orange juice and walked back into the bedroom just as Elvis came out of the bathroom. He had changed into his pajamas.

"Don't ever do that again, Joyce," he snapped.

"Do what?" I was taken aback.

"Leave the suite without telling me. I want you there sitting next to me."

"I only went to the lounge with Janice and those girls to listen to some music. I wasn't gone very long."

"Why'd you go at all? Were you bored or something?"

"You're making a big deal out of nothing." I got up from the bed with my drink still in my hand. "I really don't feel like having an argument. I'm going to take a shower."

I slammed into the bathroom, stripped off all my clothes, and threw them down on the floor. I gulped down the rest of the drink. *Damn* him for taking that tone with me! And on this night, of all nights. I stepped under the soothing warmth of the shower.

By the time I got back into the bedroom, Elvis was fast asleep, *The Impersonal Life* laying across his stomach.

Just as well, I thought; his mood had hardly seemed receptive and now mine was foul. I picked up the little book and placed it on his night table. On my own were the Placidyls left for me by my sleeping prince. I swallowed them and crawled under the covers.

The ringing of the telephone woke me the next day.

"Hello?" I mumbled.

"Joyce." Janice's voice resounded through my skull. "What are you doing?"

"Huh . . . trying to sleep? Why?" I realized Elvis wasn't in bed with me. "What time is it? It must be late. Elvis isn't here."

"I know. He's in the showroom with the band, working on a number or something. Get up."

"Okay, okay. Come up to the suite."

I raised myself into a sitting position. The room was dark, the curtains still drawn tight. My head ached, my body felt numb, and my stomach had begun acting up again. The tension, the anxiety and, no doubt, the baby. God. I put on my robe and peeked cautiously out of the bedroom to make sure no one was in the suite. There was a knock at the door and I opened it.

"You got here quick."

"You look awful." My sister stepped into the room. "What's the matter? What did he say?"

"My head and stomach are what's the matter . . . and he didn't say anything. Because I didn't tell him. *Couldn't* tell him. He was too busy telling me off about going out to the lounge. Then, by the time I'd finished in the bathroom, he'd fallen asleep. God, I feel as terrible as I must look."

"Sit down, honey," Janice ordered. "No, get dressed and let's get you some juice and breakfast."

"I can't eat. But I'd better get dressed. What time is it anyway?"

"Three-thirty."

"I'll hurry."

By the time I was ready, Elvis was just coming into the suite, with the entourage, of course. I was too late. My announcement would have to wait until after the shows that night.

For once, the shows seemed to drag, as did the time I spent sitting by him after each one, corroborating and embellishing his stories for the rapt throng of guests. For Elvis, it was business as usual. For me, playing hostess and straight woman, it was a barely endurable hell. I got through it because I knew that at the end I would at last unburden myself to him.

It was well into the party that followed his late show when Elvis got up and walked over to the stereo to play a record. There was something in his manner that made me watch him closely.

He dropped the needle and a song began to play that brought back warm and wonderful memories of those lovely days in April during my second visit to Graceland. His voice filled the room as he sang "The First Time Ever I Saw Your Face."

"Oh, Elvis, you recorded it! It's beautiful! I love it."

I was on my feet and going to him.

"Whoa . . . don't get too excited! It's just a demo album. It's not released yet."

When the song ended, he took the album off and wrote something on it. "Here, honey."

I read: "To Joyce, with love." He didn't date it. If he had, it would have read August the sixteenth—exactly six years to the day he was to die.

"It's always been for you. I wanted you to have my very first recorded rendition of that song. If you hadn't insisted I sing it over and over that day, I might never have recorded it." He reached over and while I held the album, scratched out some of the other titles listed on the label. "But promise you won't play these cuts. They're terrible; they need a lot of work."

"Elvis, I . . . I don't know what to say. Except, thank you, for thinking of me."

"Of course. You had to have it. It belongs to you. You're my girl . . . and I love you."

"Do you, Elvis? Do you really?"

He placed his hands on my shoulders. "Silly little girl, you know I do."

The love in his eyes swept away all my fears. I knew then that somehow, it would all work out. If only I could have told him then and there.

Elvis signaled Sonny that the night was over.

"Come on, honey, let's go to bed."

"Go ahead, Elvis, I'll be right in. I want to see Janice for a minute."

I walked over to where my twin was standing by the door.

"You two looked so engrossed in each other I didn't want to interrupt . . ."

"It's going to be fine. I know it is. I'm telling him tonight for sure."

Janice kissed me, hugged me tight, and left.

I took a deep breath and walked into the bedroom. Elvis was still in his bathroom. I went into mine and washed my face. When I came out he had a table spread with food waiting for me.

"Come on, honey, let's have a bite to eat."

"I'm not really hungry, but you go ahead," I told him. "I'll just have something to drink."

"Ya know," he said, digging in, "there's one other cut on that demo I really like. 'Until It's Time For You To Go.' I think that's gonna be a good one, too."

He continued to make small talk, but I had a hard time listening. I was preoccupied with what I had to tell him. I just needed the right opening.

"How long have you had it?"

"Hmmm . . . what, Elvis?"

"Your car, it's pretty old, isn't it?"

"No, it's not old."

"But I think you should have a better one, a bigger one, maybe a Mercedes or a Caddy. You know, so I'll know you're safe."

"Oh, Elvis, you are wonderful, but my car is fine. You don't have to buy me expensive things. You don't have to buy me anything. Besides, the main thing is how in the world would I explain to people what I'm doing driving a Mercedes."

"Okay, little girl. I understand what you mean. We'll drop it for now. But I do worry about you, though."

And I was worrying about what I had to tell him! I prayed silently for the right words.

"We just won't worry about it now." He laughed at me affectionately, stroking my hair and cheek, taking my hand.

When we were settled in bed, he handed me my Placidyls and reached for a book.

"Elvis, I—"

"Honey." He turned to me. "Ya know what, I'm having a little problem with my throat."

"What do you mean? Is it sore? Do you think you're coming down with a cold or virus or something?"

I reached over and put my hand on his forehead and then my cheek to his cheek to feel if he had a fever.

"Poor baby, this would be an awful time for you to get sick."

"I don't think it's really anything. Probably just 'Vegas throat.' Ya know, from the dry heat?" He cuddled up to me. "Yeah, it's probably nothin', but I love when you baby me."

"Elvis you are a baby . . . *my* baby. By the way," I said, obeying the little voice in my brain that was repeating over and over: Now or Never, "how come you never talk much about your baby?"

"Oh, Lisa Marie. She's a great little girl. Three years old now, three and a half, actually."

"And spoiled to death, I'll bet."

"Yeah, I guess I do spoil her," he said proudly.

"And what about her mother?"

"Well, she's a mama, ya know, she does the motherin'. A mother is different. Once a woman is a mama, she changes."

"I'm not sure I know what you mean, Elvis." I could feel my throat tightening.

"Well, when a woman has a child, it's a gift from God. It's God's way of telling that woman she's not a little girl anymore. She's grown up, you know? Now it's time to be respected and all."

"I don't think I'm getting this. Are you saying you didn't respect Priscilla until she had a baby?"

"No, I always respected her. But now it's different. I don't think a mama should be tryin' to be sexy and attracting men. It's not right."

"But you could have a baby when you're only twenty-six . . ." I caught myself. "I mean, lots of women have babies young. Some, when they're really young, even in their teens. Think how hard it would be on them to have to stop being thought of as lovers."

"Well, I don't know about them or what'd be hard on 'em or what wouldn't. All I know is a woman's not attractive in that way after she's a mama."

My heart and my hope were sinking fast, but I forged ahead. "There are all kinds of women, though, right? Not every woman would lose her appeal just because she had a baby."

"It's just not exciting and it's not *supposed* to be. Trust me on this, Joyce, I know I'm right."

I couldn't believe my ears. The lump in my throat became a knot, a hangman's knot. I did not know what to say, could not think of a word to utter. Elvis leaned across and kissed my silent, sealed lips. I could see he was having trouble keeping his lids from closing.

I reached over and took more Placidyl, swallowing greedily, gratefully.

"Elvis . . ." I began, trying to choose my words carefully. "What you've been saying about women once they have a baby, well, are you speaking generally? What I'm trying to get at is . . . you don't mean that you, yourself, specifically would . . . couldn't be attracted to a woman just because she . . . ?"

I looked down and saw that he had drifted off to sleep.

Which didn't matter. Because I knew the answer to my own question. It was stupid to even have asked it. I lay my head back and let the tears flow through my closed eyelids and felt them stream, warm and wet, down my cheeks.

Well, he had made it clear, without my having to come out and ask. I could not have a baby and have his love. In the one thing our love had created, we could not be together. Elvis was telling me that if I had his baby there could be no "us"; there would be only me. Alone.

Chapter Eighteen

There isn't a lot to say about having an abortion. Unless you're someone running for political office, maybe. For a woman, it's just bloody trauma that stays with you a long time no matter how hard you try to get over it.

The first thing, though, was to have the pregnancy scientifically proven.

It was Janice who took me to the doctor, naturally, as it would be Janice on whom I would have to lean throughout the ordeal. On the drive to the doctor's I expounded for the first time in detail on what Elvis had said that night.

"My God, I can't believe it," Janice replied when I'd finished. "He actually said those things? He can't possibly mean them. What's *wrong* with him?"

"I don't know. Maybe something to do with his being so crazy about his mother . . ."

"Oh, that Freudian stuff, like, he can't make love to *any* mother then, because it would be like making love to his own—like committing incest? My God, is his head in *trouble* . . ."

"No, *I'm* the one who has the trouble," I replied ruefully. "Only it's not in my head."

"Damn him! I hate him for this."

"Sure, but if *I* start hating him, how do I not hate myself as well?

"Actually," I admitted, "I *have* started hating myself. I feel like I'm going crazy. I hate the idea of the lies and ugliness I'll have to live with—and what I especially hate is feeling that now I'm left with no choice."

"You should have told him anyway."

"No. I couldn't. After what he said? It would have been the end of us. I couldn't take that."

On the nineteenth of August, we sat in the doctor's waiting room while I stared at the opposite wall. In a strange way I found staring at the wall comforting. I aspired to be just like it was— blank. I wanted to know nothing and feel nothing. I wanted to be blank inside.

Janice saw the nurse approaching and squeezed my hand. "Maybe you're wrong about the whole thing. Maybe it's something else."

I shrugged and patted her hand. "Sure, I'm wishing for a miracle, too."

The young woman in the starched whites took a urine sample and then led me to the examining room where she handed me a hospital-style gown.

"Take everything off and put this on, please. The doctor will be in shortly."

And he was, to ask even shorter questions. especially once I told him I thought I was pregnant. Then he examined me and asked me to return to the waiting room.

"What did he say?" Janice's anxiety level was only slightly lower than mine.

"Nothing, really. All very cut-and-dried so far. Until they get the results from the specimen."

"Miss Bova?"

I followed the nurse down the hallway and into the office.

The doctor was seated behind his desk and, before I could even sit down, he said, "Well, you're right. You're pregnant."

He had merely verified what I had been telling myself all along, of course. But his was the voice of medical science personified, sitting there in his white jacket with the stethoscope blooming out of his breast pocket and confirming my worst nightmare, making it real, official—final.

I fell into the chair. "Another prayer unanswered," I mumbled under my breath.

"Excuse me?"

"Nothing. Are you sure?"

"Yes, I'm quite positive."

"But I can't be . . . I mean I don't *want* to be," I mumbled. My eyes felt heavy and half shut.

"Are you saying you don't want to have this baby?"

"That's right." My voice was strained and I cleared my throat. "I am."

"Well, I can abort it, if that's what you really want. But wouldn't you like time to think about it and let me . . ."

"No. I've taken all the time I need. I don't want to think about it. I don't *have* to think about it. When can I have it done? The sooner the better." I looked down; my hands were clenched into fists, the nails digging into my palms.

There was a calendar on his desk and he glanced at it. "I would say in around two weeks. The fourth of September is good. Let me check my appointments and see . . . Yes, I'm available."

Janice stood up and started toward me as soon as I reentered the waiting room. I put her off until we were outside and walking to my car, but of course she knew the truth the minute she saw my face.

"This shouldn't happen to someone like you," she was saying as I started to get behind the wheel. "It just isn't fair. It's crazy! Honey, maybe I should drive, you've got a lot—"

"I can drive. Being pregnant doesn't make you an invalid."

"No, of course not; I was just thinking you've got a lot on your mind, you know, things to weigh . . ."

"I've already arranged to have an abortion."

"Oh, no, Joyce! Wait. Think about it!"

"There's nothing to think about. I won't change my mind. There *is* no real choice."

"Yes, there is. Maybe you *should* have the baby. It would be *your* baby. And, really, if you think about it, you don't *have* to tell Elvis. Ever."

"Janice, you're being ridiculous," I snapped. "What would I do with a baby? And without a husband? No way. I'm not bringing up Elvis Presley's child by myself. I'm going to have this abortion and that's that."

I turned the key in the ignition.

The next two weeks were perfect—a perfect preview of purgatory. My bouts of nausea came back full force, and so did Janice's husband. I had been so wrapped up in my own problems that I was neglecting to give her the emotional support she was counting on from me. Vince lost no time in stepping into the breach and, drained from the demands made on her by my inner turmoil, she couldn't bring herself to turn away from the aid and comfort he offered.

"Joyce?"

Janice was silhouetted in the doorway of my darkened bedroom.

"Are you asleep?"

"Be serious."

Just before she'd gone out on her date with Vince I had gone to bed—but to hide, not to sleep. Actually, that had become my daily routine: following each miserable day at work, I would spend a miserable night at home, hermiting myself away in my room, not wanting to go anywhere or see anybody. I had developed an almost pathological fear that someone would sense I was pregnant. Especially my mother. It would have killed her, the thought of her daughter committing *the* mortal sin.

Janice shifted uncomfortably and I could see her face in the light drifting into the hallway from the living room.

"Joyce, don't hate me. Please."

"What are you talking about?"

"Vince . . . please forgive me. I told him. I couldn't help it. It just came out."

"Oh, no. How could you? *Why?*"

"Joyce, *please,* I'm so sorry. But he swore he wouldn't tell anyone. And he's so worried . . . really. He's so concerned about you. He wants to do anything he can to help."

"I wish you hadn't."

"I know, I know, I wish I hadn't either, but I did."

"Well, it's done." I shut my eyes.

When I opened them again and saw my sister still standing in the doorway, I almost felt sorrier for her than for myself. "It'll be all right," I assured her. "Maybe he *can* help."

By the next time Elvis called, my unexpressed anger toward him and toward myself, as well as my self-pity, had reached a level that almost prevented me from communicating with him.

"Joyce, what's wrong? I can tell something's wrong."

"It's nothing, really. I just have some problems at work and they've got me down, I guess."

"Who's givin' you trouble, baby? I'll take care of it. Just tell me, I'll make some calls."

"No, Elvis. You can't help. There isn't anything that can be done. I'll take care of it," I added, trying to keep the bitterness out of my voice.

"Well, I'll come in and see you after I finish here in Vegas."

"No . . . no, please, Elvis."

"But I don't want you feelin' upset."

"I'll be okay. Really, there's nothing you can do about it."

I could tell by his voice when he said goodbye that he was

hurt because I didn't think he could help, hurt that I didn't *want* him to help me. I knew how he could be about something like that, knew it might mean not hearing from him for a time while he sulked. But there was no way I could tell him what was really happening. And I knew I wasn't ready to see him—not until it was over.

It was Janice and Vince who took me to the hospital after I finished at the office on that dismal Friday, the third of September. When my sister asked to bring Vince, I just couldn't be so selfish as to deny her someone whose shoulder she could lean on. God knows, I had nearly worn hers out.

They waited while I checked in and filled out the necessary forms, then joined me in my room where we made desultory conversation until it became obvious my eyes were starting to shut.

"Joyce, I really don't want to leave you," Janice said.

"It's okay. And *I'll* be okay . . . tomorrow. Tomorrow it will all be over."

Morning was a blur of bright white light. I was placed on a white-sheeted gurney and wheeled down a gleaming white corridor into a floodlit operating room where I stared into faceless eyes peering down at me over white masks. Chemicals were pumped into my body, and icy numbness began to pulse through my veins. I counted: "100 . . . 99 . . . 98 . . . 97 . . ."

As soon as the anesthetic wore off and I could think at all, I told myself I had to forget what I had just done. What I really wanted was to burrow back down into the comforting black hole of the anesthesia and stay there forever.

As we know, however, I didn't. I lived to tell the tale. It took me a long time before I did tell it, partly because I wanted it to be the whole truth, but mostly because I had to find the guts to *face* that truth—the truth that I didn't have enough faith in myself to bring a life into the world alone. An even tougher truth I had to face is that I wanted Elvis more than I wanted a baby. Even his baby.

"Joyce . . ." I gradually became aware of Janice and Vince standing over me, smiling kindly, and I tried smiling back, but it took too much effort. "Joyce, I'm sorry, but I won't be able to pick you up and take you home tomorrow. Mommy is insisting I take her to church and I couldn't think of an excuse off the top of my head that would cover both of us. I just told her you weren't feeling well . . . that you had your period. Funny, hunh? But don't worry. Vince will pick you up."

The trip home with Vince was painful and only increased my depression. Not that he didn't try hard to be considerate and helpful, it's just that I was beyond the reach of any kind of consolation. I wanted only to crawl into my own soft, warm bed and bury my shame under the covers.

My demeanor probably discouraged any attempt at small talk on Vince's part, but just before we pulled up to my building, he was kind enough to ask if I wanted to get something to eat.

"No, I'm not hungry, thank you," I answered. "I ate a little in the hospital."

He parked and, taking hold of my arm with one hand while carrying my bag with the other, he walked me to the apartment. "Janice told me to tell you she would be home as soon as she can," he said.

I nodded and opened the door.

"Joyce, I know you don't feel like having company," Vince said, putting my bag down, "but if you need me for anything, just call."

I closed the door behind him, leaned back against it and sighed in relief. God, I needed to be alone. I picked up my bag and carried it into my room where I unpacked. I could hardly take my eyes off the bed. It looked so inviting. I felt weak and very sorry for myself. Instinctively, I reached for the Placidyl.

It must have been hours later when I heard my name being called and felt myself being shaken.

"Joyce, wake up."

I opened my eyes and saw it was my sister.

"You're having a nightmare," she said and shook me again. "Are you all right?"

"I guess so . . . No, I'm not. Janice, I was in Vegas."

"What?"

"Yes, in Elvis's booth, and he was onstage, singing."

I sat up.

"Janice, the rest of that huge showroom was empty. Elvis was singing only to me. Then he started to throw stuffed teddy bears, but only to the empty seats—not to me. I stood up and yelled to him to throw one to me. Finally, he did. But when I caught it and sat back down, I saw that it wasn't a teddy bear at all. It was a baby. I had a baby in my arms."

"Oh, honey . . ." Janice reached out and took my hand and squeezed it.

"Suddenly, Mommy was there standing in front of the booth screaming at me that I had sinned and would be punished forever and that nothing could save me."

"Joyce, everything is going to be all right. I promise."

"When? When will it all end? It'll never go away!"

"In time, it will," she promised. "It'll just take time, that's all."

"Janice . . . this dream? Am I losing my mind? What's happening to me?"

"No. The dream is really pretty natural, if you think about it. I wouldn't mention it to anybody else, though, if I were you," she joked, trying to lighten my pain.

"Don't worry." I tried to smile. "Nobody would believe it, anyway. It's too perfect, like some symbolic scene in an arty movie."

"That's right," she said, and this time the tears were in her eyes.

"Oh, Janice . . ." I put my arms out to her. "Promise me we'll never mention . . . what happened, to anyone. Not even to each other. I want it never to have happened. Promise me, please?"

"I promise."

We held each other and cried for a long, long time.

It was only a week later that my Elvis Phone began to ring. Much too soon for me; I just stared at it until it stopped. After that it rang regularly every few days, but I was still not ready to talk to him.

A couple of weeks later, as I came out of a long meeting about an inquiry into allegations that defects and deficiencies in the design, manufacture, testing, and administrative controls of the navy's new F-14A were the real cause of its crashing on only its second test flight, I received a message that Charlie Hodge had called twice. I didn't return the calls. I was feeling stronger physically every day, but emotionally, I was not healing as rapidly as I'd hoped. If I was going to break my silence, I wanted it to be with Elvis himself, not an intermediary, however nice and well-intentioned.

It took a few days, but when my Elvis Phone did finally ring again, I picked it up, ready to talk. Only to find it was Charlie on the other end of the line.

"Joyce? Elvis has been calling and having me try to get hold of you. Where've you been?"

"I've been staying with my mother. She's been ill."

"Oh, hope it's nothing serious?"

"No. Thanks."

"He wants to see you."

"I can't . . . now. I . . . started coming down with something."

"Well, he'll be calling . . ."

Charlie hung up. I hated lying, but there was no truth in me for Elvis at that point. And damn little of anything else. I could speak to him when he phoned—in fact I needed to hear his voice—but as for seeing him . . . not yet.

I still carried something inside me. Not life . . . not any longer. No, what was still eating away inside me was anger. In fact, if depression actually *is* anger turned against oneself, then I had an awful lot of anger left to deal with. Because I certainly was depressed as hell. Carrying a grudge against the man you love will do that to you. Especially when the man has no idea of the reason why. A real Catch-22, self-inflicted punishment: I could not express my anger without telling him about our child and, not having told him while I still had it inside me, I felt I had forfeited the right to lay the whole thing on him now, after the fact.

Oh, Elvis! I would lacerate myself time and again, locked away in my little bedroom where I had taken to hiding and shutting out the world. Elvis, why are you the way you are?

Self-pity? You bet. It oozed from the wound in my heart. I wallowed in it until I nearly suffocated. Scenes from my youth flashed before me in the classic tradition of someone going under for the third time: my adolescent self rushing to buy his latest release; standing in line to see his movies over and over; those CYO dances in overheated gyms, his voice piercing me to the core.

Always his voice. I played his records more obsessively than ever. Every solitary moment I could find, I immersed myself in his sound. I hunted down his earliest recordings, the now legendary Sun Sessions. Listening to them over and over, I tried desperately to find some clue in their pure, sweet, joyous innocence as to why he was the way he was, tried desperately (I now realize) to find a way to forgive him. For something he wasn't even aware he had done.

Reliving his music as I did, as if hearing it for the first time and truly concentrating on his sheer, raw emotional power, from the country and blues beginning to the hits, I began to imagine that I, too, was wringing every ounce of emotion from those words and music along with Elvis.

After all was said and done, wasn't *this* the quality more than anything else, that made him so magical? No one ever got more out of a song. The hackneyed phrase "heartfelt" came alive to me as it never had before. Elvis sang from his heart and made people the world over feel the same emotions in theirs. Other performers pronounced the words and described the feelings. Elvis reached deep inside to somehow produce them. When he sang, he actually made you *experience* the emotion his song conveyed. And it seemed to me he could do that because he *believed* in his song. How could he not? A song is a dream and Elvis's life was a dream come true—the dream of a poor, white trash kid who grew up pretending he was the hero of the comic books he read and the movies he saw. Only Elvis did it! He fulfilled the yearning, soared free, became the caped crusader of his fantasies.

Who couldn't identify with that? How could you not love him for it? Imagining him as he must have been when it first started happening for him, the sneering, bad boy greaser who was outraging every daughter's father, I have this image of him as a modern-day Mark Twain character, swaggering into American history, swinging his hips instead of a dead cat like Huckleberry Finn.

Huck, Brando's Wild One, James Dean—Elvis was greater than them all and most perfectly captured the imagination of a generation of Rebels Without a Cause. Paradoxically, Elvis was fascinated by power and had an almost slavish respect for authority. And I knew firsthand that for all the blatant sensuality that had made him famous, he could also be a shy and modest mama's boy. These multiple aspects of his personality seemed to enhance his image, accounting for the way his appeal bridged cultural, economic, and generation gaps all over the world. Women could lust after him or want to mother him or be his little sister. He was macho enough for young studs to admire, but he was also devoutly religious and believed in family values. In a strange way, Elvis had become Everyman. There was always some part of him that struck a responsive chord in the listener—as if he had become a part of you, or you of him.

Like me. During those lonely, solitary weeks, I more than once found myself standing in front of the mirror, the stereo blasting out his voice, creating a barrier of sound to shield me from the outside world. In my tight black pants I'd stand kind of limp, like I was clinging to the microphone for support, my legs spread wide. Then, my lips curled in the sneer, my make-believe guitar hanging casually down to my groin, I'd suddenly snap one leg out. Then, the other jackknifed at the hip and my pelvis pumped pistonlike to the big beat as I whipped my throbbing guitar around—

"Joyce?"

"Oh . . . Janice. I didn't hear you come in."

"What the heck are you doing?"

"What does it look like?"

"Like you've got Saint Vitus's Dance."

"Very funny."

I walked over and lowered the stereo while my sister went to hang her coat in the closet.

"If you really want to know, I was doing Elvis."

She nodded. "Well, you *dance* better than he does, anyway."

"Try telling that one to the world." She glanced at the mail I'd placed on the table and, finding nothing of interest, turned her attention back to me. "I guess it wasn't just my imagination then. I've heard him singing at all odd hours of the night lately."

"I'm going to see him again, Janice. You know—we both know—that."

"He called?"

I nodded. "But I told him I had the flu."

"That's a lot of times you've put him off. What makes you so sure he'll call back?"

I shrugged. "It's just something I feel."

"I know what you feel," she said sharply. "What do you *think?* Are you thinking? Hasn't any of this made you *think?*"

"I've done nothing *else* but think about it for days . . . weeks! And do you know what I think, now? That this isn't *about* thinking. It's all about feeling and intuition. Which is really okay with me, because that's what *I'm* about. It's what Elvis is about. Emotion and poetry. It has to be. It's there in his music."

"I'm not asking about the performer. You don't sleep with him on a stage. What about the *man?*"

"From the beginning," I answered, "I sensed they were the same, really. A decency that's real, not staged; the need to be admired and praised endlessly without reservation; to delight you and control you all at the same time; also a certain wild something inside that *he* keeps controlled."

"Oh, come on, will you! For God's sake . . ." Janice walked out of the room, shaking her head. After a moment I followed her to her bedroom, but stopped at the open doorway. She was pulling her dress up over her head and, as it cleared, she saw me. "You're just doing the traditional, time-honored woman's number. You know that, don't you? And he's playing his own surefire role that's made him so beloved: the Bad Boy who's really good at heart and whose little woman always forgives him, whose little woman asks no embarrassing questions, because she *loves* him. Ecchhh."

"He really needs me, Janice," I said simply.

"He needs only one thing, Joyce. Since he was nineteen and knocking them dead at county fairs and high school auditoriums, he's been frozen in time, getting and needing the only thing he needed then, needs now, or ever *will* need: applause, adulation, and fame beyond anybody's wildest dream. And you can't give him that. You can only give him real life. And that only brings him down; don't delude yourself, Joyce."

"No," I said slowly. "I'm past all that." I left the doorway and walked into the room. I stood close to her, trying to make her see. "The irony is that in the beginning I would've been *thrilled* to hope that Elvis Presley wanted me. Now that I know it, I'm still thrilled. But I'm also *scared* to death."

Chapter Nineteen

Sunday, October thirty-first: Halloween. Janice and I spent it entertaining the various little neighborhood ghouls, ghosts, and goblins who stopped by to "trick or treat." The Witching Hour, however, found me already in bed and plugged into "The Late Show," another of my futile attempts to block out the evil spirits who haunted me every night, lately—adult-type evil spirits, the kind who couldn't be mollified with Hershey bars and apples. At one A.M., still wide awake, I was reaching for another Placidyl when my Elvis Phone rang.

"This is James, calling for Elvis. He's coming to see you tomorrow, Joyce."

"When tomorrow? Where?"

"In the morning sometime. He'll call."

I hung up and had to laugh to myself. Would he ever change? His assumption, as always, was that I had only one responsibility—to accommodate him. His timing was perfect, though. I was ready to see him again at last. I downed the Placidyl and fell asleep, trying to dream up a good excuse for another conspicuous Monday absence from work.

Elvis, sounding bright-eyed and bushy-tailed, called at seven A.M.

"Joyce, I should be in your town in a couple of hours. Can you meet me at the Hotel Washington by nine?"

"I'll be there."

"That's my girl. See ya then."

All during the drive into town I could feel myself coming alive again. How terrible, I thought, to need another person that much, to only truly come alive when you were with him. How terrible? No, how *beautiful!*

"Honey—am I glad to see you!"

I was barely inside the door of the suite, had barely quelled that queer mixture of excitement and apprehension at again being face-to-face with him, when he charged across the room and threw his arms around me.

Well, if he wasn't going to bring up the subject of my having avoided him for weeks, I certainly wasn't. A great, warm glow began to spread inside me as I nuzzled against his chest. It was in part the old familiar chemical response, but it was also something more—a sense of starting over, a feeling of rebirth that could fill the cold, dark void that had been hollowed out of me.

"Hey, Joyce, how ya been?"

Sonny's big, hairy, friendly face was beaming at me between Elvis's hugs and kisses.

"Hi, Sonny."

"How's Janice?"

"She's doing all right." I smiled back, feeling like family again. "She might stop by a little later." Just a simple exchange of the amenities with them made me feel better, somehow more secure. "And how are you, James?" I asked of the quiet lad who hovered in the background as usual, ever at Elvis's beck and call.

"Fine thanks. Nice to see you."

"Honey, you really should've stayed in Vegas with me."

I turned my attention back to Elvis.

"You really missed somethin' this time," he went on, obviously still flushed with his most recent triumph at the International. I continued looking at him as he went on to tell me that he had a tour upcoming.

"Elvis?" I asked when he paused for breath. "What's different? There's something different about you but I can't put my fing—"

"Now, listen, little girl," he interrupted. "I want you to come with me."

"What, on the tour?"

"Yeah, I want you to see how hard I work. Don't want you thinkin' it's all fun and games." The crooked grin was getting broader as he talked. "And don't forget to bring along some of that enthusiasm of yours. I'll be needin' it for sure on this one."

"How long do you want me to stay?"

"For as long as you can make it. Or stand it." He laughed. "Joyce, seriously now," he said, taking me by the shoulders. "I want you to be with me on this tour. We're going to spend a lot more time with each other."

God, he looked so sincere and loving at that moment, I was like a puppet on a string, dancing to whatever tune he played. I tried to interject a little humor to regain some sense of perspective. "I don't know," I said. "I'll have to weigh my options, carefully." I stepped back and looked him over. Let's see, now. I can either spend those days working at my job in my stuffy office, or going from city to city and from fabulous show to fabulous show with the most handsome and adorable man in the world. It's a tough choice—but when do we leave?"

"Real soon," he said, grabbing me and giving me another hug.

"The weekend?" I suggested hopefully, the old nagging worry about my job kicking in.

"In a few days. Don't worry, we'll work it out."

"Elvis, your tour includes Baltimore, doesn't it?"

"How'd ya know that?"

"Are you kidding? It's been advertised all over the place. I want to bring all my friends and relatives to the show so they can see how great you are. Of course, there's no auditorium that *big*. I'll have to cut the number down a bit."

"You're a silly little girl," he said, sitting down on the sofa and pulling me down alongside him. "Tell you what, we'll rent a theater and I'll do a private show just for your family. Hey, let's get something ordered up from room service, you guys."

Sonny immediately joined James in looking over the menu and I scrutinized Elvis once more. "I swear there is definitely something different about you," I declared.

"How far is Baltimore, anyway?" he asked, once more evading my observation.

"From here, downtown D.C.—about forty miles. From where I live, about twenty. Why?"

"I worry about you drivin' back and forth to work. You should have a big car—a Caddy or a Mercedes."

"Please, Elvis, I've already told you I don't need one. I really don't want a big car; I like my Ford. Besides, like I told you, how would I explain to everyone how I got a Mercedes? You know how Washington is," I kidded him. "They'll think I'm accepting gifts from lobbyists."

"I'd be makin' your work easier for you," he kidded back. "You could investigate yourself. Okay, okay. I know how you feel. That's one of the reasons why I love you."

There was a knock at the door and Sonny went to answer it. "Are we expectin' anyone, E?"

It was Janice. She had brought our friend Peggy with her and as we heard my sister introduce Sonny, Elvis and I got up to greet them.

"I was afraid you weren't going to make it."

"Well, Peggy had to come downtown to pick up her kids," Janice explained, "but when I told her who was here, she figured, what the heck, they could wait on a street corner out in the bitter cold for a few hours as long as it meant she wouldn't miss the opportunity to meet Elvis."

Elvis, his hand already extended to shake Peggy's, halted it in midair to stare at her in amazement, bless his ingenuous heart.

"I'm kidding, only kidding," Janice said quickly as Peggy blushed to the roots.

"Janice is incorrigible," said Peggy, taking the hand Elvis was again offering. "And I'm embarrassed to fall back on such a shopworn cliché, but I actually *am* one of your biggest fans. And that *is* the truth."

"I see they coached you good." Elvis smiled. "C'mon and sit down. We just ordered up somethin' to eat."

"I'd love to, but I really do have to run. Janice?"

"And I have to go with her, darn it," my sister lamented, standing on tiptoe to kiss Elvis goodbye. "Seeing Vince tonight," she whispered when I gave her a quick hug at the door.

It wasn't until after James had let room service in and the refreshments were laid out on the table where we all sat down together, and I was about halfway through my sandwich (I had for once eschewed the ubiquitous burgers for a tuna salad on toast) that it hit me. "It's your hair, isn't it?" I sputtered through a mouthful of bread and albacore. "That's what's different! It's down on your forehead more. But I think I liked it better back off your face. What's so funny?"

Still grinning, Elvis reached up, grabbed his hair, and yanked it clean off his head.

"A wig!" I was so startled I almost went backward right over my chair. "I can't believe it," I said, righting myself while Elvis and Sonny doubled up laughing at my reaction.

"Joyce, if only you coulda seen your face."

"Okay, okay, enough is enough! And how come a wig, anyway?"

"It saves me time. I don't always get a chance to have my hair done when I'm real busy, y'know?"

"Elvis, that was great, man." Sonny was still looking at the wig and shaking his head. "Joyce," he chuckled, "your expression was . . ."

"Honey, what's your favorite color?" Elvis asked abruptly.

257

"What do you mean? Favorite color of what?"

"Just your favorite color. Of anything."

"I don't have one."

"Everybody has a favorite color . . . 'specially women."

"Okay. Orange." It being just after Halloween is the only way I can account for having blurted that out.

"Orange?" Even Elvis was taken aback by that. *"Nobody's* favorite color is orange."

"Why not?" For some reason I decided to defend the choice I'd made off the top of my head. "Why do you need to know, anyway?"

"Just curious," he said cagily. "Uh . . . colors tell a lot about a person, y'know. Red means you're warm, blue means you're cold . . ."

"Yeah, well, what does orange mean then?" It wasn't lost on me that he hadn't given me a straight answer to my question.

"It means you're strange . . . or a pumpkin."

I had to laugh even if the joke was on me. "You're in rare form tonight, aren't you?"

"Yeah. I think we should have a party. Why don't you get some of your friends over later?"

"I'd really like that, Elvis. But remember, only a very few of them have ever met you. And even they don't know the whole truth about our relationship."

"Joyce, I never told you not to tell anyone, did I?"

"I know you didn't. It was my own idea. It just didn't seem good for either of us to have everybody know . . . to have it in the papers or on television."

"You're right, baby, and I appreciate you thinking that way. But don't worry, it won't be like that much longer."

"Actually, I *don't* worry about it much anymore," I said, walking over and picking up the telephone. "You and I don't need to go 'public,' Elvis. What we need is to go *private.*"

"What do you mean?"

"Well . . ." I tapped the phone with my finger. "There's no

doubt my friends would love to come and of course I'd like that, but . . ." I paused meaningfully."

"But what?"

"But then they'd be here."

Elvis laughed. "Forget it, then." He gestured to put the phone down. "I want to be alone with you. Alone with you is nicer."

"Great idea." I settled back down on the sofa. "Oh, I almost forgot. I have something for you." I reached over for my purse and rummaged around inside it. "These were taken in Vegas," I said, handing him a set of photographs. "From the time when Janice was out there with us?"

Elvis took the photographs and began to look through them. "Yeah, I can see that. The ones of you two are really great. Sonny, man . . . here. Take at look at these and see if you can tell me which one is which?"

"That's easy." Sonny gave the photographs a passing glance. "I can pick you out every time, E."

"Yeah." Elvis had to chuckle. "Right. I'm the big dude with the shades. I'm keeping them." He turned back to me. "Along with the ones you gave me before."

"Sure. I had an extra set made."

"But you didn't bring a suitcase. Why didn't you?"

"I didn't know you were staying. You didn't say anything; I thought maybe you were just here for the day."

"I'm not. And I want you to stay here with me. Okay?"

"I'll have to get some things from home . . . and clothes for work tomorrow."

"All right, when the guys get back from whatever they're going out now to do," he said pointedly with an obvious good-bye-glance in their direction, "we'll drive out to your apartment and you can get your things."

"Great. I'd love to drive around town with you." Sonny and James were already taking the hint to leave us alone together.

"*After* we go out to dinner," Elvis added.

"What?" I couldn't believe my ears. "*Out* to dinner?"

"Yeah, out to dinner. Where can we go? This is your town, after all."

"Well, what kind of food do you feel like having?"

"Actually, what I'm hungry for right now is you," he declared softly, leaning in toward me so that his lips were close to my ear.

"I might not be as nutritious as the coq au vin at the Rive Gauche," I flirted.

"But you'll sure be a lot sexier than any coco-whatever-it-is," he murmured, taking my hand and leading me into the bedroom.

"It's chicken, Elvis," I whispered as he laid me across the bed. "Just chicken."

"See, I knew I was right." He growled the words softly before dropping gently alongside me and pressing his mouth to mine.

He slowly removed one piece of my clothing, then another, and another . . .

"Do what you did that first time . . . that first time you came here looking for me," I whispered. "Our first time."

For an answer I had only the sweet silence of his warm breath in my ear. I helped him slide one arm at a time out of his shirt.

There was a fairness, a light, boyish blondness to him which made the Elvis that the world knew seem dark and almost saturnine by contract.

"Talk to me Elvis. Tell me things," I moaned. "I want to know you."

But he had begun to drift off, to pull back, shying away from that magical moment I longed for—and also dreaded. For months, what he'd said about Priscilla becoming a mother had haunted me. I had a split second of paranoid madness in which I thought: he's going to treat me like a "mama," like it isn't proper for me to have sex! But he didn't know—and his sleepy, sexy drawl calmed and reassured me.

"Joyce," he murmured, "I love you. You're beautiful and you're sweet and I need you. I just want you close to me now."

Was it something he'd taken that did this to him, I wondered, that made his desire surge and then ebb so abruptly? Well, he never failed to reassure me of his feelings at the crucial moment, anyway . . . and as long as he *needed* me, I was content. At least for the time being. So content that after watching him sleep for a while, I dozed off myself.

When I woke, the space alongside me was empty and Elvis was on the phone asking Sonny to call for the car.

"Come on, little one," he said when he saw my eyes open. "Let's get dressed. We're goin' to get your things and then go out to eat."

Well, dining in public with Elvis would almost compensate for ecstasy denied, I told myself.

But not quite! Because it had been months—and I *needed* him. Somehow, making love would make everything right and new again, might even wash away the guilt I still harbored inside.

But at the same time that I longed for him, I also dreaded that intimacy, haunted by an irrational fear that then he would *know!* That he would be able to tell that I had aborted his child. . . .

This ambivalence I felt about physically expressing my desire for him made it possible for me to accept the fact that he had stoked a volcano, only to let it smolder and die instead of bringing it to eruption. Everything was all right, I reassured myself, as if I didn't deserve to feel any disappointment or resentment. Everything was just fine. We had made a new beginning. We were starting over with a clean slate. That was the important thing.

When we drove out to my apartment, Sonny came in to wait with Elvis while I got my things together.

"You do have a real nice apartment, Joyce," Sonny remarked, walking around and checking the place out. "How long did you say you've been here?"

"About three years. The owners are talking about converting to condominiums, so, if I can work it out, I just might buy it."

"Joyce," Elvis interjected. "Whyn't you get all dressed up? We're going out to dinner, remember?"

Sonny's antennae shot up. "What are we doin', E?"

"I told Joyce we're going out to dinner."

"Where should we go?" I asked quickly, ignoring Sonny's dour, apprehensive look. "Let's pick someplace special." I was starting to feel really excited about the prospect. "Elvis, it'll be our first time out to a restaurant together."

"You pick it, Joyce. What's your favorite place?"

"I don't have one, really. What would you like? How about Italian? Do you like Italian food?"

"The kinda food doesn't matter. Just make sure it's . . ."

"Do you think this is a good idea, E?"

". . . a quiet place." He turned to Sonny. "I'm sure Joyce knows a quiet little out-of-the-way place."

"Where nobody's gonna notice Elvis Presley, boss?" Sonny looked at me. "You know anyplace that quiet, Joyce?"

"No." I sighed and shook my head. I knew when I was licked. "I'm afraid I haven't been any place quite *that* quiet lately."

Sonny gestured to Elvis. "Wherever, you're gonna attract a crowd and all, y'know."

"Maybe you're right, Sonny." Elvis smiled apologetically and said, "Honey, we'll just have to order from room service when we get back to the hotel." My disappointment must have shown in my face because he shrugged and added, "Y'know, if Sonny's right . . . I'm just not up to a crowd."

It was getting late by the time we did finish with the dinner we had sent up to the suite and, after the room service porter had carted away the dishes and the debris and Sonny and James had made themselves scarce, I emerged from the bathroom to find Elvis in the bedroom, rummaging around among his religious and philosophical books and treatises.

"Elvis," I said. "I'm concerned about getting to work late

tomorrow morning. I can't let that happen again, especially if I'm going to take more time soon to go on tour with you."

He glanced up, nodded, and reached for the Placidyl.

"No, that's what I mean, Elvis. I'm afraid I'll oversleep. It'd be better not to sleep at *all* than to be late."

"No, Joyce, you have to take something," Elvis protested. "I don't want you not sleeping when I am."

"Elvis, you're not listening. I may be overtired, but I still think I'm better off not—"

"Okay, baaaaby . . ." he coaxed gently, expertly. "Come on, just take these . . ."

I gave in, swallowed, and fell asleep in his arms.

I came out of the bathroom the next morning, still fumbling with my clothes, and was startled to find Elvis awake. Not exactly alert, but awake.

"Honey," he mumbled. "You'll be back after work, won't you?"

"Yes, but . . ."

"But what?"

"I feel awful. I can hardly move a muscle. Elvis, I'll never make it through the day."

"You're a little hung over from the pills, that's all. Wait a second."

He reached into his arsenal of pills, took one out that I'd never seen before, and handed it to me.

"What is it?"

"Just something to help you get going."

"I don't think—"

"It's all right. I know what you need. I promise you, honey, it'll make you feel better real soon."

"All right." I closed my fist over it. "I couldn't feel any worse."

I wasn't at the office an hour before my nerves began to practically twang like the strings on a cheap guitar. By the time another thirty minutes had passed, every muscle in my body began to alternate between aching and burning. This increased right up until noon when the smell of food started me retching.

When I came out of the bathroom, I called Elvis.

"I'm sick as a dog, Elvis. What was that you gave me?"

"Nothing that could hurt you, honey."

"Well, if it gets any worse I might have to just go straight home from here."

"Believe me, you'll be okay. Just get back here. You have to."

"I'm not sure I'll be able to," I said. "I'll call you later."

I started to dial Janice almost as a reflex, then thought better of it and put the phone down. Only to have it immediately ring.

"Joyce? This is Sonny. You *have* to come back tonight. Elvis has a little surprise for you and he's pacing the other room like a caged tiger for fear you're going to disappoint him."

With that little message ringing in my ears, I went to the first-aid room and lay down for a while. By late afternoon, I was feeling so much better that I called Elvis and told him that not only would I be there, but that this time I was going to act on his suggestion of the day before and invite a couple of my girlfriends over.

"Bring anybody you want. Just be here."

Karen, who had accompanied me on that awful trip to Vegas when I had stalked out of his bedroom, was the one who I brought that evening and Elvis greeted us at the door by turning us around and leading us right out again.

"C'mon, I want to show you something," he said. He turned and gave some orders to James and then, with a broadly grinning Sonny bringing up the rear, led Karen and me into the elevator.

"What is it, Elvis?" I asked as the elevator doors slid open on the mezzanine level.

"Just follow me."

And we did. Around a balcony overlooking the lobby and through the door that led to the garage.

"Elvis, what's going on?"

"Patience, little girl, patience."

The hotel garage was cold, colder than it had been outside and, as we proceeded single file through the rows of parked cars to the back, I could see my breath.

"Are we going somewhere?" I looked around but Ben's limo was nowhere in sight.

Elvis stopped and turned to me. "Yeah, we're going for a ride—in *your* car."

Then I saw it. A shiny new car. We had stopped right in front of it.

"It's all yours, honey." He was handing me the keys.

"But, Elvis, I . . ."

"Joyce, it's for your birthday next month. And it's a *little* car, not a big one. Just like you said."

"You are wonderful," I said, reaching up to hug and kiss him.

"And it's your favorite color. Orange."

"Yes," I said, letting go and settling back down on my heels. "Yes, I can see that."

"It was the only orange car we could find. You'd have saved us a lot of time if your favorite color was black or white or red."

"Well," I said. "Well, I really appreciate your going to all the trouble to find me this . . ."

"It's a Pinto, which is a little wild horse. Although I don't think I ever saw an *orange* horse."

". . . orange *car,*" I said slowly.

There followed a moment in which Elvis, Sonny, and I all stared at the car. Then we looked at one another and broke up.

"Come on, Joyce," Elvis said, seeing the blank expression on Karen's face and putting his arms around us. "You've gotta take us for a ride."

We all piled in and I drove out of the garage, around the block, and down F Street to 12th and then over to 16th and onto Pennsylvania Avenue. All the while I was holding onto Elvis's hand and every time I looked over at him he was beaming with pride and pleasure.

"Thought we ought to take in your friend's place," I kidded as we passed the White House.

"Yeah, let's stop in and visit the Prez, man."

Because with Elvis you never knew, I shot him a look to see if he was serious. There was a glint in his eye as he squeezed my hand reassuringly.

"Joyce, drive by the Capitol, okay? Man, I love that building."

I went by slowly. Elvis shook his head at the sight. "That's where it all happens, doesn't it, Joyce? That's what this country is all about."

"Have you ever been inside, Elvis?"

"Inside? No. Maybe you could take me on a tour sometime?"

"Sure, I'd love to. Only," I added dryly, "what about the mob scene you'd cause? There's no out-of-the-way spot *there* where you wouldn't be noticed or draw a crowd."

Neither Elvis nor Sonny made any response and I continued.

"Even better than taking you there, I'd just love to take you to my office. I can just *see* everyone's face! And imagine the reactions . . . wow!"

"Well, now, little girl, you just might be surprised some day," Elvis said. "I've been known to do a lot of crazy things!"

I had no sooner parked in the hotel garage and turned off the ignition, when Elvis suddenly said, "Come back to Graceland with me tonight."

"What?"

"Come back to Graceland with me tonight."

"But . . . uh . . . why?"

"Because I want you to."

"But I have to be at the office tomorrow."

"I'll get you there in time."

He turned and looked over the back seat at Karen.

"Wouldn't you like to come, too?"

Startled, she blinked once, and then blurted, "Oh, I'd love to. But Joyce . . ." Her eyes found mine. "What do you think?"

"Think? Who's thinking? Who has a choice?" I turned to Elvis. "Obviously my friend would kill to go and as for you . . . you just happen to be too adorable to refuse. But this time," I looked him straight in the eye, "I *must* be at work in the morning."

"Me, too," Karen piped up.

"Sonny," Elvis said. "Arrange for the plane."

Later, as we were all getting into the limo for the ride to the airport, I realized I had some arrangements of my own to make.

"Why don't you all follow me to my office? That way I can park my beautiful new car in my garage space and it'll be waiting there for me to drive it home after work tomorrow."

"Okay, honey. But James will drive your car. I want you right next to me. You just tell Ben where to go."

The security guard at the Rayburn Building garage, not recognizing Ben's limousine, stopped us and demanded to see a House of Representatives ID. I produced mine and was explaining what we were doing when I realized that the guard was paying absolutely no attention to me. He was staring, wide-eyed, at the figure alongside me. He didn't say anything, however, and after finally glancing at my ID, allowed us to proceed.

James joined us in the limo and as we passed the guard on our way out, Elvis gave him a barely perceptible nod. I turned around and saw through the back window that he had taken off his hat and was scratching his head. Everyone laughed, but with one eye on Elvis.

He was unfazed. "Probably thought I was a congressman," he said finally, looking ahead with a straight face.

"National Airport, Ben," Sonny directed.

And away we went.

At her first sight of Graceland, Karen's face made me wonder if *I* looked as awestruck the first time I saw it.

Elvis and I took her on a grand tour around the home of which he was so proud. We ended up in the Blue Room, a trophy room which housed all of his gold and platinum records along with innumerable awards, plaques, and other memorabilia.

Karen shook her head. "This is incredible," she gasped as Elvis related how thousands of articles about his career, information that could have taken up an entire warehouse, had been recorded on microfilm and was now stored in just one part of that huge room.

When he had finished, I couldn't help exclaiming over a beautifully framed picture that caught him in motion onstage.

"Elvis, this is great, the way it captures your energy and vitality and . . ."

"And what?"

"And . . . I don't know. I just love it."

"Then it's yours."

"It's mine?"

"Yeah. If you like it, you can have it." He stepped up to the wall and began to remove it.

"But—you mean you're just going to take it right off your wall and give it to me!"

"There's that enthusiasm I love! Here, let me put it in a safe place till you're ready to leave."

Then, as he moved away with it, he asked how Karen and I would like to take a tour of the grounds.

Our answer to that was exactly what you would expect.

After a good fifteen minutes of playing "Grand Prix Bumper Derby" in the golf carts Elvis provided for the tour, Karen and Sonny in one, and Elvis and I in the other, he suddenly veered away and drove us off on a course of our own.

"Elvis, where are we going? You know it's freezing out here, don't you?" I said through chattering teeth.

"I'll keep you warm." He laughed and put his arm around me. "I want to show you something," he said in the low tone of voice he reserved for something he felt strongly about, and in another moment we were bouncing along to the far end of his domain.

"Look, Joyce," he exclaimed, stopping the cart and pointing. "Look at that. Isn't that beautiful?"

The air was crisp and clear and looking up to where he indicated, I saw the Tennessee sky lit by a host of shimmering, silvery stars.

"Oh . . . that _is_ lovely, Elvis."

He put his arm around me and held me close.

"This is one of my favorite places to be on a clear night, honey. It relaxes me. I come here often and look up and listen to the sky."

"What does it say to you, Elvis?"

He didn't answer immediately and I saw his gorgeous face, pensive and far away in the pale moonlight.

"Tell me, Elvis, please."

"Oh, you'd be surprised. If you just relax and open up your mind, the heavens can tell you all kinds of things. Sometimes I can even hear my mama talking to me out here, Joyce."

"You must really miss her," I said softly.

"You have no idea how much. She was really somethin'. I wish you could've known her. She would have loved you; I just know it. She's the reason I got as far as I have in life. She was always there for me. She understood me. Losing her was a terrible loss, Joyce . . . just terrible. But, you know . . . sometimes I think God wants me to be greater than I am."

"Seems to me most of the world thinks you're pretty great already." I was afraid that thinking of his mother had made him not only sad but morbid, and I tried to lighten things up a little. "Just the way you are."

"No, I don't mean as an entertainer," he explained. "I mean as a person. I truly believe, Joyce, that God has a greater purpose in mind for me. That's why I was the twin that survived. To carry a message for Him. I could have been a preacher. Maybe that's what he wants from me now."

"You touch an awful lot of people now," I told him, trying to allay his doubts. He seemed in such inner turmoil.

"Not enough, though . . . not enough." He shook his head and was silent for a moment. "You should read those books I gave you, Joyce. It's all in there." He tightened his arm around my shoulder. "I can feel you shivering, honey." He smiled. "I'll take my little girl inside . . . unless . . ." He gave me one of his searching looks. "Unless you can stand it just a little longer? There's something else I want to show you."

"Go ahead. It was your words more than the cold that made me shiver like that. I'm not really that cold," I fibbed.

Elvis started up the cart and drove until we reached what looked to me like a corral. He helped me out of the cart and we walked over to the fence.

"There he is. Isn't he beautiful, Joyce?"

Standing stock-still as though he thought so, too, and had decided to pose for us, was the biggest horse, a Palomino, that I had ever seen.

"I call him Sun. He's my favorite. I'll let you ride him one day. You can ride, can't you?"

"Well, actually . . . no. Well, not really. That is, I tried it once."

"Well, I'll just have to teach you then," he said, smiling at my nervousness.

Just as we started to get back in the cart, James appeared. He was holding a large glass of water in one hand and just stood there silently.

"What's James doing?" I asked when I realized Elvis was not going to acknowledge him.

"His job. Just his job," Elvis replied, starting up the golf cart. "He thought I might be thirsty from being out here so long."

"He must be a very thoughtful person," I said with a straight face.

Elvis didn't bother to acknowledge that, either.

It was after three A.M. when we started getting ready for bed and Elvis immediately downed his sedatives. This was something of a disappointment for me. I knew I wasn't going to do much sleeping—not with a chartered plane for Karen and me to catch at six-thirty—but I certainly wouldn't have minded a little close companionship for the next hour or so. But Elvis was already showing signs of drowsiness, his lids getting heavy.

"Elvis." I put my arms around him, knowing I wouldn't have an opportunity in the morning. "I just want to thank you for everything. This has been a wonderful day."

"You don't have to thank me. I *want* to do nice things for you. If you'll only let me. You sure fight me a lot, though."

"Oh, no, Elvis, that's not it . . . not at all. I . . ."

"Remember when I asked you about movin' in here, Joyce?"

"Well, yes . . ."

"I asked you to think about it, right?"

"Elvis, honestly, I have to tell you . . . I wasn't sure you really meant it. There've been times in these past months when I just about convinced myself that I had dreamed it, that you'd never really asked me."

"Well, you better pinch yourself, Joyce, 'cause you aren't dreaming. 'Cept for making a dream come true, maybe."

His speech was starting to slur.

"Elvis," I said quickly. "Is that what it would be to you? A dream come true?"

"That's what it's about."

"What? What do you mean?"

"Elvis," he said thickly, "is about making people's dreams come true."

He tried to give me my pills, but for once I was adamant and refused. And for once, he was fading too fast to make me give in.

I began to tuck him in, thinking to myself that I was starting to feel at home in Graceland, that perhaps I *did* belong there, that maybe, just maybe I could make it work.

"Joyce?"

Elvis had managed to half open his eyes.

"Don't go in the morning. Let your friend go . . . but you be here for me when I wake up."

"I wish I could," I whispered fervently. "But I can't."

"Why can't you?"

"You know why, Elvis. My job is very important to me."

"Your *child!* What do you mean, your child?" He tried to raise his voice to a shout, but it came out a hoarse croak.

"I didn't say my child," I cried. "You know I don't have a child. I said my *job.*"

"You have . . . child . . ."

"Elvis, damn it, you know . . ." There was no response other than his breathing. I shook him, but to no avail.

Look at the silver lining, I told myself, as I gritted my teeth. Now I wouldn't have to worry about falling asleep and missing the plane. I lay back and stared up at the ceiling. I *knew* I hadn't said "child" instead of job. I couldn't have, I never would have made that mistake. Never. Not to Elvis. Not ever.

Chapter Twenty

Despite not having slept the previous night, despite having done a hard day's work straight upon disembarking from the chartered plane, despite the promises to Janice, when I crawled into my own bed that night, my hand shot out for my little pills . . . just one last time. After all, I *had* promised Janice I would stop, so those really *were* the last ones I would ever have, which meant they didn't really count . . . I comforted and buttressed myself with one rationalization after another in the classic manner of a person with a growing dependency; I needed to pretend that I was still in charge.

Accordingly, my rude awakening the next day was even more rude than it might have been. Especially since it came at one o'clock in the afternoon. In my chemically induced slumber, I had slept right through the alarm. Not that I was ready to face that last fact in all its implications. Me, an addict? Addicts were street people, skulking in ghettos and dealing with shady, underworld characters to obtain illegal substances. They were pathetic, sweating, runny-nosed burnouts.

How could such caricatures of doom bear any resemblance to a respectable, competent staff member of an important congressional committee? For that matter, was it any more likely that an addict would be the girlfriend of the most popular and beloved entertainer in the world, a man who was well known for his abhorrence of drugs and the drug culture, a man who did not even *drink!*

All this notwithstanding, I found myself glancing anxiously from the telephone to that damned, relentless clock. No matter how hard I stared, however, it kept getting later. God, in all the times (too many times, *many* too many times, it came to me with a sickening jolt) I had phoned the office to say I couldn't make it, I had at least called first thing in the morning. I picked up the phone, wondering just how many more lame excuses it was possible for me to get away with.

At least one more, apparently.

I was still breathing periodic sighs of relief and thanking my lucky stars while I tried to throw something together in the kitchen for dinner when I heard the front door open and shut.

"Janice." I called. "I'm in here."

The second I saw her face it was obvious that even if my office was still inclined to tolerate my irresponsibility, my sister was not.

"What the hell happened today that you weren't at work when I called?"

"A lot, actually, Janice. A lot happened today. Which I'm about to tell you."

"Yeah?" She looked around the apartment. "Did you even get out at all?"

"I . . . uh . . . didn't have time." The truth was that I had moped around the apartment all afternoon because I did not have the *energy* to go out—and that *did* bother me. But I wasn't going to scare Janice with that admission.

"It was really too bad," I said, assuming an exaggeratedly casual manner. "Because I *definitely* need to get some new clothes."

"Well, then," she asked, staring hard into my face, "Why didn't you? Do you know you don't look so terrific, either?"

"Well, that's why I needed a day of rest," I said blandly, and slid the casserole I had managed to laboriously piece together from one of my mother's old recipes, into the oven.

"What are you, seventy years old? I know you, Joyce. On your list of priorities, *eating* comes after buying new cloth . . ." She stopped, her mouth still open, her eyes narrowing shrewdly. "Why do you suddenly need new clothes?"

"That's what I've been trying to tell you. He called."

"Elvis? When?"

"I hung up just before you came in. It's all set. I'm going on tour with him. Janice, I'm so excited!"

"Joyce, that's great. I guess."

"Please don't. Don't bring me down. Janice, really, if you'd been here . . . talked to him . . ."

"What did he say?"

"Well, nothing really." I laughed. "It's just that it was him. I don't know. The sound of his voice . . . All I know is my adrenaline started to pump and I felt alive and happy after moping around here the whole day." I brought a bowl of the salad I'd made earlier into the living room.

Janice had kicked off her shoes and was sprawled on the couch. "Honey, don't you understand that's part of what I'm worried about? That your whole life is starting to revolve around him? That's not healthy. Oh, I know you'll love being on the road with him; it'll be new and exciting and Elvis will feel good about having you there, but—"

"I know. It's incredible, isn't it?" I sat down across from her. "I'm meeting him in Cleveland the day after tomorrow. Then we're going to Louisville and then Philadelphia."

"Joyce?" Janice had raised up on one elbow. "Please, please keep your promise to me. That's all I ask."

"I said I would. Now stop worrying."

"Stop worrying!" Her voice went up an octave or so, a sure sign she was really upset.

"Right, stop making such a big deal of it."

"It *is* a big deal . . . and the first big deal is *your life*. The second big deal, if you're interested, is whether you're prepared to lose a damn good *job* over this man. Just remember, in case things don't end up like in a fairy tale, you'll still have to support yourself. So don't be stupid. It's not easy to get a job on the Hill. And I know you wouldn't want to be dependent on Elvis Presley . . . or on anyone."

"Okay, Janice." I held both my hands out, palm up, in a gesture of capitulation. "I know you're right. Please, let's not fight."

"I don't want to fight with you, either. And I'm not, not really. It's just that you're the most important, dearest person in my life and I couldn't bear to see even one hair on your head hurt. I'm just trying to prepare you, to cushion you in case things don't work out."

I guess I must have looked pretty devastated at that moment because my sister suddenly stood up and held her arms out to me.

"Aw, come here. Give me a hug, Bov," she said.

"Hey," Janice said later, munching away, "this salad is really crisp."

"Of course. I kept it in the refrigerator. I'm no dope."

"Right!" She squinted her eyes and pointed her finger at me. "So no more . . ."

"Pills!" I said in unison with her.

My plane landed about six o'clock in the evening, Cleveland time, on that Saturday, November sixth, 1971. There was a wet snow falling and the limousine sent to pick me up moved slowly through the crowded, slushy streets. It was bitterly cold outside, with an ugly wind blowing in off Lake Erie. But it was warm and wonderful inside Elvis's arms.

He wrapped them around me as soon as he saw me walk into his suite at the Statler-Hilton. He held me for a long time and then I walked around and got reacquainted with the entourage that included most of the regulars and old hands with whom I had long since been on familiar terms.

The only one who seemed uncomfortable was Elvis himself. He was even more jittery than usual before a performance and could not seem to sit still. I had noticed, however, that one familiar face was missing from the group and when I was informed Joe had gone ahead as Elvis's advance man on the tour, I wondered if perhaps in his absence, Elvis might not worry more than he normally did about things going smoothly.

The next time he lighted next to me for a few minutes, I observed, "You seem really on edge. You're not nervous, are you?"

"Aw, you know, I'm always a little shaky before I get out there."

In this instance, "a little shaky" manifested itself in his pacing incessantly back and forth across the room and barking orders to his men, not all of them exactly comprehensive or even necessary. On the next loop he made around the sofa where I was sitting, he halted midway and said, "Look at these nails, would ya, Joyce. Can you file 'em a little for me?"

"I guess I can . . ." I looked up at him. He was unbelievably tense, his attention already drifting off somewhere else. I patted the sofa. "If you sit down and stay still."

He smiled and sat and I filed. His hands never stopped shaking, even while I held them. He also never stopped talking and after the third or fourth time that he interrupted the operation by getting up to pace around the room, I gave up.

The next time he walked past, he reminded me that I hadn't finished his nails.

"They're hard to do when you're a moving target! Calm down. You'll be great," I assured him. "As usual."

He leaned down toward me. "You know, playing the road is different," he said, very much in earnest. "It's not like playing Vegas, Joyce. The *real* fans come to these shows. They're not people away on vacation or fillin' in time till they can get back to their gamblin'. These people leave their houses and buy tickets. They're here because they wanna see me. They expect a lot . . . and they deserve to get it."

"More than the crowds in Vegas?" I asked. "I mean, you know I've never seen your show anyplace else, but those people there in the International stand in awfully long lines for an awfully long time for those reservations, I can tell you that. I have seen them actually *fight* for a reservation."

I had gotten his attention with my chance remark and I decided to try to take advantage of the opportunity and lighten his mood somewhat.

"And God knows what they tip Emilio for a good table," I added with a grin. "What greater proof could there be? You can't get much more enthusiastic than that. It proves the people in Vegas love you, too, Elvis."

"Oh, yeah, I love playin' Vegas, but this is different . . ." He looked up and nodded as one of his men signaled it was time to leave for the auditorium. "Well, you'll see," he said and gave me his hand to get up.

During the ride in the limo, Elvis seemed to get more hyper. He talked continuously, but more *at* the rest of us rather than *with* us in conversation.

When we pulled up to the huge Public Auditorium, Elvis gave me a quick kiss and prepared to head backstage with Charlie and the bodyguards. He smiled at me and waved two of the boys over to my side to escort me around to the auditorium entrance.

"Make sure you don't lose her in the crowd," he said and reached out to give my shoulder a reassuring pat.

"Elvis, I . . ." I hesitated, but this was the last chance I'd have to speak before he actually went onstage. "I want to ask you something."

"Uh-oh." He grinned. "Sounds tough."

"Not really. I was just wondering if you're going to sing 'The First Time Ever I Saw your Face' tonight?"

He chuckled. "You really like that song, hunh?"

"I really, really do. But, also . . . it's just that it's special. To me, Elvis. Will you sing it?"

"We'll see," he said and was gone, whisked away as he was so often for the sake of security. His answer upset me and burned in my ears as we made our way among the thousands and thousands of people hurrying to get inside, or to push their way through to the concessionaires to buy the souvenir books and photographs they were hawking.

By the time my two baby-sitters and I took our places, it seemed to me that every single one of the rest of the Public Auditorium's fifteen thousand seats was filled. We were situated about ten rows back, but directly at center stage. It was exciting . . . at their first sight of him the entire audience had gasped and caught its breath . . . and it was frightening.

Elvis had been right. This *was* different.

Looking around at the sea of screaming flesh that surrounded us, I could not help but wonder if, in spite of the solid phalanx of armed guards that walled off the stage from the people someone would do something crazy and a riot would explode, putting all of us—including Elvis—at risk.

Being in the midst of this crowd was like being in the belly of some great, thrashing, primordial beast who was guided only by the most primitive instincts and illusions.

And there, above us, onstage in a cone of light was Elvis, ready to live them out for us, however briefly. The creature of a million fantasies relived: in his look, his stance . . . his sound. His voice took off then, and soared, and the beast was, in turn, mollified, enthralled, captivated.

As his performance drew to a close, Elvis abruptly motioned for the audience to quiet down. He put one of his hands up to his forehead, shielding his eyes from the spotlight and then tilted his head upward in the general direction from which they were beamed down upon him.

"Hey, man!" he called. "Up there wherever you are. Put the house lights up."

With that done, he was able to look out and survey his audience. "You've been lookin' at me all night, now I wanna get a look at *you.*"

By showing his appreciation for them, Elvis sent his loyal fans into an adulatory frenzy of gratitude and for one hairy moment it looked like the stage would be stormed in a human tidal wave of reciprocal appreciation. The guards cooled the situation by sluicing a tiny but steady flow of customers off the mainstream and allowing those to pass close enough to Elvis so that he could present each of them with one of his coveted sweaty scarves, dutifully handed him in rapid succession by Charlie Hodge.

He was sauntering back and forth across the stage, nodding half to himself, half to the audience, offering appropriately humorous and self-deprecating observations, and obviously just enjoying the hell out of himself and grooving on the rapport he could establish with his "real" fans, when one young woman eluded the guards, jumped up onto the stage, and flung herself at him, ensnaring him with a hammerlock around the neck. In a flash, massive Sonny was alongside, but Elvis spread both his arms out wide to indicate he was perfectly all right—except for being smooched to death. That poor young girl, her blonde beehive hairdo bouncing up and down in time with her body, leapt off the floor over and over again to plant big, wet kisses on his face until Sonny finally pried her off. Once they realized she was not going to let go of her own free will, the crowd began to roar approval and encouragement, while Elvis, his eyes still fixed on his audience, kept his arms outstretched to show that he had no intention of responding to her advances.

The aisles remained flooded with exuberant fans, dancing and singing and clapping with the beat of the music even after the young woman had been led off, while Elvis himself merely shrugged his shoulders, made an inaudible comment as the house lights dimmed, and launched into his next song.

"Good audience, hunh?" Elvis asked with a wry little smile when we were back having dinner in the suite.

"You were right, Elvis, it *was* different. I never saw an audience that loved you like that one did," I confessed. But then I added, "One blonde bombshell in particular."

"Oh, yeah." He shook his head. "Some bombshell . . . man. She bit me, y'know."

"Well, I wanted to get her off ya right away, E," Sonny declared, "but when you didn't say nothin' I just followed your lead."

"Well, man, I didn't say nothin' because I couldn't talk. She was holdin' onto my lip! Goddam, she had teeth just like a barracuda," he announced, holding his lip gingerly between thumb and forefinger and breaking everybody up.

It was only a few minutes later that Elvis noticed me pushing away my plate of creamed potatoes, black-eyed peas (the kitchen at Cleveland's Statler-Hilton must have been pretty accommodating), and overroasted meat.

"What's the matter, honey?" he asked. "Is there anything wrong?"

There was, of course, but I had no intention of bringing Elvis down by showing him how disappointed I felt.

"No, not really, 'wrong.' " I smiled, and put on my perkiest face. "It's just that you didn't sing the song, that's all. It's nothing really, I was just looking forward, I guess, to hearing and seeing you perform 'The First Time Ever I Saw Your Face' in front of an audience . . . Maybe sometime soon?"

Elvis chewed and swallowed before answering. "Sorry, honey. I guess I should've told you before. I don't think it fits in the show. You know what I mean?"

"Well, I guess so," I said. I glanced quickly around, but as usual when anyone was being refused by Elvis, the entourage automatically, almost instinctively tended to look right through them as if they didn't exist. I laughed and shrugged and said, "Be kind of presumptuous for me to be telling you what you ought to sing."

"I know you don't intend nothin' like that, honey," Elvis said. "Besides, you've always shown me you have good taste." He chuckled. "And there are times I *will* rely on it, but when I know something is right—or wrong—I really know it."

You couldn't argue with that, so I nodded and he turned to his guys. "Hey, man, where are we tomorrow?" he asked of no one in particular.

"In Louisville," James answered.

"Where, man? Where'd you say?"

"In Louisville, Kentucky, E," Charlie Hodge said. "For a matinee."

"A matinee?" Elvis repeated. He turned and looked at me.

So it turned out to be early to bed (relatively speaking) for us that night.

"They're my people out there," he called into the bathroom where I was getting ready for bed after everyone had gone. "Baby, you know, I don't wanna disappoint 'em."

"And you don't." I emerged to tell him, "Elvis, you give them more than enough."

"Mmmm . . . They still like me," he said, getting under the covers. "The people, I mean."

"Like you! They *love* you." I crawled in beside him.

"They're my people out there. I wanna give what they want. In Vegas well, sure, it's great. But, uh, you know, some of the people out there come to see me just so they can go back home and brag on how they had the pull to get in. That's what I was tryin' to tell you before 'bout the difference. Most of my real fans couldn't even get past Emiliero or whatever his name is, to see a show in Vegas. It's uh . . . a different type crowd, if ya know what I mean. Hell, a lot of these folks that were here tonight, they couldn't afford to *go* to Vegas even if they could get in to a show."

"I know that's true," I said. "It's too bad you couldn't do your own Woodstock, just once, with everybody allowed in, free."

"I'm not kidding about this, Joyce."

"I wasn't, either."

"Well, it's the kind of thing wouldn't be practical enough for the Colonel. It'd be important to me, but it's strictly business to him."

He turned away from me as he said that last, but I could never forget the expression that flashed across his face, one I had never seen before—one of resentment. It only lasted a microsecond.

"These are the people, honey, you know, the ones who gave me what I got and I want 'em to know I'm grateful."

"They do, Elvis. Believe me, they do," I said, trying to calm him. But it was no use, there was no stopping him. He took my hand between both of his.

"I really love doin' these shows. It's the live audience . . . they make *me* feel alive. I can feel em . . . and I communicate with 'em. There is nothin' like it. You know, all those years makin' them lousy movies. What a damn waste. But the Colonel . . . he made me do 'em."

"I know you don't like them, Elvis, but they were all big hits. And I'm sure they made a lot of money."

"Yeah, sure. Parker's shrewd, honey. Yeah, we made plenty of money. But that's not what's important to me. I need to feel good about what I do. But I need him, too, ya know? Hell, I'd probably work for nothin' if I felt good enough about the audience and what I was doin'. But the Colonel, man . . ." He laughed. "He'd probably have a heart attack. He'd never go for that. Y'know, I remember when he wouldn't let me do Dick Clark's show, "American Bandstand." 'There's no money in it, Elvis,' he'd say to me. Ya know, Joyce, before I played the International, I was really scared . . . scared I couldn't cut it anymore. But after that, I knew I still had it. I captured 'em, didn't I?"

"And me."

He tightened his grip on my hands and stared into my eyes.

"Yeah, what about you, little girl?" he asked after a long moment. "How you holdin' up?"

"Great. I'm loving all of it, every minute. But I can't wait for Tuesday in Baltimore."

"Whoa! We gotta get through Louisville and then . . . uh, Philadelphia on . . . what is it? Monday. Monday night, first."

"Elvis, I can't stay that long," I protested. "I have to leave tomorrow night. I thought you realized . . . I have to be back at work. I have to prepare for a hearing on Tuesday. I'm sorry."

"What? Damnit, Joyce!" He pulled his hands away from mine. "Can't you *ever* put yourself out for me?"

I was hurt. "How can you say that?" I cried. "I have gone for days without sleep for you. I run practically every time you call, even when you don't give me any notice." I could feel a hot stabbing sensation in my chest and a flush spreading up to my cheeks. His mood had changed so dramatically; he caught me off guard when he'd turned on me with so much anger. But it was my own anger I fought to control. After all, I told myself, even if it is selfish on his part to behave like this, it's a selfishness that emanates from his desire for me. To be with me. And that's what I want, too. To be with him.

I cleared my throat and said as evenly as I could, "I really do the very best I can under difficult circumstances, Elvis."

"But I want you with me on this tour." He had calmed down, too. "It means a lot to me and you said that you would."

"And I am. I'm here with you now, but you know I can't stay indefinitely. That's something I just can't help. Honest. I really can't."

"All right, all right . . . all right." He nodded and accepted it one more time but from the look in his eye, it was only a temporary acceptance. He reached out and took my hand again. "But stay till Monday morning. I'll get you back in time then. Just stay with me tomorrow night in Philadelphia, okay?"

"All right," I said and squeezed his hand, feeling the heat of a familiar flame begin to lick deep down inside, and wanting to let him know, wanting him to respond, wanting his passion to burn away any bitterness or resentment that still remained.

"Hey," he said, dropping my hand. "What about your tickets? For your family and all. How many do ya need for Baltimore?"

"It's already taken care of, Elvis," I said. "You have so much to deal with, I didn't think it was fair for you to have to concern yourself with that, too. We already have our tickets."

"I told you I'd take care of that for you." He reached his hand out again, but this time it was merely to place the little pills into my palm.

I brought them up to my mouth and hesitated. I thought of the promise I had made to Janice. I couldn't keep it—not tonight. Not when we were scheduled to leave early in the morning and I needed to sleep. Even though I wanted him to make love to me . . . I put them in my mouth.

While I was preoccupied with making my ritual excuses to myself, Elvis was rummaging through his books. Dozens of them were always stacked near his bed, even when he was on the road, as well as dozens of pairs of sunglasses and an arsenal of handguns.

"One of the main reasons I need you with me," he said, bringing one of the books with him as he turned back toward me, "is that I need somebody who can understand the things I am about. Somebody I can talk to. You know I have to reach people, Joyce. That's what it must be about . . . what *I'm* about."

"I realize that, Elvis. I appreciate that. I really *do* try to be there for you," I said.

He went on as if he hadn't heard me. "There has to be some

master plan behind it for me to have the chance to reach so many people. That must be part of why it happened to me . . . that's what I was trying to get across to you about paying back my people for everything they've given me."

I scooched over and cuddled up against him. He opened the book and seemed to be searching through it as he spoke.

"A new type of person is evolving, y'know, slowly reaching a higher plane of development. It's the way to salvation, but people have to be reached . . . taught, really."

I could feel the pills kicking in, my eyelids growing heavy. I picked my head up and tried to read the book's title *The Secret Doctrine*. I'd never heard of it.

"That's where my music comes in, Joyce." His words were starting to slur very slightly. "We've always known of Wise Men, right? But there are also Masters of Wisdom, and they will teach not from authority, but from experience. Do you see it? My music is from experience, from life, from the heart. I can form a spiritual oneness for my people who truly hear my song because it does not push and lay down rules on people, it frees them . . ."

My head felt as though it weighed fifty pounds. The opportunity for love was slipping away. I forced my sandbag of a head up and kissed his shoulder and then his neck. I felt the warmth and weight of his body on mine and his soft, moist lips on my mouth. He began to kiss and caress me in his old-fashioned, gallant, romantic, courting way, lovingly letting me choose my own pace, slowly . . . slowly . . . too slowly. I felt his flame flicker and die as he faded, with a last sighing attempt to quote me one more theory.

Chapter Twenty-one

It was a nifty little Fairchild 28 that taxied down the runway of the Cleveland airport shortly after we boarded her around ten o'clock the following morning. A moment or so later there was the abrupt lurching sensation as the jets flamed on and off we roared for Louisville.

I don't think we were airborne fifteen minutes before Elvis jumped up and, grabbing me by the hand, said, "Come on, how'd you like to go into the cockpit?"

We navigated our way slowly through the narrow walkway, the Fairchild 28's rather streamlined fuselage being crammed to the bursting point with a full complement of guards and gofers. When we reached the front cabin Elvis opened the door, gestured me inside, and introduced me to the pilot.

He offered his hand and I gave it a quick shake. "Thanks for the really smooth takeoff," I told him. "That must be quite an accomplishment in these stiff winter winds."

"I have all of your records and I've seen every one of your movies."

I restrained myself from telling him I'd never cut a record or been in any movies when I saw his glassy-eyed gaze still fixed on Elvis. It wasn't a case of his mistaking my identity, merely a case of his being star-struck and a little rude. I was finding out that an incredible number of people were affected in this way by the presence of a star. Of *the* star.

"You know what one I really liked?" the pilot went on. *"Kid Galahad,"* he said, answering his own question and picking one of Elvis's least believable roles. "You know, the one where you're a boxer? You must have really had to train for that." He shook his head. "Yes, sir, that's really one of my all-time favorites."

Elvis responded to all this, of course, by thanking him and being modest as only Elvis could be.

"When was that, though?" the pilot continued. "I can't remember the year offhand."

"Honey?" Elvis looked at me. Somehow, in his mind I had become his own personal walking encyclopedia of Elvis lore and he loved showing it off. "When was it?" He turned back to the pilot. "Joyce will know," he assured him.

"Kid Galahad came out in nineteen sixty-two," I shot back immediately, assuming a blasé and confident tone. And why not? I was just taking a wild guess.

"I can't believe it." Elvis shook his head. "That long ago."

"Yeah." The pilot nodded. "I loved that movie."

"I knew that Joyce would know," Elvis reminded him, beaming proudly.

It was almost as cold in the sunny southland city of Louisville, Kentucky, as it had been on the frozen shores of Lake Erie and I was grateful for the limousine driving directly from the ramp where we landed to Freedom Hall for Elvis's two o'clock matinee performance.

The show soon warmed me—and I needed it. I needed to know his performance could still produce an intoxicating, visceral excitement inside me, even in the context of one-night stands and matinees in city after city. Nothing was more central to Elvis's being than his talent. I instinctively sensed that from the beginning: he was his image and that image was both "ELVIS" and Elvis.

It would have been impossible for that matinee audience to match the dramatically emotional response Elvis had received the night before in Cleveland, but just as the show ended, events took a tragicomic turn for me. When Elvis went into his last song, my baby-sitters and I started out in order to get ahead of the crowd and meet him on schedule. Suddenly, two women left their seats and jumped in front of me, cutting me off from my two escorts.

"Priscilla!" they yelled in my face. "Please, please! Give us your autograph."

Then one of them shoved a souvenir book at me and from somewhere flashbulbs began to pop and flash.

"No," I told them, trying to shield my eyes. "I'm not Priscilla."

"Come on, Priscilla," the other one snarled, "don't be a bitch."

My face flushed and now the bulbs had me half blinded.

"Sit down!"

I looked around. My two tormentors were blocking the view of some of the audience and people were yelling and pointing.

"DOWN IN FRONT!!!"

The two women hesitated, then backed off a few steps. It gave me an opening and I slipped quickly through and past them, quickening my pace until I caught up with the guys.

All the way back to the Louisville airport it ate at me. For a long time I had blocked Priscilla out of my mind.

Elvis had made me feel that I was the only woman in his life. Looking over at him, sitting beside me, still in costume and trying so hard to unwind, I made a choice even before we got back to the plane. I decided not to say anything.

Once on board and jetting into the sky, I tried to keep my mind off what had happened and on *him*—and on what could or should happen with us. Needless to say, it wasn't difficult at any time to make Elvis my focus of attention.

"I just don't have any appetite," he said and pushed aside the platters of delicacies that had been set out waiting for him when we came aboard.

"Oh, come on," I said, a little concerned. "You have to eat something. Look, how about these shrimp? They look delicious."

"No, honey, I'm really not hungry. I'll just have some chips. Anyway, I don't like shrimp. Not much on seafood."

I nibbled away awhile longer, not feeling too hearty about food myself, but finally I was unable to ignore his continual fidgeting any longer.

"Elvis, what's wrong? You can't seem to relax these past couple of days."

"I'm okay, I guess." He shrugged and crunched another chip. "Just didn't sleep good."

"How come?"

"I don't know. It happens sometimes."

I was still nibbling, but he stood up abruptly and took my other hand. "Let's go, Joyce."

"Go? Where? Should I get my parachute?"

"Very funny, Joyce." He chuckled. "No, just to the back of the plane where we can be alone."

When we reached the last door toward the tail, Elvis opened it and we stepped inside a small cabin furnished with a couple of seats and a cot. One of the guys I didn't really know was resting on the cot, but he rose immediately on our entering and left without a word.

Elvis and I sat down in the seats facing each other.

"I felt like gettin' away from the crowd and being alone with you," he said.

"This has really been a fantastic time for me, Elvis," I said with unabashed enthusiasm. "I mean, it's really exciting and you are just something to see, show after show like this. You have so much . . . so much to give . . ." I shrugged, unable to put my thoughts into words anymore.

"What?"

"I don't know . . . just thinking of you being able to do this whenever you want . . . It can be such a wonderful life." I laughed. "You know, you're very lucky."

Elvis didn't laugh back. He looked me straight in the eye and spoke with great seriousness.

"Oh, yeah, sure I'm lucky. But, you got to remember I was born in poverty and grew up with nothin'. And I could live without all this luxury. If I had to, I could go back to that poverty."

Suddenly, he snapped to his feet, muttering, "Damn, man, aren't we there yet? I'm ready to get off this plane. Come on, honey, let's get back up front and see what's goin' on."

His fantasy of returning to the simple life had evaporated into thin air as abruptly as it had come over him. It was just as well, because the only response that had come to mind was: "What would you *do?* You can't function anymore unless there's an army of retainers available to run and fetch you everything, from me to a glass of water." I think Elvis really believed what he'd said, though; he had looked totally sincere.

"Come on, honey."

He was still standing impatiently, waiting for me.

"Just a second, Elvis. I want to ask you something first. Now, don't get mad or anything, and I *am* having a wonderful time, but have you figured out yet how I'm going to get home tomorrow?"

"You're not. I'll take you home when we go to Baltimore."

"Oh, Elvis, honey, don't make it any harder for me, because you know I can't do that. I hate to miss even a second of this, and . . . and I really want to be with you . . . but . . ." I tried to look stern. "But you knew I had to get back in the morning."

He threw his open palm up in the air as if exaggeratedly warding off a blow. "You can take that nasty ol' look off your face and stop narrowin' your eyes at me." He grinned. "I'm only kiddin'. You're goin' in the mornin'. In the Colonel's plane, and

George Klein's gonna go with you so you won't be by yourself."

"Colonel Parker's plane?"

"Yeah, he'll be there in Philadelphia tonight. Now, c'mon, let's go. We oughta be gettin' pretty near ready to land by now."

The presidential suite of Philadelphia's Bellevue Stratford was, as the phrase goes, "tastefully appointed." That is, everything from the furnishings to the color scheme had been chosen to enhance the overall, elegant effect, while not intruding upon or intimidating the inhabitants of any given room.

All of this subdued, tasteful elegance had little or no effect on Elvis Presley and his Merry Men of the Memphis Mafia. If anything, Elvis had grown even more hyper since setting his feet on solid ground and the revelry and endless adolescent pranks that formed the core of what today would be called their "male bonding sessions" seemed to me to be aggravating his tension, not dissipating it.

Elvis had me sitting, as always, right by him. I was on the verge of whispering that I wanted us to go to bed, but before I could make up my mind to speak, the room suddenly hushed and I became aware that Elvis was staring over my shoulder.

I turned and saw a man standing in the doorway. He immediately headed for us. He was a stocky man, rather nondescript, actually, though looking to be easily past his fiftieth birthday. He wore baggy pants into which a rumpled shirt had been carelessly stuffed and had a pair of shabby slippers on his feet.

Ordinary-looking though he might have been, the extraordinary silence that greeted the man's unannounced (unheard of in that security conscious world) entrance aroused my curiosity and I kept my eyes glued to him so that I sensed, rather than saw, Elvis rise and take a step toward him.

"Joyce," he said. "I want you to meet Col . . . the Colonel, Colonel Parker."

"Hello, Colonel," I said.

He nodded in the tenth of a microsecond his eyes took to

register where I might—or might not fit—before they returned to what they were interested in: Elvis.

"You look tired, son," he said.

"Aw, just a little."

He put his arm around Elvis and walked him away from me.

"Well, why don't you get some rest now . . ." I heard him say before they got too far for his voice to carry. They stood out of earshot talking quietly for a few minutes and then the Colonel left. Was it my overwrought imagination or did the man make a point of not saying goodbye to me?

It was *not* merely my imagination that I saw Elvis, for the first (and last) time, defer to another person.

Elvis walked back to me. "Come on, Joyce," he said. "I think we should get to sleep."

Well, the Colonel could decree that the night's frivolities should end, I thought to myself when Elvis and I were alone in the bedroom, but he can't decree the tension out of Elvis's head. Since he still seemed to be every bit as wired as before, I couldn't help but wonder if having his outlet shut off so abruptly wouldn't do Elvis more harm than good.

He had disappeared into the bathroom for about ten minutes before I heard him calling.

"What?"

I went over to the closed door and knocked softly.

"What is it?" I could hear water running in the sink.

"Joyce, come in here."

"What do you want?"

"Want ya to see how I keep my sinuses clear."

I opened the door and took a step or two inside. "What are you talking about, Elvis?"

"It's so I can sing . . ."

He was bent over the sink in his pajamas.

"Watch, now. This is a good thing to do . . ." Cupping his hands under the water, Elvis leaned down, stuck his face into his water-filled palms and inhaled the water through his nose.

"Elvis—"

He sent a long, arcing geyser out of his mouth and spattering into the sink.

"What are you doing?" A stupid question, I have to admit, since he had already told—and shown—me. It didn't make any difference, anyway, as he ignored me and repeated this startling procedure not once, but over and over.

"Elvis, come on, enough . . ."

He stopped then, twisted around, saw the expression on my face, and burst out laughing.

"All right." I laughed. *"You* are having a good time, making me sick, but I'm not having a good time *being* sick." I turned around and started back into the bedroom.

"Don't ya wanna know the secret to keepin' my voice in condition?" he yelled after me, still laughing.

I was just fluffing up the pillows when I heard him calling again. "Joyce!"

"What is it now?"

"Come on back. I wanna show you something else."

"Oh, no, I've seen enough, thank you."

"Joyce, get back in here." He was laughing harder than ever.

"All right, Elvis," I said, taking a couple of tentative steps through the doorway and into the bathroom. "What've you got in mind for an encore?"

He doubled over then in a fit of laughter, probably because of the shocked expression on my face.

I couldn't help it. Seeing Elvis Presley standing perfectly naked (and I do mean, perfect) in front of me was a shock, mostly because it was totally out of character for him to display himself like that. He had taken off his pajamas and hung them on the towel rack.

"What are you doing?"

"Look at this," he said, taking hold of himself with his left hand.

"I've seen it before," I said dryly. "Are you feeling all right, Elvis?"

"I want you to watch this?"

Still holding himself with his one hand, he pulled his foreskin back with the other and washed himself with soap and water.

"Elvis, I can't believe you want me to stay here and watch you do this. I'm going back into the bedroom."

"You're not embarrassed, are you, baby? I'm not tryin' to embarrass you, y'know. Just have to do it. Want ya to know I'm clean."

"Well, I *am* embarrassed! I can't help it, I'm sorry."

Actually, it wasn't so much embarrassment I felt as astonishment. This was not the Elvis I had come to know, not the man who was modest almost to a fault. It was disconcerting to see him cavorting like that.

I left him still doubled over, laughing at me and scrubbing at himself, and walked back into the bedroom.

"Come back here! I want you to watch this." And then, employing the partly sarcastic, partly peremptory tone he sometimes used to give orders to his men, he said, "I might need your help, y'know . . ."

I sat down on the edge of the enormous bed. I didn't answer him. Instead, I tried to think things through. He might need my help, all right. He certainly needed *somebody's*. I knew his behavior must be the result of whatever drugs were being prescribed for him. I was beginning to feel really frightened. Not frightened *of* him; frightened *for* him.

"Why didn't you come back when I called?"

I looked up to see him standing there, dripping water on the rug, but pajamaed once again. I opened my mouth, but before I could respond, there was a loud knock at the door. Another startling occurrence; no one ever dared disturb Elvis once he was in his bedroom. Elvis, however, moved immediately to answer it. I picked up my negligee from the bed, put it on over my nightgown, and turned to see the door opening.

Elvis stepped aside and a total stranger walked into our bed-room.

"Come on in, Doc," said Elvis to a middle-aged man in a gray suit, carrying a black bag.

"Doc? What's a doctor coming here for, Elvis?"

"Don't worry, it's okay." Elvis was reassuring. Except it wasn't *me* he was reassuring, it was the doctor, who was eyeing me suspiciously.

Elvis didn't even look at me, just sat down on the other side of the bed. The strange doctor then reached into his little black bag and brought out a rubber tube and a hypodermic needle. Elvis rolled up one sleeve of his pajama top and the tube was tied around his bare arm.

"Elvis, what are you taking . . . what is that?" I asked nervously.

"Just wait now, Joyce, it's okay. You go ahead, Doc."

Elvis held his arm taut and the doctor slid the hypodermic needle into his protruding vein and pushed in the plunger. I turned away, unable to watch anymore. My face was still averted when I heard Elvis say, "All right, Doc, give her one, too."

I turned around to see the doctor pulling the empty hypodermic out of Elvis and looking at me.

"No! No!" I jumped an involuntary step and a half backward. "I don't *want* a shot of anything. Elvis, why are you . . ."

"Joyce, take one of these. I'm telling you, you'll feel better . . . and sleep better."

"No . . . no, I won't . . . because I won't take it. No way, absolutely not . . ." I continued to back away from them.

Finally, Elvis acknowledged that I was too upset and adamant to be persuaded. "Doc," he said, "think maybe you better go now."

Once he had shut the door behind this strange figure, Elvis wheeled on me. "What's wrong with you, Joyce? You know I'm not going to do anything to hurt you."

"How can you say that so certainly?" I cried. "What did he give you? Do you even know for sure?"

"All *you* need to know is that *I* say it's somethin' you need," he told me as he got into bed.

"You knew that 'doctor' was coming up here all along, didn't you, Elvis? Who's idea—"

"But if you don't want to listen to me," he went on, as if I had never spoken, "if you think you know better'n me, well, forget it."

"I wish I could," I said as I approached my side of the bed, "but I'm not sure I should, Elvis."

"Uh . . . Joyce?"

"What?" I hesitated, one knee up on the bed, one foot still on the floor.

"Would you do me a favor?"

"What . . . what kind of a favor?"

"I want you to take something with you when you leave tomorrow."

" 'Take something'?" "What something?" I asked.

"I want you to take this with you," he said and held up the needle the doctor had just used to inject him with the unknown drug.

"The needle? The used needle?" My head started to spin.

"And I want you to throw it away after you get home, okay?"

"Why? Why don't you . . ."

"It's nothin'. Just don't want anyone to find it. Here, wrap it up and put it in your bag."

"Elvis, I don't think I should . . ."

He reached over and without getting out of bed, put it in my bag. He rolled back and we were facing each other. "Just do it for me?"

I sighed and settled under the covers, automatically putting my hand out to him. Before I realized what I was doing, the little pills were nestled in my palm. But, of course, I wanted them. I needed them. They would help me forget what I had seen and enhance the fleeting illusion that when I woke in the morning I would discover it had been only an ugly dream.

But the only thing they enhanced the next morning was my resentment. I woke in slow motion to an icy November dawn trying to claw through the fog in my brain. The first thing I managed to do was knock my watch off the night table and saw it fall, also apparently in slow motion, to the floor. I then discovered that my hand was too numb to pick it up.

I felt Elvis stir next to me in his sleep, his breathing so shallow that the incredibly handsome face seemed almost like a death mask, so peaceful, so like a young god that it came to me with the incredible clarity an insight has only when everything else is a muddled mess—how his innocent arrogance could kill us. He certainly was killing himself with it.

Terrifying. Like the needle. The long, cold needle he wanted some stranger to stick into me. My eyes began to focus and my head to clear slightly and I remembered who had the empty needle *now*. What I still didn't know was what it had been filled with last night. That was what I could not find out. That was what you were not supposed to ask.

Pills, on the other hand, were no problem . . . pills were a piece of cake.

I felt his leg pressing against mine. God, he was clammy. The damned air conditioner. But he would demand air-conditioning even in a goddamned igloo!

I groped my way from the bed and made it to the bathroom where, leaning heavily on the sink for balance, I splashed cold water in my face and forced myself to face the hard, grim truth that stared back at me from the mirror. A serpent had reared its ugly head in my garden of Eden.

"Joyce, are you almost ready? It's gettin' late." The voice on the other side of the bathroom door was Sonny's.

"Be right out," I mumbled, my tongue thick, my mouth dry, my stomach aching. I pulled myself together somehow, packed, and tiptoed through the bedroom, already getting my perky, cheerful false face ready for the world.

Chapter Twenty-two

Shortly after dawn, Colonel Parker's plane, the Falcon, taxied the length of the airport runway and lifted gracefully into the cloud-rimmed, gray morning. It fleetingly sought the edge of the continent etched in the dirty-green surf below, and then banked sharply south for Washington.

George Klein, who had been waiting dutifully for me in the Bellevue Stratford lobby as Elvis had insisted he would be, was the only other passenger. A small, slight, dark-haired man, he tried so very hard throughout the flight to be a friendly, pleasant companion that I did my best to make small talk back, even though my stomach was turning over and my brain kept switching channels from confusion to hurt to anxiety and back again.

"You must be an awfully good friend to Elvis, Mr. Klein."

"George, please."

"George . . . to get up at such an ungodly hour and fly me home just to turn right around and go back."

His big black eyes lit up. "Yeah, Elvis and I have been friends since high school. We graduated Hume High together. I'd do anything for the man. Not that escorting a beautiful young lady is my idea of a sacrifice."

"Thank you," I said. "And I'm aware how much he thinks of you, too. Whenever I've been in Graceland and your program has come on the air, Elvis always makes a point of calling attention to it. He'll say: 'There's my man!'"

"Well, you know, even after high school we stayed close."

"Mmm." I nodded. "I remember that when Elvis had his eye infection, you kept track of his progress for all his fans. It was like you gave them a forum for wishing him well."

The Memphis radio personality seemed touched at my recalling the incident.

"That's right. That's just the way it was! Elvis has always been there for me—know what I mean? And I'll always be there for him."

Under ordinary circumstances, talking with a man who had been close to Elvis for so many years, who knew the entire Presley clan intimately, and who seemed to love and appreciate Elvis as both an artist and a human being, would have been exactly the tonic needed to perk me up.

But on that particular morning it was all I could do to restrain myself from telling Mr. George Klein that he *wasn't* always there for Elvis. He wasn't there when anonymous doctors arrived in the middle of the night and injected him with needles. Needles that he then insisted had to be disposed of by another person in another city. Needles like the one nestling coolly in my bag even as we spoke.

Yeah, George, I wanted to tell him, that's really terrific that you've known Elvis for so long and love him so much. But, do you know what? There's a good chance you won't know him much longer.

Because you don't love him enough to stand up to him and make him stop trying to kill himself.

I didn't say anything of the kind, of course. Besides, I told myself, as I rode in to the Rayburn Building from National Airport, it would be a cop-out to lay that guilt trip on anyone.

Because it had an intimidating corollary: if I loved Elvis so much, wasn't it up to *me* to prevent him from destroying himself?

I made it to the office on time, which was fortunate since I wound up needing every minute of that long, hard day to prepare for a hearing that was now scheduled to begin the following morning.

When I finally called it quits it was almost evening and Janice was waiting for me, sitting in her parked car, on the horseshoe-shaped drive at the South Capitol Street entrance to the Rayburn Building.

"Well, how did everything go?" she asked the second I was settled in the passenger's seat.

"It was great. Everything was as fabulous as you might hope or expect."

"Really? *Every*thing?" she asked pointedly. "No pills? Nothing like that?"

"Janice," I said, looking straight ahead out the windshield. "You would have been proud of me. I did real good."

"And you can't imagine how different it was from Las Vegas," I babbled as we drove home. "The crowds were different, the makeup of the audience, just like Elvis had said they would be. And huge, naturally. I even met Colonel Parker; in fact, I flew back on his jet, with George Klein, Elvis's old friend . . . the disc jockey? Elvis had him escort me."

If I talked fast enough and kept talking, Janice would have less chance to ask any more embarrassing questions and hopefully I wouldn't have to tell any more lies.

"Joyce, do you mean Elvis didn't do any drugs himself, or did he take them but let you—"

"Janice, you have no idea how completely different he is when he's on tour. And of course, Colonel Parker, his manager was there and . . . oh, yeah, I almost forgot! What's going on with Mommy? About the show and all?"

"Well, first of all, she's waiting for us now at the apartment.

She's going to spend the night. That's partly so we'll all be able to go together to see Elvis tomorrow."

"I hope she isn't going to give me a hard time," I said. "I'm really not up to it tonight. It was a tough day."

"I think it'll be all right. We had a long talk last night and I told her how happy he makes you."

I took a quick, sideways glance at my sister, but no irony or sarcasm showed in her expression. Though she herself was ambivalent about Elvis and me, she had naturally put the best face on the situation when talking to our mother.

"She'd die rather than admit it, but I think she's really excited about going to the show and meeting him." Janice made a right turn and we drove into the apartment complex. "She even bought a new dress for the occasion."

"Sounds like you've turned her attitude around a little," I said as Janice parked in front of our building.

If that were ever the case at all, it was, unfortunately, a turnaround that barely lasted through dinner. By the time the dishes had been loaded into the washer, Mom was ensconced at the kitchen table, her gaze cast dramatically at the floor like the long suffering heroine in some old silent movie melodrama.

Not that *silent* films could ever have been Mom's medium.

"None of your cousins live like you do . . ." she started.

"Probably no one else in the world lives like me, Ma," I answered as calmly as I could. "That's because they're *not* me. They're *them. I'm* me."

Being in the kitchen with her, being yelled at by her, brought it all back, beginning with the first stories she had told us about ourselves, how she knew we were going to be twin girls no matter how much the doctor insisted she was going to have one very big boy. Over time, I began to think she actually believed she willed herself to have twin girls that bitter cold December afternoon in St. Agnes Hospital in Baltimore. We were born almost a full month before our due date (which was, incidentally, January eighth, Elvis's birthday) and ever since Mom has insisted that Janice and I are always in too much of a hurry. Perhaps this perception of hers helped lead to our eventual (and fairly rapid) estrangement. Somewhere in our adolescence, Mom began to invoke a rigid set of rules regarding our conduct and whether she was inspired in this by her fear about our being "too much in a hurry," or her own Sicilian Catholic upbringing, it conspired, together with the escalating marital turmoil between Mom and our almost always absent (but easygoing) father, to drive Janice and me out of our family home as soon as we could find jobs that would make us financially independent.

Mom went on undaunted by any attempt at rational discourse.

"Why do you have to embarrass me like this?" she said. "Good girls don't go away with a man, not even if he *is* a big shot movie star. My own daughter, running around the country with a married man. You know you two weren't raised that way."

She gave a little scornful shake of her head.

"I'll bet you've stopped going to church, as well, and as for *him* . . ."

"Listen," I said, determined to interject some sanity into the conversation. "Does any of what you've said matter very much compared to the fact that he's good to me and makes me happy?"

"Ma, listen to her." Janice came to my defense. "Listen to what she's saying and leave her alone. She's a grown-up woman."

Ignoring that bit of sound advice, my mother kept at me. *"You're* happy? What about *me?* Knowing a married man is ruining my only daughter? How can he make you happy while doing that?"

There was a moment of stunned silence in which I tried to catch my sister's eye. Her gaze never left our mother.

Finally I said, "What do you mean 'only daught . . .' "

But Janice waved me off. "He makes your 'only' daughter happy," she said, laughing, "by singing to her over the phone.

And he's even sung the same way to your 'only' daughter's twin sister. Me."

No levity for Mom, however. She got up and headed for the living room in full scowl. "There may be two of you in body, but there's only one of you in spirit and mind. The two of you stick together like glue. No wonder I can never win an argument, no matter how right I am."

I stayed in the kitchen while Janice followed after her. "You let up on Joyce right now, Ma," I heard her say. "If you want to go to the show tomorrow night, you've got to stop this stuff right now. I don't want to have you do or say anything that will embarrass Joyce or Elvis or me."

For an answer, Mom chugged back into the kitchen. "Okay," she said. "You win. I want to meet him. I have to meet him . . . to see." She looked me squarely in the eye. "I only hope you know what you're doing," she said and huffed off into the bedroom.

After a moment, I came out into the living room.

"Thanks," I said. "I think that really did the trick."

Janice looked up from the magazine she was reading. "Well, you know, regardless of anything she might say, I can tell Mom's excited about the prospect of meeting Elvis."

"What the heck was that 'only daughter' stuff?"

"I don't know. She's been under a strain with the divorce and everything. Maybe she's losing it a little."

"You really handled it well, Janice, better than . . ."

"Well, you two. What do you think?"

Our mother had reappeared from the bedroom, wearing her new dress and pirouetting into the room to show it off.

"How does it look? How do I look?"

Janice and I exchanged a quick glance and even quicker smiles. This was our mom, all right.

"Fantastic, Mom," said Janice.

"Fabulous, Mom," said I.

"It's really cute."

"It's you."

After we had done our filial duty, I announced, with no exaggeration, "I am totally exhausted and need to get some sleep immediately. Tomorrow is going to be another big day."

"And an even bigger night," my sister said, smiling at our mother.

On the big night, the ninth of November, Peggy arrived at the apartment, on time, for once, and I drove all four of us out to the Baltimore Civic Center in the little orange Pinto Elvis had given me.

It had been another tough day at work, beginning with an executive session hearing that had been long and quite grueling. On the twenty-sixth of October, a Cuban airliner had landed at New Orleans Moisant International Airport with twenty-one Cuban nationals who announced they had come to attend a technological conference on sugarcane. The Cubans had no U.S. visas, nor had the plane filed the required flight plan. This day's session, as well as two follow-up hearings, had been scheduled to determine just how a large aircraft from an ostensibly hostile country could so casually penetrate United States air space without detection.

During the last break I had been gathering up my papers, preparatory to leaving the hearing room, when I heard behind me the deep southern drawl of Congressman Hebert.

"How are ya doing, Joyce?"

I turned. "Oh, fine, thank you, Mr. Chairman. How are you?"

"Good, good. By the way, I hear ya been taking quite a few sick days lately. Hope you're doing better now?"

There was a twinkle in his eye, but I wasn't entirely sure it was all benevolence on his part. I knew my absences could be a sore spot. "I am, sir. I'm fine . . . At least I am now, sir."

"Good. Like seeing you 'round here."

"Thank you, sir, for being concerned. I . . . uh . . . like being here."

I was embarrassed and obviously fumbling for the proper response, my guilty conscience showing.

"Glad to hear it. I wouldn't want to lose you because of your health . . . or for any other reason," he added pointedly.

I stared at the hearing room door as it closed behind him, the not so subtle warning echoing in my brain. "Wouldn't want to lose you." There was no question I was now walking a very narrow line.

The implications of that brief but ominous run-in with the powerful head of the House Armed Services Committee continued to reverberate as we headed that night for the city of my birth. And Elvis. From the time we left Greenbelt Road and drove onto the Baltimore-Washington Parkway, I couldn't stop turning over and over in my mind all the most negative aspects of our relationship. It was obviously jeopardizing my career, and with it the independence I had fought so hard to maintain, but it also seemed to be wreaking havoc on the person closest to me in the whole world.

Before getting ready ourselves, my sister and I had done our mother's hair for her and, while she was in the bathroom examining the result of our efforts, Janice took the opportunity to inform me that I looked like hell.

"What do you mean?"

"I mean that I'm not as convinced as you are that this relationship is good for you. Do you realize how jittery you've been since you came back from that tour with him?"

"No, I don't," I said defiantly. "It sounds to me like you *want* it to be doomed. I really don't need to hear this right now. You know what a big night this is for me. I need to feel good, not—"

"That's what I'm talking about. Look at yourself. You *don't* feel good, do you? Your eyes are dark, you're losing weight."

"But I'm happy, Janice," I insisted. "And I need you to be happy for me."

"But I need to *help* you when I feel you're not being realistic. Being in love isn't always good for you, you know. I *want* to be happy for you, but I can't necessarily be happy about the things you *want* me to be happy about."

"What is this all about, Janice?" I demanded. "What are you getting at?"

My sister shook her head impatiently. "It's what's getting at *you*. I'll bet you still can't go to sleep without those damn pills, can you?"

"Don't be silly," I protested. "Of course I can."

But my mind flashed back to the night before. After admiring my mother's dress, I'd made a beeline for the bathroom and my stash of Placidyls hidden beneath the sink, greedily gulping down enough to get me the sleep I craved.

As if on cue, that guilty image was interrupted by the bathroom door opening behind Janice. "Mom's coming back," I said.

"Please, Joyce," Janice whispered, "I'm scared. Please, please don't take any more."

"Joyce . . . you teased my hair too high."

Mom's trivial accusation was a relief. Recalling it as I drove into the Civic Center temporarily staunched the torrent of fear and doubt racing through my mind and brought me back to more mundane problems. The dozen friends and relatives I had invited were already congregating expectantly at the main door, and I knew they were too many to take backstage to meet Elvis before the show. At that moment, knowing I'd have to cause anyone else hurt or disappointment was more than I could bear. Just anticipating their pained reaction, I could feel my stomach tense.

When Janice and I went off by ourselves to the stage entrance to meet Marty Lacker, one of Elvis's main men, he suggested we all get seated first. A few minutes later he appeared at our seats and leaned over to whisper in my ear.

"Elvis would like you to bring Janice and your mother with you," he said. "The three of you follow me, please," he added, emphasizing the number.

I shrugged and smiled apologetically as we passed by the group. They had heard Marty and I was off the hook.

Jerry Schilling was standing at the door when we got to the dressing room. That seemed a favorable omen. I had never forgotten it was Jerry who helped Elvis find me that first time in Washington after I had given up all hope of ever seeing him again.

The room itself seemed tiny, possibly because it was filled with people. Sonny and Red were there (I had seen and spoken to Lamar Fike outside), along with George Klein, Doctor Nick and, of course, Elvis's dad, Vernon, as well as some faces I hadn't seen before. There was a makeup table on which someone had left a huge basket of roses. The roses looked painted and false in the hideous overhead fluorescent light. Next to the basket was Elvis's long, black flashlight. In the full-length mirror that hung on one of the lightly paneled walls, I finally saw him. He was dressed in a white jumpsuit bedecked with jewels and accented in red. I turned from the image and looked for the man. At the same time he saw me and came toward us.

"Oh, you don't have to tell me who this is," he said with a broad smile. "This is your mama." He took her hands in his and leaned down. "You're as beautiful as your twins, ma'am."

At that moment, my four-foot, eleven-inch mother simultaneously floated up high as the ceiling and melted down to a puddle. She stood on tiptoe to offer her cheek to his lips. In ten seconds flat, the charm that had beguiled audiences from Tennessee to Tipperary to Tokyo, had turned my puritanical, uptight, judgmental mom into an adoring, worshipful, weak-at-the-knees schoolgirl.

"How are you, little sister?"

He and Janice hugged and kissed, but then she pulled back and plucked at his sleeve.

"Aren't you hot in this getup, Elvis? I can't believe how heavy this material is! How can you stand it?"

Before he could answer, Mom whipped out a Kleenex and wiped the perspiration from his brow.

She got the curled-lip smile. "Thank you, ma'am. And now, for this lovely daughter—"

The kiss I got made up for being last. Elvis put his arm around my waist and turned back to face Mom. "And you do have a lovely daughter here," he drawled.

Mom—my mom, the Spanish Inquisition Mom of only the night before—merely beamed modestly: "I always did tell my twins how much I liked your singing." I swear, if he had casually stated his intention to ravish me behind the curtain a few times before the show started, she probably would have giggled and curtsied. Elvis had made another convert.

Elvis, his arm still around me, took me aside. Janice proceeded to shepherd Mom over to the other side of the room.

Elvis was perspiring again and I put my hand up to his forehead. "Elvis, you really do feel clammy," I said.

"I'm warm in this suit, that's all."

"Honey, you don't look well. Really. You're pale."

"I want you to come back to Philadelphia with me after the show," he replied, ignoring my concerns about his health.

"Please don't, Elvis. I can't. Honestly."

"But, Joyce—"

"I have to tell you," I burst out, "that last night there in the Bellevue Stratford, when the doctor came in with that needle, was scary. We have to talk about that."

Across the way I could see Janice introducing our mother to some of the guys. My sister was taking out her camera.

"I don't know what to make of it . . ." I couldn't seem to make the words and thoughts come out any way but clumsily. But I couldn't stop, either. ". . . but I think . . . Elvis, I *know* you have to do something about all the . . . uh . . . about all the medication."

"I don't need a sermon, Joyce," Elvis said firmly.

"Oh, honey, I'm making a mess of this." I whispered. "I know that it isn't the time or the place but I'm so scared, the fears just came out. And Elvis—they come from my heart. You've got to know that."

"I just want you to come back with me." His voice was soft and I could almost feel the hurt that had come into his eyes. "Won't you? Please?"

"I'm sorry, it's just im—"

"Elvis!"

I looked over at the sound of Mom's booming voice.

"Elvis," she called again, "we have some people outside who are waiting to meet you. Can we get them now and bring them back here?"

"No!" I said, before Elvis could reply. "Ma, no, it's late and Elvis has to get ready to go onstage."

"Well, how about taking a picture with me?"

Elvis walked over to my mother, Janice clicked her trusty camera, and he said, "It was a real pleasure meeting you, ma'am. I'll try to do a good job out there for ya. I hope you'll enjoy it and I'll be seein ya'll again."

Then he had his arms around me and his voice was soft in my ear. "Are you sure, Joyce, sure you can't . . . there's no way?"

"God, Elvis, I would if I could. Please don't look that way."

"What way?"

"The way I feel."

He smiled sadly and gave me one last hug: "See ya, little sister," he called to Janice, and suddenly, Marty Lacker was there and we were being led once more through the crowd.

When we were inside the auditorium I cocked a suitably blasé eyebrow and inquired archly, "Well, Mom?"

"He seems like a nice boy."

"We actually have a Jewish Mother," I said to Janice out of the corner of my mouth.

"Ma," snapped my sister, "you loved him. I knew you would. Admit it. You thought he was a real gentleman and crazy about Joyce."

"Well . . . I've always liked him as a singer."

Janice shrugged as if to say, "what can you do?"

"He promised he would try to be extra good tonight because I was here," our mother explained to the group as we found our seats.

"But he looks terrible," Janice whispered to me. "Do you think he's ill or something?"

"Probably just tired. This touring is a real strain, you know," I said, hoping my real concern was hidden.

"The two of you looked pretty intense when you were talking back there, alone in the corner."

"We were." I nodded. "I'm worried about him."

"I could see," Janice said. "Especially when I snapped your picture."

"When was that?" I started to ask, but was drowned out by the opening chords of his deafening overture.

Which brought the twenty thousand people who had packed the Baltimore Civic Center to their feet and screaming.

And they didn't stop screaming until Elvis, after singing over them for his first few numbers, stepped directly to center stage and, gesturing for quiet, abruptly stopped the show. He stood stock-still and waited for the screaming, the stamping, the whistling to stop.

When you could hear a pin drop, he looked toward where he knew I would be seated. He brought the microphone to his mouth.

"Joyce, this is for you."

The music began.

"Stop. Please, stop." He held up his hand. "That's not right. I want this to be perfect . . ."

The music began again, this time swelling to perfection as the most compelling voice of our time rose out over the vast, hushed throng.

When he came to the end of the song, the crowd applauding, the friends and relatives buzzing, my sister took my hand. And held it until the final curtain. She knew I was numb, adrift in a reverie of love and gratitude.

"Better wipe your mascara. It's smeared all over from your tears," she whispered with the understanding of a twin who knew when her other self needed to be left to her own thoughts.

Only minutes after we got home, my Elvis Phone began to ring and I raced for the bedroom.

"Elvis! I knew you'd call! Where are you?"

"Back in Philadelphia. But, little girl, I had to find out what you thought."

"What I thought! You must know how happy you made me. I loved it. It was so beautiful. Elvis, you can be so wonderful."

"Try all the time. You should've come back with me."

"Maybe, but please, Elvis, don't make me feel like any more of an ingrate than I already do. And you . . . you're right, you really can be a great actor. All those phony excuses about why you couldn't sing that song in any of the shows before. I'll never forget that you waited to sing it especially for me in front of all my friends and relatives in the town where I grew up, where I listened to your records, never thinking some day I'd . . ."

My voice had begun to break. Elvis, out of kindness or embarrassment, or both, said, "It was still a little rough around the edges. Haven't really rehearsed it enough yet. But I had to do it tonight. I gotta go now. Just wanted to hear your reaction. I love you."

"I love you, too, but take care of yourself, pleeeease."

He hung up.

Well, he had done it again. Just when the negatives of our relationship had provided enough impetus for me to stand up and be strong with him, he had undercut me with one sweet, magnificent gesture. He *is* wonderful, I thought to myself as I went to sneak my Placidyls from their secret cache.

It wasn't until I had gone back to humming and basking in the warmth of our song, of that sun that "rose in your eyes," that it dawned on me. Being thwarted and attacked was exactly the time when Elvis *would* make such a romantic gesture; of course. No statesman on the Hill was any craftier at brinkmanship than Elvis at rising to a crisis. And control.

It wasn't until after the Baltimore show and after Elvis's phone call that night that I told Janice about the needle he had given me to throw away. Janice had been so insistent that I admit to not having taken any pills, I just couldn't bear telling her before then. Now, I couldn't keep it from her any longer. The night had been so perfect, I was sure we would be able to talk about it rationally.

I had hidden the needle way back in the cabinet underneath my bathroom sink when I unpacked the night before—probably because I was afraid of being caught by Janice or Mom while trying to throw it away. Now, Janice sat scrunched on the bathroom floor beside me as I removed it from its hiding place. I told her the whole story and how scared I was.

Janice was furious. She thought we should have the needle analyzed to find out exactly what substance had been injected into Elvis. But I was adamant. I wanted to throw it away. I didn't want to know what had been in it. So, I securely wrapped the needle in a brown bag and went outside, down to the bottom floor, and threw the bag into the big garbage barrel.

Chapter Twenty-three

I was just stepping out of the shower that Sunday evening, the fifth of December, when the Elvis Phone rang. I wrapped a towel around myself and ran to answer it, the bare, damp soles of my feet making little slapping sounds across the cold floor.

"Hello?"

"Hi. You sound out of breath."

"It *is* you. Yeah, I just ran out of the shower."

"Got you out of the shower, huh? Bet you look pretty."

"Pretty? I hope so. Damp . . . definitely. How are you?"

"Okay, I guess."

"What do you mean, you 'guess'?"

"Well, a few days ago I fell and hit my head."

"You fell? Did you hurt yourself? Are you all right?"

"Yeah. But I had to have a few stitches."

"Stitches! How did it happen?" I asked.

"Oh, I was gettin' up out of bed and I . . . uh . . . guess I couldn't see too good in the dark or somethin'. Tripped and hit my head on the furniture. But it's okay now."

"Why didn't you call me?"

"Didn't wanna worry you. But I'm fine now. Honest. And I'm plannin' to come see you on your birthday."

"It's still a week away," I replied. "You're giving me that much notice? I'm impressed."

"Didn't want you to make your celebration plans without me," he kidded. "Anyway, I miss you."

"Elvis . . . God, every day that goes by I want to be with you more and more. Do you realize it's almost a month now since I saw you last?"

"Could've been a lot sooner. If you woulda come and met me last time I called."

"I wanted to," I said. "You know I did. But you can't call me on Friday and expect me to be able to book flights from Texas that will get me—"

"Utah."

"Right, Utah. The flight was *to* Texas, but I would've had to return *from* Utah. Anyway, the point is that you've got to give me enough notice so I can arrange to be back in the office when I'm needed."

"Like the notice I'm giving you now," he said flatly.

"Right. But what day are you coming?"

"Not sure yet. I'll let you know."

Four days later, I was at the office, having just come out of a hearing, when Charlie Hodge called.

"Elvis will be coming in Saturday night, the eleventh," he said. "About nine o'clock."

Saturday morning, Janice and I were about to embark on a quick shopping expedition when I decided to get her opinion on the outfits I planned to take to the hotel that night. She sat on my bed, dutifully offering her comments while I went through the first half dozen.

"How about this black one?" I asked, noticing her glance impatiently at her watch. "He's never seen it and—"

"Enough . . . please," she said, stretching out on the bed and resting her head on the pillow. "This is more tiring than shopping and not as much fun as a fashion show."

"Okay, okay, but let me just show you one . . ."

"What's gotten into you? You're as giddy as if this was your first date with him."

"I almost feel like it is. I've been feeling that way for a while now. I can't explain it. He just has a way of getting to me."

"I don't know why you care about what you wear, anyway. You never leave the damn hotel. Nobody sees you."

_"He_ sees me."

The phone rang. I looked at Janice.

"Right on cue," she said.

I reached across her and picked up the receiver.

"Elvis?"

"Plans changed, darlin'."

"What?"

"I want you to come here."

"Why? I was looking forward to you coming here."

"Sorry, honey. I can't work it out, so you'll have to come to Memphis."

"When?"

"As soon as you can. Check on the flights and call me back."

"All right. Oh, wait. If you'll hold on, I'll use the other phone and check right now and tell you."

"Okay, go ahead. I'll hold."

I put my hand over the mouthpiece and turned to Janice. "I'm going there instead. I've got to check on the flights."

I laid the receiver down on the pillow next to her and went out to the kitchen to call.

After making a reservation on American Airlines for a five o'clock flight, I hurried back to the bedroom and found Janice still lying there, her head next to the receiver. I started to reach for it but she shook me off, putting her finger to her lips in a signal for silence.

"Janice, what are you . . . you're eavesdropping!" I whispered.

"Wait till I tell you," she whispered back. "Here." She handed me the phone. "Finish talking first."

I took the instrument. "Elvis?"

"Honey?"

I told him my flight number and time of arrival.

"Good. I'll have the ticket prepaid and Joe will be there when you land. See you then."

I hung up. "Janice, I can't believe—"

"I didn't really mean to," my sister explained. "It was just that I all of a sudden heard their voices. My ear *was* pretty close to the phone."

"Oh."

"Now, come on. I didn't *expect* to hear a person who was just holding on start to talk. But only a saint would have been able to resist listening after that. Anyway, what's the difference? You want to know, don't you?"

"Well, what did you hear?"

"Joe must have picked up an extension and I heard Elvis tell him that he was holding on for you. Then Joe asked Elvis if he'd told you yet. And Elvis said, 'No.' "

"Told me what?"

"Just listen, will you? About the divorce. Joe said: 'Have you told her yet about the divorce?' "

"Divorce?"

"Right. Then Elvis said, 'Not yet. I want to tell her when she's here with me in Graceland.' "

I don't think my head stopped spinning until I was actually on the plane to Memphis that evening. Any number of times he had assured me his marriage to Priscilla was over in all but name; nevertheless, the imminent reality of something as official as a divorce still had the power to shock.

It was a cold night in Tennessee.

And dark.

Looming ahead, a beacon in the chill night, mythic, stately, and ethereal in its corona of blazing light, the white magnificence of Graceland beckoned.

I floated up the steps to the great front door.

It opened before I touched it and I entered.

Joe Esposito had brought me and was walking just behind, carrying my suitcase. He put it down, smiled, and motioned casually toward the stairs. I looked, and there was Elvis.

He seemed somehow bigger, stronger than ever as he came down the stairs, so handsome with his hair coal-black and his perfect teeth, carrying with him a kind of glow that immediately welcomed and warmed me.

Elvis was always larger than life, but somehow that night he made everything else larger and more splendid, too.

"Hi, birthday girl."

He wrapped his arms around me.

"Let me look at you," he said after a moment and, gripping me by both shoulders, took a step backward as an artist might to get a better perspective on his canvas.

"You sure you're gonna be twenty-seven? Damn if you don't look younger than you did when we met."

"Yeah, yeah."

"Must be me that keeps you young." He grinned, sliding his right hand to my waist and leading me toward the dining room. "I'm hungry, honey. Hope you're ready for dinner."

When dinner was finished, Elvis took me by the hand and, leaving the entourage behind, ushered me into the den. He sat down on the sofa next to me and said, "I have something to tell you."

"Sounds serious," I said, playing dumb, not wanting to spoil it for him. "Is it good or bad?"

"It's good, honey." He reached for my other hand and, now

holding both of mine in his, said, "Priscilla has given me . . . has given *us* . . . the best Christmas present ever. My freedom."

"Elvis . . . do you mean you're divorced?"

"I mean we're getting a divorce."

"When?"

"Soon. We just have to work out the details."

Even though I was prepared for it, his news left me speechless. I was experiencing mixed emotions. Suddenly, and for the first time, I felt sorry for Priscilla, felt a sadness for the pain she must be experiencing.

"You don't look happy. What's wrong?"

"Nothing, really. I was just thinking, that's all."

"Well, don't think about anything sad. Think about movin' into Graceland."

That shouldn't have been a surprise, coming then, but it was. I wasn't prepared for it.

"Well," I said finally, "you did say you have details to work out."

"Joyce, what's the matter? You won't have to worry about anything. I want you here."

"Please, Elvis." I put my hand up to his lips. "It's just that I'm in a state of shock. I have to think about what it would mean, how it would change things. I know I'm not making much sense. Just please give me some time to think. I need time for it to sink in."

He stared at me for what seemed an eternity.

"Okay, you've got thirty seconds," he said, breaking into a smile and looking down at an imaginary wristwatch.

I smiled back in relief. "I do love you, Elvis, you know that. It's just . . ."

"Okay, little girl. I don't mean for you to call the moving man today. It's just that I thought you'd be happy to hear about it."

"I *am* happy . . . as long as you are."

"Good. Now come on upstairs with me. I've got a little somethin' for you."

We mounted the main staircase to his bedroom and he closed the door behind us. He went to his nightstand, opened the drawer, turned and handed me a plain white envelope.

"Not that good at pickin' out presents. This here's a little somethin' for your birthday."

I held the envelope in my hand and could tell it was stuffed with money.

"A little something? Elvis, this feels like a whole lot of something to me. You didn't have to do this. I mean, the *car* was for my birthday. I mean . . . you're wonderful."

I threw my arms around his neck.

"Don't ever lose that enthusiasm of yours." He laughed. "Gettin' so excited like a little girl. I just didn't know what to buy you, so you get whatever you want with it."

When we got back downstairs to the den, his guys were there lounging around.

"You lazy bums are gonna get fat sittin' round like that," Elvis declared. "Let's go out and do some shootin'."

"Shooting? Shooting what?"

It seemed like a legitimate question to me, but I was ignored in the mad scramble to get out the door. Elvis led the way, gun in hand, the rest of them rushing to catch up. It occurred to me I had not actually seen him get the gun. It just suddenly seemed to appear in his hand.

Sonny had stayed behind and I looked over to him.

"Where are they going?"

"To the shooting range, Joyce," he said and left, just as the first crackle of gunshots sounded from outside.

Well, I thought, sitting down on the sofa, at least it would give me a little time in which to think about things. Joyce, I lectured myself sternly, what is it with you? You knew he was going to tell you about the divorce. Common sense, or just sheer imagination, should have told you he'd bring up your moving in again. Still, you were caught without a solid, practical, intelligent answer. Maybe, I answered myself back, that's because right now there *is* no solid, practical, intelligent answer. Well, then, let's begin at the beginning. Could I really make the move into Graceland? Could I fit into this life . . . into his world? Do I even *want* to?

In perfect time with my questions, as though punctuating them, came the crack-crack-crack of the gunshots from outside.

I realized that Sonny had come back into the room and was standing there in front of me.

"Joyce, you ought to get out there. He's puttin' on this show for you, y'know."

"Sonny, it's freezing out there," I protested.

"Yeah, but Elvis doesn't know that. He's just havin' a good time . . . but most of all he wants to show off for you. For your birthday and all."

I nodded, got up, and walked to the door. I opened it, took a step outside, and quickly took two steps back in, my teeth chattering. Keeping most of my body inside, I chanced opening the door again and leaned out while exposing as little as possible and shouting encouragement and appreciation to my prince—who apparently couldn't hear me, since the only response I got was more gunshots and the cackle of his laughter wafting back to me on the freezing gusts of wind.

After about ten minutes of this charade, he came bounding back inside, the rest of his posse on his heels.

"Well, if it isn't Wyatt Earp. What brings you to Graceland, Marshal?"

He broke up at that.

"What's the matter?" he asked, still laughing. "Don't you wanna see how good a shot I am?"

"But I did, Elvis. I was watching you from the door. And you're good, very good. I was really impressed and I'd love to see you do more—but in the daylight and maybe in the summer?"

"Okay. I guess you had enough."

He plopped down on the sofa, stretching his arms out over

the back. I started to sit down next to him when he bounced right up again.

"Hey, ready to take in a movie?"

"As long as we'll be indoors," I answered.

By eleven-thirty we were in the Memphian Theater along with about a half dozen of his friends and the guys. The first film was *The French Connection* and Elvis really got caught up in the action; his eyes were riveted to the screen, especially during the famous car chase.

After it was over, and while the projectionist was changing reels, he asked me what I thought.

"It was exciting," I said. "I was actually holding my breath during that car chase under the elevated subway."

"Ya know, Joyce, this is a true story," he explained excitedly. "That cop that Gene Hackman played really exists. Yeah, old Popeye Doyle is based on a real cop named Eddie Eagan."

"Well, I really like movies filmed in New York," I said. "There's something special about that city. Popeye Doyle—or Eddie Eagan—he was a tough cop, all right. But I don't know how factual it all was, though. From things my father's told me I doubt it could happen like that in real life."

"But it did, Joyce, believe me. Ya really gotta have a lot of guts to be a cop in that city."

"I'm just saying that I think the filmmakers took liberties in a couple of places," I argued.

"Well, you *have* to, making a film, y'know. I mean, they must've had some rough time shooting Hackman chasing the subway. Y'know they use special stunt drivers and even have special units with their own directors for those kind of action sequences, guys who are experts in just that. They do that kind of stuff . . . with a lot of multiple camera setups and all."

"I can see you wouldn't mind being a director or a producer/director, would you, Elvis?"

"With the right script . . . ya never know, little one, ya never know."

I smiled. "This was a real 'man's movie' I'd say, Elvis."

"Yeah. My kind of movie! I knew it'd be good. But the next one is a lot different. It might be kind of weird, even. But if we don't like it, we'll watch something else."

About halfway through that second picture, which happened to be the low-budget sleeper entitled *Joe,* I whispered to Elvis that I was going to the ladies' room.

"Honey, if you don't wanna see this, there's plenty other—"

"No, I like it, really."

I started up the aisle only to realize he was following me. "I know where it is, Elvis. I'll be right back."

"Just wanna make sure nobody bothers you."

"That's very nice of you, but who's going to bother me?" I teased. "The people you invited? They're the only ones here. And you'll miss some of the movie."

"It's okay, I wanna wait."

I could tell there was no dissuading him. He was faithfully guarding the door when I came out and immediately alert to the fact that I yawned as we started back down the aisle to our seats.

"Are you tired, Joyce?"

"Actually, I am. But I don't want to leave. I just don't know if I can stay awake."

"D'you want somethin' to help you?"

"No, I'm okay. I mean, I don't need anything," I said hastily.

And so, even without Elvis's "help," I was able to sit through a third picture, *Carnal Knowledge* before we made our way back to Graceland.

I crawled wearily into bed while Elvis, still excited by a night with a medium he felt he had failed to conquer, could not stop discussing the attraction and fascination that film held for him.

"Damn movies, they can really get to you . . ." He was still going on as I got under the electric blanket. "Even when the hero's a jerk like this Joe character that Peter Boyle played, they can still grab you. That ending knocked you out, didn't it, Joyce?"

"It really shocked me," I admitted. "I didn't expect it."

"I could tell you didn't have a clue." He laughed.

"And neither did you! You were as surprised as I was."

"Nah, I had that script figured all the way."

Aware that he'd been linked romantically with Ann-Margret, I couldn't resist hearing what he might have to say about her performance in *Carnal Knowledge*.

"Ann-Margret really is beautiful," I prompted. "Don't you think she was good in her part?"

"Yeah, she did a good job. As for beautiful . . . yeah, I suppose she was," he conceded. He reached over to squeeze my hand. "A lot better to look at than Art Garfunkel. Man, that is one goofy-lookin' dude. That haircut of his! Whoa. That boy's gonna have a hard time of it without Simon, lemme tell ya."

"You really like Paul Simon, don't you?"

"Man's got talent. Really like 'Bridge Over Troubled Waters.' "

"I guess so, since you perform it in your shows."

He reached for one of his books then, but I knew that my pills had already started to kick in and that I wouldn't be able to handle anything as esoteric as his philosophy.

"Elvis," I said, hoping to deflect him into an area of nice, juicy, mundane gossip, "tell me. How was it working with Ann-Margret in *Viva Las Vegas?*"

I should have known better than to try. He was too gallant (or too shrewd) to utter anything more than prudent platitudes. "She was lots of fun. Even in a silly Elvis Presley movie, you could tell that she was gonna be a good actress. Some nice girl."

I drifted off into blissful oblivion as he was contrasting Ann-Margret's attitude toward outdoor filming with that of Mary Tyler Moore. MTM, he insisted, would avoid it because sunlight was pitiless to her skin, possibly exacerbated by a diabetic condition.

About an hour later I woke with a start. I had been dreaming that I was walking through an open field in a blizzard and had fallen to my knees. The stinging snow blew relentlessly into my face until I was suffocating. Even my eyelids were frozen shut. I could not move or open my mouth against the driving wind. I knew I was freezing to death.

That was when I woke. I was still half asleep as I reached for the electric blanket control dial and turned it up. I lay back down and, in a few minutes, began to shiver. It was now even colder.

I looked over at Elvis. He seemed sound asleep, though I thought it odd that he had kicked his blanket off. I shook my head and turned the control dial up still another notch. It had no more effect than the first time. I was still freezing, only now I could hear and feel Elvis stirring alongside me.

"Joyce . . ."

"What?" In a Placidyl haze, I barely got the word out.

"Can you turn down the temperature on the blanket?"

"Turn it down?" I slurred indignantly. "I'm freezing."

"Well, I'm on fire."

"What?"

"Hmm," he said after a long moment. "Better get up, Joyce. We'll fix it."

I dragged myself off the bed and joined him in stumbling around the huge thing trying to figure out what to do. Imagine a scene from a comedy in which a couple of drunks attempt to execute some simple task. Make it a silent slapstick comedy, in fact and that ought to put the finishing touches on your picture of what Elvis and I must have looked like.

Finally, alternating between falling giggling into each other's arms on discovering that the electric blanket, specially constructed with dual controls for that enormous bed, was twisted around so that Elvis had my controls and I had his, and bumping awkwardly into each other as we maneuvered the damned, bulky thing back into its correct position, we actually did "fix" it.

"C'mon, Joyce, I'm hungry," Elvis said then and steered me out of the room.

How the two of us managed to negotiate the narrow back staircase down to the kitchen without one of us breaking his or her fool neck, is beyond me. It was definitely another classic movie scene though—the one where the hero and the heroine climb down the impossibly sheer side of the mountain to escape the evil villains. Except that, as is usually the case in real life, there was just goofy us—no heroes, no villains. Unless we were both.

The kitchen was dark, but Elvis didn't bother with a light. He made his way across to the refrigerator while I got myself over to the table and sat down. I was really groggy by then and rested both elbows on the table, supporting my head, now weighing in at about a metric ton, in the palms of my hands.

Elvis threw a little light on the situation by opening the refrigerator. "What would you like, honey?"

"A roaring fire, about five fur coats, and a muffler."

"Hunh?"

"Nothing, really, Elvis. I'm not hungry . . . maybe a little thirsty," I said through chattering teeth. I got up and, staggering from object to object for support along the way, found the sink. Hearing clanging sounds, I peered through the gloom and saw that Elvis was groping in one of the drawers. When he came up with a large spoon, I turned my full attention back to the faucet handle I was trying unsuccessfully to manipulate. Unbelievable as it seems, I simply could not turn that damned faucet on. I gave up and limped lamely back to the table where I shivered even more pathetically watching Elvis finish off the container of ice cream he'd found.

"How 'bout some yogurt?"

I snapped my head out of my hands, blinking and trying to focus. "I must have fallen asleep," I mumbled.

"Here. Take the spoon and try this yogurt."

"What happened to the ice cream?"

"Finished it."

"My God . . ."

He held the spoon out to me.

"I can't, Elvis, really. No thanks." I waved the spoon away

from under my nose. "Doesn't that make you cold, eating all that freezing stuff? Why aren't you ever *cold?*"

"Honey, you are out of it." He chuckled. "I better get you back to bed. Now, get up . . . easy now. Okay, that's it, that's my girl. Hold onto my arm and just lean on me."

I hung on to one of Elvis's arms (the one attached to the hand that was attached to the yogurt container) for dear life. I remember that we both did a fair amount of bumbling and tripping on that return ascent up the magic mountain; nevertheless, I do believe that my prince never spilled so much as a single drop of his yogurt.

Chapter Twenty-four

Elvis placed his hands around my waist, leaned down, and kissed my mouth. "It's the twelfth of December. Happy Birthday."

It was after three o'clock in the afternoon by the time we'd wakened, showered, and dressed that next day. We had just been about to go downstairs together when he stopped me.

"Thank you, Elvis," I said, kissing him back. "You've made this a wonderful birthday. Exciting, too," I kidded. "There were moments there last night where I wasn't sure I was going to make this one. Thought I'd either freeze to death or break my neck."

"I was with you, silly thing. You know I won't ever let anything happen to ya."

We left the bedroom and started down the main staircase, headed for the dining room and breakfast when a thought struck me.

"Elvis, I'd love to call Janice and wish her a happy birthday."

"Sure, go ahead."

"I won't be long."

I started back up the stairs.

"Hey, hold it. What would you think of us goin' to Washington now and both wishin' her a happy birthday in person?"

"Do you mean it? I'd *love* that! But I thought there was some reason you couldn't leave Memphis."

"Nah, I just told you that 'cause I wanted you here with me first."

"Cute, Elvis, real cute. You are a master manipulator, you know that?"

"Yeah, but don't forget, I also figured out you'd want to be with your twin on the twelfth."

"Then you're forgiven and I'll just call her now and let her know we're coming."

As I started again for the bedroom I could hear him ordering somebody (Charlie, I assumed) to set up our journey.

Another surprise was in store for me when we arrived at the Memphis airport and I discovered we were taking a regularly scheduled commercial flight.

"How come?" I asked Elvis.

"Why not?"

Why not, indeed, I said to myself. I could certainly handle going public with our relationship as long as that was what he wanted. It bore testimony to his new freedom, confirmation of his avowed intention to end the marriage to Priscilla.

We boarded the plane from the rear and walked up the long aisle to the first-class cabin. Needless to say, Elvis did not go unnoticed and soon I felt all eyes upon us as we made our way to our seats. Elvis and I sat down together in seats to the right, about three rows back, while Charlie, Sonny, Lamar, and young Ricky Stanley took the seats around us. After a moment, even the pilot came out and stopped by to pay his respects before returning to the cockpit.

As soon as the plane had climbed to cruising altitude and the "Fasten Seat Belts" light went out, people began drifting in from the rear cabin and attempted to approach Elvis. Initially they were stopped by the flight attendants, but Elvis, in an expansive mood, and generous as always with his fans, told them that he didn't mind.

In no time at all he was signing dozens of autographs and joking with everyone over the salutations they requested, even going so far as to think up messages for those who suddenly went tongue-tied in his presence.

Once his admirers left, things quieted down. Which, apparently, didn't suit Elvis, and it wasn't long before he and the guys began cutting up. The highlight of their clowning was some parodying of a few of the less memorable Presley hits. I feel honor bound to point out, however, that it was The King himself who led the way in this, otherwise such liberties would have been strictly verboten.

He finished up by inserting some comic lyrics into "Jailhouse Rock." "That was somethin', man," he said at one point. "Singin' and dancin' cons, a warden who throws parties and has a jailhouse band! Man, that must be some crooked warden! That dude was obviously on the take. Even the title don't make any sense. Only rock those poor sons of bitches in jail know about is the rock they're bustin' their asses over all day on the chain gang. Only realistic line in the whole damn song is number 47 comin' on to number 3, tellin him he's the cutest jailbird he ever did see. I do believe I have heard rumors to the effect that some of that does go on behind bars."

"Elvis, how about singing me a song," I coaxed.

"Okay, silly, what do you want me to sing?"

"How about. 'All That I Am'?"

"Don't think I remember that one," he demurred. But there was a teasing twinkle in his eye.

"Now who's silly. Come on, I'm serious."

He started humming, then tried a lyric or two and stopped. "I don't seem to know the rest of it. What're the words to it, honey? Sing it for me."

"Oh, no you don't. I couldn't carry a tune if it was in my purse. And I sure wouldn't try to in front of you!"

"Okay, okay." He laughed. "What's it from, anyway?"

"Well, I'm not sure. But it's on the flip side of 'Spinout,' so I guess it's from 'Spinout.'"

"Yeah, I remember it now. Pretty song. Okay, tell me the words as we go along. And you don't have to sing 'em."

I cleared my throat, rolled my eyes, and spoke the first lines of the song.

He began to sing.

He was into it now, taking my hand and gazing into my eyes.

When the song was finished, he leaned down and tenderly kissed the tip of my nose.

At that moment, all my fears and doubts and mixed emotions evaporated and I felt I was as loved and cherished as any woman could ever want to be.

It was about an hour and a half later, while we were all still getting ourselves settled into the suite in the Hotel Washington, that Elvis started complaining that his stomach was upset. As soon as the words were out of his mouth, Lamar wheeled on the poor stepbrother, Ricky Stanley.

"Hey, boy," he ordered, "you heard the man. Get on the phone and get some Alka-Seltzer up here—now!"

Ricky leapt to the phone.

I had to cover my mouth with my hand not to laugh out loud at the sheer, puerile tyranny of this display. Then, noticing that I was the only one who saw any humor in it, I said, "C'mon with me, Elvis, I think I might have a Rolaid in my bag."

He followed me into the bedroom, closing the door behind him as I rummaged in vain for the antacid.

"Sorry, Elvis, I can't seem to . . ."

"It's okay. I need to talk to you anyway."

I looked up quickly at the somber tone of his voice.

"What now? I can't take any more surprises—good *or* bad."

For once my attempt at levity failed to evoke even a smile.

"I'm only kidding, honey," I said. "What is it?"

"It's Lisa Marie. I feel I should spend as much time as I can with her. Over the holidays and all. Problem is, that's not goin' ta leave much time—if any—for us. I feel really bad, Joyce, 'cause this is the time I figured we'd start really bein' together. But Christmas, for a kid and all, with her bein' so young, not even four years old yet . . ."

"It's all right, Elvis," I said after a moment. "I understand that you need to be with her, especially now."

"You're right, Joyce, and that's really understanding of you. I really appreciate how you're always bein' that way with me. I know it isn't easy. And little Lisa Marie's gonna have to accept what's happenin' between her mama and me and that won't be easy, either."

"You just love her, Elvis, and don't worry about me. I'll be fine," said the noble, self-sacrificing heroine of practically every novel I'd read or movie I'd seen.

The thing was, though, I really meant it. Every word. And believed it, believed that Elvis's desire and my sacrifice was right and natural.

Elvis's eyes grew misty and he held me and pressed his cheek to mine.

"Thank you, honey. Lisa Marie is just so important to me . . . Brrummmpph."

You can bet *that* broke the mood, his stomach announcing itself like that.

"Didn't that Alka-Seltzer get here yet?"

"Let's see," I said. I opened the door to the sitting room and found my sister standing there.

"Janice, when did—" I started over to greet her and almost collided with little stepbrother Ricky who was rushing forward at the sight of Elvis, carefully balancing a glass filled with fizzing liquid.

"Thanks, man." Elvis nonchalantly plucked the glass from Ricky's hand, simultaneously acknowledging Janice's presence with a wink and a smile. He gulped down the Alka-Seltzer, belched, and sighed: "That's better, much better. Hi, Janice."

"Hi, Elvis. How's your tummy?"

"Okay now. I needed that. Hey, Rick, go down and get a supply of that stuff. Might need more later."

"Boy, that was great timing, your opening the door just when you did." My sister grinned at Elvis and then at Ricky Stanley, as he hurried off to execute his master's latest order.

"Okay," I said, taking her aside. "What's so amusing?"

"That boy, Ricky, is a riot. He's so frantic he'll displease Elvis. That's why when the Alka-Seltzer arrived—same time as I did, incidentally—and Elvis was with *you,* he panicked."

"Why?"

"Because the two of you were in the bedroom and he knows not to disturb you . . ."

"Oh."

"You see, as soon as the Alka-Seltzer came, he immediately plunked a couple of tablets into a glass of water. Then he stood there a nervous wreck with a fistful of fizz. I could see him sneaking little looks at me, knowing that I'm just a friend, but that I'm also *your* sister, which might give me a special enough status to knock on the door. Only he was afraid to ask because Sonny and Lamar were standing right there and he's almost as intimidated by them as he is by Elvis."

"Poor baby."

"Yeah, well, anyway, just then, big ol' Lamar barks at him: 'What're you doin' standin' there with that in your hand?'

" 'I'm waitin' to give it to Elvis,' answers poor Ricky, already beginning to shake in his boots.

" 'Well, it ain't gonna do him any good if the fizz is all gone, is it?' Lamar roars back at him.

" 'What should I do?'

" 'What should you do?' Lamar thunders at him. 'Make another one, boy . . . and keep on makin' em till he comes out.' "

By now, I noticed, Elvis and all the other guys had stopped their own conversation and were following my sister's narrative.

"Joyce," she said, "I swear to you, that was at least the fifth fizzing glass he was stuck with before you and Elvis came out. He reminded me of those mythological creatures who is sentenced to do the same thing over and over through all eternity for having offended the gods."

That last struck a nerve and Janice couldn't stop from breaking up again. For about three awful seconds, the only sound in that room was the sound of her laughter. Not until Elvis joined in did a chorus of laughter and wisecracks rise up from the ranks, all at the expense of Ricky, who picked that moment to return, his arms overflowing with boxes of Alka-Seltzer.

Unfortunately for poor Ricky Stanley, his night's ordeal had not yet ended. As it happened, he was to be put to yet further tests.

But first Elvis turned his attention to Janice, giving her a big Happy Birthday hug and kiss. "You're a year older and you look younger and more beautiful than ever, just like your twin here."

Janice was invited to stay for dinner, and afterward cornered me while Elvis was doing his usual television number which consisted of intermittent attention to the picture on the tube and continual flicking of the dial back and forth between channels.

"What did he say about the divorce?" she asked. She listened intently through every detail of this latest trip to Graceland, interrupting only when my recounting of the Comedy of the Absurd of the previous night became too much for her.

"Comedy?" she said. "Sorry, but I don't think so. It's not Laurel and Hardy you and Elvis remind me of, staggering dopily around in the dark. It's Jack Lemmon and Lee Remick, in *Days of Wine and Roses.*"

"Come on, you know we don't drink . . ."

"And *you* know what I mean. Ah, Bov . . . you've got me bouncing back and forth like a Ping-Pong ball from delight to despair, from hating the guy for what he's doing to you, to loving him for making you so happy. Like you seem to be tonight."

"What do you mean, 'seem to'?"

"Ricky!"

We were interrupted by Elvis summoning his stepbrother.

"Janice, Joyce, you hungry?"

We responded in the negative just as Ricky appeared, on the run.

"Got a yen for burgers, man, and it's too late for room service. Go and get us some . . . and don't forget the french fries!" He had to yell because Ricky was already halfway out the door.

About half an hour passed, during which time Janice and I assiduously avoided any further serious discussion. We were watching television and making small talk with the guys, when the phone rang.

"If that's the kid," Elvis demanded, "ask him what the hell's taking him so long."

"E, it is Ricky." Lamar held the phone in his hand. "He says he got the burgers, but they won't make the fries 'cause it's too late. He had trouble even finding a—"

"Hey, man!" Elvis jumped to his feet. "Tell him not to come back without the fries! I mean it."

Lamar relayed Elvis's command and hung up.

I looked at Janice. Her expression was hovering somewhere between amusement and disbelief, as though not sure which was suitable.

"It's okay," I said finally. "He's probably just playacting and not really angry. Only showing off a little for us. I think."

"I hope."

"Sure, he's just having a little fun, you know?"

Janice nodded. "I ought to be used to his humor by now."

Some minutes later Elvis asked, "Where the hell is that kid?"

"He's probably not comin back, E," observed Lamar. "No fries—no Ricky."

That brought the rest of the guys into the act.

"Poor Ricky. What'll we tell his ma?"

"Lost forever out there somewhere in Washington, D.C., searchin' for french fries."

There was a knock at the door and Sonny went to open it.

In walked Ricky with a big smile on his face and a big bag of burgers and fries in his arms.

"Well, I'd love to stay for this feast," Janice said, "but it's late and I've got to get home."

I waited while she kissed Elvis good night and said goodbye to everyone else, then I walked her to the door.

"Never a dull moment, ay?" was her parting remark as I closed the door behind her.

It was two o'clock in the morning when Elvis suddenly announced he needed some things from the drugstore.

"Elvis, I don't know of any drugstore open in the middle of the night around here. I mean, are these things you have to have right now?"

"Yeah, a couple of 'em. I wanna get a new toothbrush, too."

"You need a toothbrush?" I kidded. "How odd, seeing as how you only brush your teeth six or seven times a day."

That brought a slight smile. Very slight.

"Seriously, Elvis, can't it wait until tomorrow? There isn't any drugstore that's going to be open at this hour."

"I'll bet there is somewhere. C'mon, Joyce, think about it. You must know of some place."

Sighing dramatically, I dragged out a phone book. After checking through the classified, I looked up. "You're in luck. I think I've found one. This says there's an all-night pharmacy on Glebe Road. That's in Virginia. Tell whoever you're going to send that—"

"Don't have to tell anybody. Ben'll know."

"You're going to send Ben. In the limo?"

"Nope, we're all goin'. C'mon."

I didn't really object. "Cabin fever" was always a factor in Elvis's sealed environment and opportunities to get out, even at two A.M., provided welcome relief.

Ben knew exactly where and how to go and in twenty minutes we were parking at a corner in front of a good-sized drugstore.

"I'll get whatever you need, boss," Sonny volunteered, protective as always of Elvis.

"No, man, I wanna go in and look around. Come on, Joyce, you come with me."

For the first few minutes we were inside, Elvis strolled leisurely up and down the aisles, perusing the shelves to his heart's content. It was not long, however, before I realized that the six or seven insomniac customers in the store had begun to notice him, began shooting glances his way out of the corners of their eyes, and then back to one another, obviously hoping for corroboration that he was who they thought.

Then it happened. First one person came over and then another, and then a third—each one timid in the beginning, but then, seeing him smile, screwing up their courage to ask him for his autograph. Eventually, it seemed everyone in the store would seek him out. I decided to get out of the way and position myself to observe.

Watching him during those minutes, it occurred to me that it was perhaps the Elvis scenario I enjoyed most. He was so genuinely delighted that people found him approachable and wanted to talk to him. He signed every autograph without a trace of hesitation. I wondered if maybe, just maybe, he had used the excuse of needing a toothbrush to get out into the world for a few fleeting moments.

I felt a tap on my shoulder.

"Priscilla, could I have your autograph, too?"

The next day was Monday. After the five-minute cab ride from the Hotel Washington to the Rayburn Building, and a quick detour to the cafeteria for coffee, I was at my desk opening my mail. The telephone rang.

"Hi, Bov."

"Janice. I was just thinking of calling you. I wanted to take you to lunch for our birthday, even though it will be a day late."

"As a matter of fact, that's exactly why I'm calling. We didn't really get to celebrate together yesterday."

"Let's go someplace special. How about the Monacle?"

"I'll pick you up at noon."

The trip around the Capitol Building and over to 107 "D" Street, N.E., just one block from the Senate Office Building took only about five minutes.

We were greeted upon entering by a darkly handsome young man who led us to our seats. It was a small place, dominated by its bar, a place where men far outnumbered women. They all appeared deeply engrossed in their wheeling and dealing. The Monacle was then definitely the place for anyone who was anyone in the power structure of what we all took for granted as the world's most important capital.

I ordered two champagne cocktails.

"Right." My teetotalling twin nodded after the waiter had left. "This is a special occasion. Twenty-seven years together. We're so lucky to have each other."

"I know, I'm so glad I have you for a twin," I said.

The cocktails arrived and we looked at each other, smiled, and picked up our glasses.

"Happy Birthday," we said in unison.

"This has been one hell of a year, too," Janice said, setting her glass down. "Mom and Dad got divorced; my marriage collapsed; and you're about to come apart at the seams."

"What do you mean?"

"Come on, Joyce, the truth now. You're still taking those damn sleeping pills, aren't you?"

I stared down at the tiny bubbles in my glass.

"I thought so. Joyce, honey, you . . ."

"I know, I know. And I am trying. But . . . it's not easy. I *will* quit, though, as soon as . . ."

"As soon as what?"

I didn't answer. Didn't want to answer.

"What were you going to say?"

I shook my head. "Nothing."

"Please tell me. What is it?"

"No. I wasn't going to say anything. Just that I'd only finish up the pills I have," I lied. "But I realized that was a stupid thing to say. If it's bad for me to take more, it's bad for me to take the ones I have left."

"Joyce, you know I'll do anything I can," Janice promised. "I'll rock you to sleep every night if that's what it takes."

"Janice . . . don't." I held back the tears.

The waiter came then and took our orders. When he had gone, Janice continued.

"How can you believe he truly loves you when—"

"You don't believe he loves me?"

"I believe he *thinks* he loves you, but wanting you to take that needle . . . He doesn't know what love is."

"What you really mean, is that *I* don't know what love is. But I know one thing. I know where *he* is."

"What are you talking about?"

"Janice, where is Elvis? Right now, where is he?"

"I don't know. In the hotel, isn't he? What are you driving at?"

"Exactly this: Elvis Presley, who could be virtually anywhere in the world he wanted to be and *with* anyone—in Majorca or Saint Moritz or on the French Riviera, hobnobbing with the beautiful people, having famous, glamorous women throw themselves at him, as we damn well know they do—isn't. He's in a hotel room in Washington, D.C., waiting for me, unknown Joyce Bova, who bruises his masculine ego by insisting on her independence, who often leaves him for her career when he says he needs her most, who stands up to him for what she feels is right. Still the most famous and legendary star probably of the entire twentieth century, Elvis Presley is waiting for me to finish my work for the day so that he can be with me. Now *that's* heavy. I don't care what anyone says, that has to count for *something,* has to mean we've got something powerful going for us, something solid."

Janice was shaking her head. "Why do women in love look at things the wrong way around? I say *you* are the one who is special and unique— which, of course, is why he went for *you* in the first place. Now, he's special, too, but *only* in that he's Elvis Presley. If he weren't a huge, famous star, if he was just a guy—a guy into drugs you don't even know the name of by the way— would you jeopardize not only your emotional, but also your physical health? No. I don't think you would. That's how I see it, Joyce, and if you would open your eyes, you could, too. I mean, I admit I would love nothing more than to brag that my twin is dating Elvis Presley, but I love you too much to—"

The waiter interrupted by arriving then with our food and, by some unspoken but mutually understood pact, Janice let it drop and we devoted the rest of lunch to less divisive topics.

It turned into a busy afternoon at the committee and it was after six by the time I got back to the hotel and found the guys all lounging around the sitting room.

"Elvis is in with the doc," I was told upon inquiring.

"The 'doc'? You mean a doctor, an M.D.?"

"Yeah, they're in the bedroom."

Elvis himself answered my knock, looking none the worse for wear. This calmed one fear and exacerbated another.

"C'mon in, honey. This is Doctor Lewis."

"Joyce Bova, Doctor," I said, giving him my most searching glance.

"Nice to meet you," he replied, picking up his little black bag and departing.

"Elvis, what's wrong? Are you all right? Why did you need a doctor?"

"Nothin' to worry your pretty little head about. Just wanted somethin' for that upset stomach."

"You're sure that's all?"

"Of course, I'm sure. C'mon, now, relax. Let me look at my beautiful girl."

He took both my hands in his. "Now, how was your day? Make any new laws for us poor ordinary citizens?"

"Yeah." Despite myself, I couldn't help enjoying him, couldn't refrain from teasing him even when I was upset. "Elvis, you know you're lucky that I don't make the laws, don't you? Better thank your lucky stars, because if I did . . ."

By that point he was doubled up with laughter and I gave him one last seriocomic "severe" look before going into the bathroom.

I could still hear him laughing and saying, "I know, baby, I know that's the truth . . ." I shut the door behind me, leaned back against it, and took a deep breath.

I had to get myself together. My brain was racing through the possibilities. First, of course, it *was* possible that the doctor had been here for the reason Elvis gave, to treat his stomach complaint. I hadn't challenged the explanation because I *wanted* to believe him and confrontation only made him more stubborn about insisting he was right and knew best. God, how often was this going to happen! Time would tell. If I was right and the doctor had been here to give Elvis an injection of whatever drug the other doctor had given him, Elvis would show the effects soon enough.

I leaned over the basin and splashed cold water onto my face. Please let it not be the needle, I murmured silently. Please.

When I came out into the sitting room, the guys were asking Elvis if it was all right for them to go down to the dining room and have dinner.

"Sure, go ahead," he said, not even bothering to look away from the TV he was watching. "Joyce'll order something for us from room service."

The guys filed out and I sat myself down on the sofa, next to Elvis.

Three seconds later I was sitting there by myself. Elvis had jumped abruptly to his feet and was stalking angrily across the room.

"Damn this place! You'd think they could at least have a TV that works!"

I glanced over at the set and saw the picture was "spilling."

I opened my mouth to jokingly advise him to, call his daddy, but the joke died in my throat and I shut up. I had never seen him this way. Cursing and shouting, he grabbed hold of the tuning knobs and wrenched them this way and that until I was sure they would come off in his hand. Then, as I watched in disbelief, he began to pound and kick the set, mouthing obscenities as he did so.

The door opened just as I tried to tell him I would call the desk downstairs, and the guys ambled back in. The sight of their boss mugging the furniture brought them up short.

"What's wrong, E?"

"Goddamn TV won't work. Get somebody up here to fix the fuckin' . . . What're y'all doin' back here anyway? Thought you went to eat?"

"Yeah, well, they wouldn't let us in their dining room. Got some sort of rule about wearin' coats and ties."

"That's it!" Elvis yelled at the top of his lungs. "We're gettin' out of this dump."

I sat and stared: at the guys on the phone arranging for other accommodations; at the guys packing his clothes, guns, sunglasses, and books; at Elvis relentlessly pounding the TV.

Somewhere along the line, my circuits must have glitched, because it seemed that without consciously making the transition, or physically making the effort, and without any sense of the passage of real time, I found myself sitting on another sofa in another hotel in another state, watching another television. With a different Elvis. An amazing transformation had taken place there, too. Now he was smiling and overjoyed, digging exuberantly into the dinner that had been sent up.

"I like this place a whole lot better anyway. Don't you, honey?"

"Well, it's okay, I guess."

My enthusiasm for the Marriott Hotel, where we were now ensconced, across the bridge from Washington in Northern Virginia, was definitely tempered by its bland, unlived-in ambience. Legitimately describable as Plastique Provincial, the furniture cried out to be encased in those cellophanelike coverings so popular in the suburban tract houses of that era. The rooms, of course, were larger but this was of minor significance compared to those factors that really mattered. As expressed with admirable succinctness by The King in rebuttal to my lukewarm response.

"Yeah? Well, I like it. And besides, the TV works."

Because it was Monday night. And Monday night, to the American male (at least at that time of year), means football. Now, if ever there was a group that didn't need another male bonding rite, it was Elvis's Memphis Mafia. But, doubting the wisdom of pointing this out while they were engrossed in their pigskin ritual, I hung out and endured instead.

"Great game, hunh, Joyce?"

"I don't understand a thing that's going on, Elvis. To tell you the truth, I can almost never follow the ball."

That was all he had to hear.

He turned into Howard Cosell before my very eyes, explaining and clarifying each play as it took place, never missing a chance to present me with an overview, as well.

"And that's why the quarterback is the most important man on the field in the modern football game, Joyce, where they use the T formation."

"I never doubted it for a minute, Elvis," I responded.

It did not end when the game did. He had become so animated and involved as my personal sportscaster and analyst, that he couldn't stop talking. He was too "up" to even *think* of winding down just because it was late and I'd have to get up and go to the office in the morning.

It carried over into the bedroom where he changed from Howard Cosell to . . . I don't know who . . . George Allen (one sports name I knew because he coached Washington and was a friend of Richard Nixon) demonstrating the finer points of the game. "The reason you don't see the ball, Joyce, is 'cause the center just hands it to the quarterback. See . . . c'mere, like this . . ."

"You mean the quarterback puts his hands *here?* Now I know why they all huddle around him like that."

"Football players aren't fags, Joyce."

Elvis was taking his football very seriously that night.

"It takes teamwork. No star can do it without the rest of the team. The guys in the line that don't get the glamour and the publicity. It's like me onstage, Joyce; I've got a great team, top musicians and all givin' me the backup I need."

"You really like football, don't you?" I observed.

"It's a real man's game."

"I guess so. I know I feel like I was on the losing team while you were the winning quarterback."

He laughed. "That's me."

I got into bed, pulled the blanket over me and turned to him.

"Yeah? How's your stomach?"

"Hmm? Oh, my stomach . . . fine, baby, fine. The doc took good care of me." He walked around to his side of the bed then and got in.

"I guess he did," I said pointedly.

But he was busy leafing through one of his books. He marked a place with his finger and settled in, adjusting the blanket to his body.

"Joyce," he said after a moment, "I've been thinking. I'm not leavin' early tomorrow like I had planned to originally. Gonna wait till later so I can have a little more time with ya."

"That's great, Elvis, but . . ." I was almost afraid to bring it up again. "But I have to go to work."

"I know that. But couldn't you come back over here during the day sometime? Or you could come at lunch, couldn't ya?"

"Yes, I can do that all right. But what time will you be leaving now?"

"Around five o'clock. I'd stay longer, but I can't. Want us to be together before I leave, though . . ."

He paused. I felt he was going to say something more but he hesitated again, as though lost in thought. After a moment he reached for the switch and dimmed the light.

Then he reached for me.

This time it was not his ordinary good-night kiss. This time he had the passion and the desire that had been missing lately more often than not.

It turned out those things would be missing this time, too. The surprise was that they would be missing in me.

But there was something I did want, something I did need. I slid over to where I could get my hands on my Placidyl.

Elvis, who had already taken his medication (on top of whatever that doctor had provided him with earlier), watched me take mine with a certain bemused look on his face.

"What's the matter, baby? You can't be needin' to sleep already."

"Elvis, I'm sorry. I . . . all of a sudden, I can't seem to keep my eyes open."

"Oh, you're a silly little thing, you know that?" He snuggled closer to me. "Did the game really wear you out? Nah, not you. You have more energy than any quarterback. Come here and let me hold you. Don't you love me?"

"You know I do. It's just that I'm so exhausted, Elvis, honey. Really . . . please."

He pulled me close and tried to kiss my mouth. I turned my head.

It wasn't anything I'd planned. It was just that suddenly I wasn't responding to him in the way I always had. All of a sudden, something inside me seemed to change. No, that's not quite right. It probably wasn't so sudden at all. It must have happened gradually. It was only my realization of it that was sudden, which didn't make the change any easier to deal with, either. And, as usual, I didn't *want* to deal with it, didn't want to deal with *him,* didn't want to deal with *anything.* I wanted to be left alone to think . . . or, at least to be left so alone I didn't *have* to think.

What made little sense to me was the timing. Why now? Why, at this moment, had I stopped accepting the drug abuse as part of him, part of what I had to deal with if I wanted him, Elvis Presley? I couldn't explain my own change of heart. But the more my abrupt alienation from him didn't make sense, the stronger it got. That had a crazy kind of logic to it; I knew that if I'd found some new and compelling reason, I just would have rationalized it away, coaxed myself out of it like I always had before. This way, no reason, no rationalization.

He reached out for me then and, taking my face in both his hands, turned it to him and kissed me again and again. But by then the pills must have begun to break down his conscious will and he began to fade and eventually we fell asleep locked in each other's arms.

Sitting in my office the next morning, I thought about not going back at lunchtime as he had asked. One glance at my full workload, and it occurred to me how easy it would have been just to call and tell him that the pressures of a new investigation or something were such that I wouldn't be able to leave the office until after his flight had departed.

But I didn't.

Instead, I made it a point to be back at the Marriott before twelve, deriving a kind of perverse pleasure out of finding him still in his pajamas. He and Sonny were in the middle of eating breakfast and to my relief, he was quite chipper. He got up and greeted me warmly with a kiss.

All the way over to the hotel, I thought about the night before.

I tried to examine what was actually happening with Elvis and me. But it was like exploring an iceberg. Only the tip stuck up into the light of reality. There were always the things going on beneath the surface, submerged and hidden from me. His mysterious doctors and their miracle cures operated there. It was where those drastic mood swings originated, so unpredictable that I was left to wonder if I could ever truly know him, if there even was a true Elvis left *to* know. Was he becoming a series of chemical compounds, formulated to meet the needs of the occasion?

Still, no matter how much I might be afraid for our having any kind of life together, there was something incredibly beautiful about him. I mean, there he was the morning after I had rejected him, his arm draped affectionately around me, hugging and kissing me on first sight. Some men would not have resisted retaliating with a little rejection of their own, but Elvis was too big a person to use sex as a weapon.

"Listen to this, honey," he was saying, "and tell me what you think. It's a new song I'm gonna record."

Before I could even get my coat off, he had me sitting down in the chair beside him.

With his burly bodyguard, Sonny West, providing the only musical accompaniment by humming along behind him, Elvis Presley sang, acappella and impromptu, the beautiful ballad, "I'm Leaving." To me.

"That's enough for now, Sonny."

Elvis ended the session with the last note of the song. Sonny took the hint and left the room. One microsecond later, I was in his arms and he was laughing in my ear, "Man, that was some tough number. I didn't get that last mouthful of pancakes completely swallowed before we started."

"Oh, it's gorgeous, Elvis."

"Yeah. And so are you," he said, kissing me again. "I'm gonna miss you through these holidays . . ."

Our time together that day ended on a note of affirmation. If that were the way I chose to view it. And I did.

Chapter Twenty-five

Dinner at Graceland three and a half weeks later on Saturday, January eighth, 1972, was very much like all the other dinners I had eaten there. We were dressed informally, Elvis topping his black slacks off with a blue shirt while my skirt and sweater, though new, were also casual. I was seated next to Elvis on his right; his guys were all around us, and the big television was on at the end of the table. Despite the conspicuous lack of fuss, however, we were about to experience one small departure from the usual routine.

Because this was Elvis Presley's thirty-seventh birthday and immediately after the dishes had been cleared away, the maid came back in smiling broadly and carrying a beautifully decorated cake ablaze with candles. I turned and saw in Elvis's face how embarrassed he was. The maid walked around to his left side and placed the cake down on the table directly in front of him.

He smiled shyly. "Thank you," he murmured.

"Elvis," I said, "you're going to hate me."

He stared at me. "What're you . . . ?

"Because you obviously don't want a big deal made of your

birthday. But, I'm sorry. I'm not going to let you get away with it."

I chimed my dessert fork against my glass before he could protest further.

"C'mon, you guys," I said once I had their attention. "Sing, 'Happy Birthday.' "

"Okay, you start . . ." Their response came back amidst general laughter. They knew me only too well.

This called for drastic measures. I stood up. "Before the candles burn down and scorch the icing on Elvis's cake—come on! I raised my arms up over my head and started to move them as if conducting a choir. For a moment there was only silence. Until the maid began to sing, her fine, mellow voice filling the quiet room. One by one, the rest of them straggled in and, though Elvis laughed at the cacophony, it was clear he was genuinely touched.

"Better move in there, 'Birthday Boy,' " I urged, "and blow out those candles."

He was laughing so hard as he leaned over the table it took him three tries, but finally Elvis extinguished every one of them. "Thanks," he said, straightening up. "Especially for the beautiful harmony. But I don't think you guys should uh . . . go out and cut an album just yet."

That produced the desired effect of breaking everybody up and, as the cake was cut and being passed around, he looked over and said quietly, "Joyce, I'm goin' upstairs for a minute."

"I'll go with you," I said and followed him up the staircase.

When we got to the bedroom, Elvis went into the bathroom and I hurried over to my suitcase.

"How 'bout a movie tonight?" he asked when he came out a few minutes later.

"Okay, but first I have a little something for you."

"A little . . . ?"

He stopped in midsentence when I brought the tiny, gift-wrapped box out from behind my back and handed it to him.

"Happy Birthday. I hope you like it. Even if you don't, pretend you do. I went through too much trying to find something for the man who truly has everything."

He laughed as he fumbled with the ribbon. Then, opening the box and seeing the ring, he actually blushed. He took it out, held it up to the light for a long moment, looked back to me, started to say something, but then just shook his head and smiled.

"I hope it fits," I said, still a little apprehensive.

He nodded and tried it on each of his fingers until finally, it ended up on his pinky.

"I don't have to pretend, Joyce. Thank you. You've got great taste—but I already knew that," he added with a twinkle in his eye.

"It was so hard to get you something. But I really thought a simple gold band . . . and see the word 'love' carved there?"

"I know, I saw it."

"And the tiny diamond inside the 'o' in love? I mean . . . it's not opulent, but it says what's in my heart. And I knew it would fit your pinky . . . almost. It's really a little too big . . . ."

"Naw, honey, it fits fine," he assured me.

"You really like it?"

"I love it."

"And you'll wear it?"

"Yes, yes, yes. You are a silly little girl. I love it and I love you," he said and took me in his arms and hugged me.

"Happy thirty-seventh birthday," I whispered and kissed him.

"C'mon," he said, "I'll take you out for my birthday."

"Really, Elvis? That'll be great. Where'll we go?"

"To the movies, like I said."

"Oh. Okay." For one minute there I had let myself believe that we were actually going "out" to a club or something on his home turf where he could still be comfortable.

"What's the matter, darlin'? Don't you feel like a movie?"

"Sure." I smiled, always the accommodating trouper. "Let's go."

"You're sure you're feelin' up to it?" he asked as we walked back down the stairs to rejoin the end of the celebration. "Ya looked a little tired, y'know, when you first got here."

"No, I'm fine. Matter of fact, I was concerned that you might not be feeling well. When I didn't hear from you after I called in the middle of the week, I got worried."

"What do you mean, when you called? Nobody told me you called. Who'd you talk to?"

"Charlie," I said, taking his hand, feeling very close to him after seeing him so obviously moved by my little gift. "I talked to Charlie. Didn't he mention it?"

He didn't answer. We had reached the first floor and he quickened his pace so that I had to let go of his hand or run to keep up with his long strides.

"That sonofabitch."

Startled, I actually did run a step or two, trying, unsuccessfully, to head him off. I could see his face was flushed and his nostrils flared.

"CHARLIE!"

Small, sweet Charlie Hodge appeared almost instantly.

"What's up, Elvis? What's wrong?"

"Why the hell didn't you tell me Joyce called?"

"Ya mean the other day? Oh, man, didn't I tell you? I'm sorry, E. I must have forgot."

"Forgot! What the hell do I pay you for, anyway?"

I witnessed the expression of pained embarrassment spread over Charlie's face. No more pain and embarrassment than I was feeling myself, however. I was torn between walking away to save Charlie some small measure of humiliation and sticking it out to intervene on his behalf.

I opted for the latter. "Elvis," I said, "it doesn't matter now—"

He didn't seem to even hear.

"You're fired, man. Get out!"

"Elvis . . ." I reached up and tugged at his sleeve. "Are you . . . ? You're kidding, right?" I mean, they were always clowning around with each other. Then I saw the expression on his face.

"You heard me, man. You're fired."

"Elvis, no . . ." But he wasn't paying any attention to me.

After a second that lasted an eternity, Charlie turned and walked away.

"Elvis, please don't, don't let him go like th—"

"Dumb sonofabitch."

He walked away, still making a show of his anger and calling for Sonny to arrange for the theater and someone else to take care of other details. Ones that were normally Charlie's responsibility? I didn't know, but dreaded that it was so.

Finally, just as we were almost ready to leave for the Memphian, I cornered him where we could talk without being overheard which, I knew intuitively, was eminently preferable. It would eliminate any necessity for Elvis having to save face. Another thing I knew intuitively was that Elvis must be regretting his rash and hasty action already. It was up to me to provide the channel through which he could express his basic decency and good-heartedness and bring Charlie back into the fold.

"Elvis," I began almost off-handedly, "Charlie's always been so helpful and perfectly on the ball in arranging things for me, I wish you could overlook one mistake. I'm sure it was one of those accidents that won't happen again and everyone is entitled to *one* mistake, don't you think? I mean, to err is human, right?" Then I socked it to him with the punch line. "And to forgive . . ."

"Is divine, hunh?" I could see him trying not to smile at the ambush I'd set for him. But he wasn't going to give in without letting me know I'd been in a struggle. "Listen, Joyce, I pay my guys good money and I expect them not to mess up," he huffed and puffed. "Especially not to forget something as important as a call from you."

He had lobbed the ball back in my court.

"There's that, too, Elvis; it makes Charlie losing his job *my* fault."

It was easier and easier to get through to him. He had blown off steam, was cooling down, and probably hoping for a way to rehire Charlie without appearing to relent completely.

"Well, honey, if you really feel that way; there could be maybe . . ."

"You don't know how terrible I feel. God, he's not just your employee, he's your *friend*, too. Please take him back."

And so it came about that Charlie also sat through that night's double feature at the Memphian Theater. The nature of his firing together with my success in getting Elvis to recant occupied my thoughts, however, and *Cactus Flower* and *Such Good Friends* were just images that passed across the big screen. Granted, I had merely persuaded Elvis to do something he wanted to do anyway. Nevertheless, I was encouraged that I had persuaded him to act out of his own best instincts and felt the same low-key approach might work in getting him at least to discuss a cutback on the chemical substances. For both of us.

I waited until we were changed for bed and Elvis was settled in. As soon as he seemed to have run out of comments about the night's films (in response to which I could do little more than nod and agree) I cleared my throat, preparatory to bringing up what I planned to characterize as his "overreaction." Even Elvis would have to agree that summarily firing and humiliating a long-time friend and accompanist for so small a mistake was inconsistent with the down-home, stand-up virtues to which he ascribed, sang about and, to a large extent, lived. I would then be on solid ground in suggesting that we examine what might have caused such an uncharacteristic outburst.

Before I could begin, he reached into the nightstand, took something out of the drawer and said, "Joyce, I want you to have this. I think it's beautiful."

He had handed me a picture of Jesus, his eyes piercing, but with an expression of somber serenity on his face.

"Do you see the eyes, honey? So intense."

"It is beautiful, Elvis, but . . ." I handed it back to him.

"Just look at it. I like it a lot. Ya know, you can see so much in the eyes. Here . . ."

"What?"

"I want you to have it. To keep."

"Oh, thanks, Elvis. But, if you like it so much, I don't want to . . ."

"Nah, it's okay. I've got plenty of 'em. And, Joyce, I really want you to read those books I gave ya."

"I will, Elvis. I *have* looked at them. But tonight I don't want—"

"There's stuff in 'em that can teach you about life. And about me."

"You know, earlier this evening when I told you about Char—" I tried again to reach him.

"Like this here."

He reached for a copy of *The Impersonal Life* that was on the nightstand already opened to a previously marked page. "This part is about, 'My Idea Within.' " From the tone of his voice and the expression on his face, I knew I would not be able to talk to him that night.

" 'When you begin to glimpse that Idea you will begin to know Me—your own Real Self' " he read. " 'Before you can truly know Me, however, you must learn that all things I give you are Good—and that they are for use.' "

I stuck my cupped hand out under his chin. He reached over to the nightstand with his right hand and then brought it back and dropped the two Placidyls into my upturned palm. All without missing a beat.

" '. . . only as you put them to such use,' " his voice droned on, " 'I may be expressing through you beautiful symphonies of sound, color or language, that manifest as music, art or poetry according to human terminology, and which so affect others as to cause them to acclaim you as one of the great ones of the day.

" 'I may be speaking through your mouth or inspiring you to write many beautiful Truths, which may be attracting to you many followers who hail you . . .' "

That was about it for me. The Placidyls did their job and I heard no more of the sermonette.

I was up before Elvis the next afternoon and soon discovered I had something else to concern myself about. Not long after Elvis had come down and joined me for breakfast, we were sitting in the den when we got a weather forecast predicting a snowstorm for that night.

"That makes it all the more imperative I don't miss my flight," I said. I glanced at the time. "I think I'll go up and pack, Elvis. It's almost time for me to leave."

I started to get up off the sofa and he put his hand on my arm. "Don't leave now, honey."

"You know I don't really want to, Elvis, it's just that there is my job, and with the weather . . ."

"Well, y'know, it's . . . uh . . . still kind of my birthday . . . my birthday weekend. We'll getya on a later flight." He looked over to where Charlie Hodge had walked in and just sat down. "Right, Charlie?"

"Can do, E. No problem." He got up and left.

"There, ya see?"

"Oh, yeah, I see, all right," I teased.

"Okay. What does my little girl think she sees?" He wrapped his other arm around me.

"I see you being so adorable, as usual, that I relent as usual, and you get your way. As always."

"The only reason this keeps comin' up, little one, is that you're always leavin'."

For a moment I thought he was going to bring up my moving into Graceland again. I think he thought so, too, and then thought better of it.

"And not only leavin'," he went on, "but leavin' too soon."

"And what, exactly, is 'too soon,' Elvis?" I smiled.

"Before I wantya to." He grinned and busted out laughing.

"Sorry, E . . ."

We both looked to the doorway.

"There is a problem after all," said Charlie Hodge, looking a little hangdog. "All the later flights are booked solid."

"Hell, that's no problem, Charlie."

I could tell he was going out of his way to make sure Charlie didn't feel bad.

"Don't worry." He looked over at me. "But, to tell ya the truth, honey, I think you should wait and leave in the morning."

"You know I can't. I just *have* to get home and get to work in the morning."

"I'll take care of it. You know I can. But I still think you're makin' a mistake. Charlie, charter a plane for Joyce to get her to Washington before too late tonight."

He turned and smiled at me.

The only problem with that move was that by the time we found out that there wasn't a pilot in the area who would take off in the snowstorm that was now raging with unexpected velocity, it was way too late for me to catch my original flight.

Elvis was eyeing me with his curled-lip mixture of amusement and concern and I shook my head. "I don't blame them." I gestured toward the window. "I wasn't crazy about going up in this in any small plane. But, damn it, Elvis, I really should get home tonight."

"I told ya not ta worry, baby. I'll getya home."

"I know there's no obstacle you think you can't overcome, Elvis, but a force of nature might just be too much, even for you."

He got up off the sofa and walked out of the room and I turned to Charlie who had sat down after bringing the latest pilot report.

"I hope he wasn't offended. I didn't mean it to be as sarcastic as it might've come out."

"I know, Joyce," Charlie responded. "Don't worry about Elvis. He's probably just gone to buy an airline."

"I don't want to lose my job, Charlie."

"I know that, too."

"The thing is, it's as much my fault as it is his. I should've just gone as originally scheduled. But it's so damn hard to say 'No' to him."

"I know that for sure." He sighed.

"I'd better phone my sister before she leaves to meet the six o'clock plane."

Telling Charlie I would be right back in case Elvis came up with something, I went into the kitchen and used the telephone there.

"Listen to Elvis this time, Joyce."

"What?" I could hardly believe it was my sister's voice in my ear.

"For once he's absolutely right. The weather is really bad here, too. It makes sense for you to wait until morning."

Elvis walked into the kitchen just as I hung up.

"Honey, it's all set. I told you I'd take care of it and I did. The plane'll be ready for you about eleven o'clock."

"Uh, Elvis—"

He was feeling so cock-a-the-walkish that he didn't notice my slowly reddening face. He just took me by the arm, saying, "Now c'mon in the den and relax with me till it's time for you to go."

"That's one of your song titles," I observed as he shepherded me back onto the sofa, pausing only to turn on both the stereo and the television.

"Hey, look," I said, pointing to the latter. "It's *Stay Away, Joe*."

"Turn it off," he groaned. "I hate that thing."

"Elvis, I swear to you, it's like it was meant to be. It's the only movie of yours I've never seen."

"Well, if you insist. But at least turn down the sound so I can listen to the stereo and I won't have to listen to that . . . that . . ."

"All right, if you feel that strongly about your own movie." I gave in and turned the set off. "And there's something else you can have that you feel strongly about. At least I hope you do."

"What's that, baby?"

"Me. For the night.

"How's that?"

"Well, I hate to admit it, but you're right; I think it probably *is* best if I stay here tonight and go in the morning when it'll be safer. And, to tell you the truth, I didn't want to leave you any more than you wanted me to go."

That was the truth on more than one count. I really felt I had a certain moral momentum going for me to tell him about the things that were on my mind. All I needed was the right opening.

"What am I gonna do with you?" He chuckled and took me in his arms.

"Sonny!" he bellowed, "Cancel that plane. Joyce is leaving in the morning instead, so get her on an early-morning flight. And make sure she catches it."

He led me by the hand into the living room. He sat down at the gold-speckled piano and started to do a little impromptu splanking.

"Give us a song, big boy?" I leaned across the piano in my best Mae West impression.

He looked up from the keys as Sonny came into the room.

"All taken care of, E." Sonny stifled a sneeze. "The pilot wasn't too thrilled after what we put him through," he added, in a voice that broke to a hoarse whisper.

"Fuckim. We probably saved his life." Elvis grinned, slipping me a sardonic little side-glance.

"Nice, Elvis, very nice."

"Now, honey, you know I wouldnt've let you go if there was any danger," Elvis said, looking down at the keys and then up at me and going into the first bars of "Amazing Grace." "C'mon, Sonny," he said, "join in with me . . ."

"Are you kidding? Sonny sounds like he's dying." For some

reason (probably having to do with that little zinger about saving the pilot's life by not sending us up into the blizzard) I was indignant on Sonny's behalf; I looked up at his watery eyes and red nose. "You need to take some asprin with a big glass of orange juice."

"It's all right, Joyce, I'll live." The big bodyguard grinned at me, darting a look at Elvis.

Who, having already begun the song over again, was only saying, "Sonny, come in . . . right here."

Sonny did, or he tried, before he started to cough.

"Sorry, man." He pounded his offending chest.

"Don't stop, Sonny. You'll be okay. Now, there's something I want to try with this . . . right about this spot."

They started up again and Sonny, sniffling and coughing, joined dutifully in where asked. I stood it for half an hour, but when Elvis began a new song, "He Is My Everything," I couldn't keep quiet any longer.

"Sonny sounds awful. He shouldn't be singing. He should get to bed."

"Naw, he's okay. Aren't ya, man?"

"Yeah, E. I'm fine." He smiled. And on they went, Sonny sniffling, wheezing, and coughing all the way. After another quarter hour, Elvis was ready to call it quits and Sonny looked like he was ready to call an ambulance.

As he got up from the bench, Elvis put his arm around me and started to lead me into the dining room for the evening meal with everyone. But just before we exited the living room, he stopped and looked back and said, "Hey, Sonny, man, y'know ya don't look so good. Better rest up, man. Can't have ya gettin' sick on me now."

That episode seemed to set the tone for the rest of the night. Elvis was pleasant and cheerful enough, but also self-absorbed and somewhat removed from the immediate reality around him. By which I mean me, and the issues I was anxious to raise with him. Once again, the only available time for me to broach a private issue turned out to be when we had gone upstairs to bed. That was obviously the most suitable time, anyway. My only trepidation stemmed from past experience with Elvis's uncanny knack for sidetracking us from anything pertaining to our relationship. I had no complaints when that sidetracking was for the expression of love, but lately, that express was not pulling into my station.

When I came out of the bathroom, Elvis was sitting on the side of the bed with one foot on the floor and the other propped up on the covers. My eyes darted to the dreaded open book laying next to him on the pillow, and then back again to the foot on the bed. He was clipping his toenails. I opened my mouth to say something like "how romantic"—which would only have worked against any chance for a serious discussion. But before I got a word out, he picked up his phone and was telling someone to come up and vacuum his clippings.

When he had hung up, I just shook my head and said, "Now that's funny."

"What's funny?" I could tell he didn't see it.

"Calling someone to come vacuum your toenail clippings at this hour? That beats getting them to run up and tune the TV."

He was looking at me, very serious, not even the hint of a smile.

"I don't know, Elvis, I guess I'm a plain working-class gal, not used to the ways of royalty. It's amusing to me, watching everybody fall all over you. You are just so spoiled."

"You think I am, hunh?" A half smile had begun to form.

"I know it. And I'm as guilty of spoiling you as the rest of them."

"What d'ya mean! You don't spoil me enough!" Laughing, he grabbed me and pulled me into his arms.

"Yes, I do, you're just such a little boy . . ."

"No," he said, cradling me onto the bed, "you're my little girl . . ."

I put my arms around his neck and he leaned down and kissed me.

There was a knock at the door.

"God . . ." I said.

"I forgot. The vacuuming."

We both sat up. I pulled the blankets around me.

"Come in," he said.

One of the maids entered carrying a vacuum cleaner. Elvis pointed to the floor and she plugged in the cord and began to vacuum the area indicated. Elvis picked up the opened book from his pillow. I got up and walked into the bathroom, shutting the door behind me and blocking out some of the irritating mechanical whine. I leaned over the sink and ran cold water into a washcloth and rung it out. I sat down on the toilet seat, crossed my legs, and pressed the cold, damp cloth to the vein that was throbbing in my neck. I knew when I was licked. It's hard to get yourself up for a serious, life-and-death discussion with a person who is into summoning ladies to vacuum up his toenails in the wee small hours of the morning. It was just a little too surreal for me. Next time, I told myself. Next time, definitely. When I heard the whirring subside on the other side of the door, I leaned over to splash a little cold water onto my temples, and got up and went back into the bedroom.

"Is there anything else, Mr. Elvis?"

I looked over and saw the maid about to go out the door.

"No, thanks, that's all for now."

The lady left. I shook my head in amazement. Elvis raised his book and gestured.

"Honey, look here."

I went over and sat beside him on the bed, receiving my ration of Placidyl as I did so, Elvis not even bothering to look over as he placed it in my hand. I leaned in close against him. He had his finger on a particular sentence.

"See, it refers to 'El' being another name for God."

"I know, Elvis. You showed me that before, remember?"

"Yeah, but that's really somethin', don'tya think?"

"Mmm," I said, swallowing my pills.

"Y'know, Joyce, one phase of my life is ending," he said rather cryptically. "I felt very much into myself, into contemplating things over my birthday. It won't be long until I'm forty, y'know, and that could be too late."

"Hmm?" I had already stretched out and was waiting for the pills to work. "Too late for what?"

"We have a lot to talk about, Joyce . . . I'll be wanting an answer from you soon. How soon can you come back here? Next week?"

His words were beginning to slur.

I wasn't doing too bad a job of slurring, myself, I realized. I wouldn't be conscious much longer.

"I'm past the age of Christ crucified . . ." I was startled to hear him say. "I can't wait much longer to plan the rest of my life's work. A phase has definitely ended . . ."

"What do you mean?"

"One day you'll understand. But, Joyce, I'm going to open in Vegas in February. I want you there . . . and a decision."

"I know . . . And I'll be there."

I remember him staring at the book as I was going under, and hearing his voice saying, "Man, thaaat's sommmm . . ."

Chapter Twenty-six

I had been doing it again; immersing myself in Elvis. Before I went to Las Vegas in February, I decided to make the effort again to get into him through his music, hoping to eke out just a little more precious insight, to dig just a little deeper.

Almost immediately on getting back to Washington from Graceland after Elvis's birthday celebration, the idea dawned on me again that it might be important, that it might even be fun, that it might help me get through all those defenses of his.

It was on my way to work the morning before heading back to see him that I really began thinking like this. After parking my little orange Pinto, I decided that even though it was quite cold, I'd walk a bit to clear my head. I walked very slowly through the park across the street from the Rayburn Building, and tried to think some things through.

By the time I arrived home that evening, I felt I had come up with some insights. I couldn't wait to play the Elvis albums I had bought at the record store earlier that day.

"Again? I bet boxers don't train as hard for championship matches."

"Janice! I was just getting ready. I didn't hear you come in."

"Well, the music *is* a little loud." She hung up her coat and I turned off the stereo and joined her in the kitchen. "Blizzard warnings all over the radio tonight; maybe you ought to wait and see him in Memphis when the weather might be better."

"Maybe I ought to wait until June then we could harmonize on 'Memphis in June' together."

"Oooh, somebody's a little on edge, isn't she?"

"Janice, I've *got* to be on that plane tomorrow or—"

"Or what?"

"Or I might just never go at all."

"Meaning?"

"Sit down, would you, Bov?"

Janice sat down at the table across from me.

"Remember when we had our birthday lunch at the Monacle and you were on my back about promising not to take any more sleeping pills and I said I would, 'as soon as,' and then I stopped talking and you asked what I had been going to say?"

"Sure. And you said something about stopping the pills as soon as you'd used up the ones you had."

"But that was a lie. I actually *started* to say—and it had just popped into my head—'as soon as I stop seeing him.' Now where did that come from? I *swear* to you it was unpremeditated."

Janice looked at me carefully.

"Somewhere in your subconscious you've got a little common sense, anyway."

"I mean, this is at a time when we're talking about my moving into Graceland, when he's divorcing his wife . . ."

"I'm glad you brought that up," Janice interrupted. "I've been meaning to ask you—has the magic little word *marriage* ever been mentioned, by any chance?"

"Elvis and me, you mean? No, never."

"Well, don't you think he *should* mention it? I mean, what's the big deal in asking a girl to shack up with you—to put it crudely?"

"Well, first of all, he is still *married;* secondly, he's sensitive enough to pick up on my own ambivalence about making that kind of a commitment; and finally, he's Elvis Presley. Which kind of takes it out of the "shack job" category. I'd have a pretty high profile since half the known world seems to follow every intimate detail of his life as it appears in fan magazines, tabloids, gossip columns . . . Janice, would you mind turning on the news? I'd like to keep an eye on those weather reports myself."

"Sure." She got up, saying, as she did so, "It always comes down to the glamour of being Elvis Presley's woman, though, doesn't it?" She turned on the television. "It's the old familiar story about stars blazing. They give off an almost supernatural heat. Maybe you're just feeling that false glow when you're close to him."

She came back to the table and sat down. "But where do stars go when it storms? When it really gets rough, they hide, they disappear into the clouds. But *you* won't be able to. You're not a star, you're not even of that world." Janice paused. "Anyway, he won't be glittering forever, not at the pace he's going. Brush away the stardust and what do you find? A man who's slowly sinking in quicksand and dragging you down with him."

"Janice, I love him," I replied. "So, even if you're right, it means I've got to try and help him. Nobody else can . . . or *will.*"

"He's not going to listen to you," Janice argued. "How much can he really care about you if he's trying to get you as hooked as he is?"

"But he doesn't *think* he's hooked on anything. *That's* why I've got to tell him! And, Janice, he isn't going to listen to *anyone else.* Because there *isn't* anyone else. *I'm* the only one who doesn't work for him or who isn't totally dependent on his whims and generosity. I'm the only person in the world who is in a position to take an independent stand, to keep Elvis Presley, the man I'm in love with, from killing himself."

My plane was late getting in to Las Vegas, but Gee Gee, one of Elvis's faithful men, was waiting patiently and managed to get me to the International in time for the second show. My stomach had already been in a knot when I'd boarded at Washington National (tension, no doubt, over the impending confrontation) and a bumpy flight had done nothing to improve it. But at least it hadn't exacerbated the condition; *that* was accomplished by a group of fans who surrounded me immediately after I had excused myself to Gee Gee and headed for the ladies' lounge in the lobby. Before I even got to the door they were on me, a mixed bag, both male and female, demanding my autograph and insisting I was Priscilla.

I darted inside the lounge, my stomach getting queasier by the moment, and stationed myself in front of the mirror so that I could give my makeup the once-over.

"Excuse me. You look familiar. Don't I know you?"

It was an unfamiliar voice, and when I focused on the equally unfamiliar face now reflected in the mirror, I knew she had made a mistake. I'm not Priscilla Presley, I was tempted to answer, but just shook my head instead.

"What I mean is, weren't you at the hotel party the other night with that real estate hotshot from New York?"

"No, I'm sorry. It wasn't me."

"Aw, come on . . ." She adjusted her push-up bra to accentuate her breasts. "What's the problem, honey? I'm not interested in him, anyway. Not with what I've got going for myself."

There was something in her voice that made me look up.

"Well . . ." She took the opportunity to lean in confidentially, kind of woman to woman. Kind of working woman to working woman, I began to realize as she went on.

"My friend Shirley . . ." She indicated a heavily made-up woman coming out of one of the stalls. "We do all right together, if you know what I mean."

This is really amazing, I thought to myself. This woman obviously thinks I am also a local hooker. I knew I should feel insulted, but it was too off the wall for me to be anything but amused.

"Yeah," she went on, "Shirley and I get it on together for well, what you might call the 'right people.'"

I hate to admit it, but by now I was all ears.

"For instance," she continued proudly, "we've done it for Elvis Presley."

Yikes.

"Elvis Presley!!" I exclaimed.

"Yeah, he's actually an all right guy."

"I really . . . uh . . ." I had to clear my throat. "Find that hard to believe. I mean, why would Elvis Presley need to . . ."

"For kicks, honey. Just for kicks."

"You're saying you actually . . . uh . . . when did—"

"C'mon," interrupted the one called Shirley. "We're gonna be late."

"We got another show to do," the first one said almost boastfully, smoothing down her skintight mini and giving another tug to her bra. "Seeya round." She winked as they sashayed out together.

I stared at myself in the mirror. My God, did I really look like . . . For one split second I conjured up a vision of Elvis with Shirley and Co. Hastily, I put my lipstick in my purse, got up, and dashed out the door.

Elvis had already left for his dressing room to prepare for the show by the time I arrived at the suite. I paced back and forth in front of my open luggage. But I wasn't seeing my wardrobe inside, I was seeing two overly made-up whores who had assumed I was one of them. I knew I still had time before his performance, time enough to make a decision and do something about it. I hurried out the door, into the elevator, and down to the dress shop.

When I returned, I undressed as quickly as I could, unwrapped my purchase and reached up and unpinned the long, full fall attached to my hair.

"Joyce," I muttered, "it's time to be *you*."

Because that was the real problem, of course, not whether a couple of tarts might see me as one of them, but whether *Elvis* was seeing the real me. And did he want to? Did he want the true Joyce, the woman who was an entity unto herself? I was willing to make compromises and to accept a merging of our two selves, but I wasn't willing to become an appendage, a decoration. I just couldn't allow myself to be molded to fit some preconceived image he had of what his woman should look like. That was why being mistaken for Priscilla haunted me so; it was the fear that in some part of his psyche, Elvis might need me as a surrogate for what he was giving up, that I might be another version of the woman whom he had practically raised from the time she was fourteen years old.

But not if I could do anything about it—and I could.

I leaned down and brushed the teasing completely out of my hair. Then I parted the long, dark tresses in the middle, pulling them sleekly down over my ears and off my face into a chignon. One glance in my hand-held mirror, and I smiled. "Perfect, Joyce; it looks perfect."

I faced the wall mirror again and freshened my makeup, applying a final hint of blush. Then I reached for a Kleenex and symbolically wiped off almost all of the heavy, dark eye shadow Elvis liked so much. I hurried into the bedroom, scooped my new dress off the bed, and stepped into it. A final glance in the full-length mirror there showed a black lamé gown that draped my bodice, then hung full and flowing to the floor. One invisible zipper up the front to a turtleneck provided a finishing touch of simple elegance. It was a complete departure from the form-fitting, blatantly sexy attire Elvis seemed to prefer. The thought of him then almost made me renege. Would he, *could* he like it? I struck one last pose in the mirror. "Much better," I said defiantly, stepping into my shoes and rushing out the door.

By the end of the show I was back in the suite with my stomach in even worse shape, having progressed from doing simple flip-flops to full somersaults. Naturally, it was party time and the room was already filling with those who had come to pay him homage. I was at the bar getting a ginger ale I hoped would alleviate the nausea, when he made his entrance, looked around, saw me, and made his way through the crowd until he was at my side. He pecked my cheek and taking my arm, navigated our way together to the sofa.

"Elvis," I said as we sat, "I'll bet nobody would believe that I still react so totally to your performances, even after seeing you so many times now. Each one is so fresh for me. You're just sheer magic."

And it was true. Seeing him onstage had put its usual spell over me, lulling my fears and doubts so that I almost had to make a conscious effort to recall what they were. If it weren't for my queasy stomach, even a conscious effort might not have done the trick.

He kissed me on the nose and grinned. "You're not biased, are ya?"

I laughed. "Well, it's better than being jaded. And, Elvis, the new song, the one you sang to me in Washington last time?"

" 'I'm Leavin'?"

"Yes. I was amazed what you did with it! And every choice you made seemed to enhance it in every way."

"Yeah, it's really turned into a good number," he said, looking pleased with himself.

I don't know if it was the title of that damned song, my inability to continue to make small talk on a sick stomach, or just my general determination to confront him, but my response was to ask him, "About your situation with Priscilla, the divorce and all? I haven't seen anything in the news media on it."

He stared at me for a long moment. Then he said, speaking quite rapidly for him, "Not much to say; it's movin' slow, y'know?

Funny thing is, she's here. In Vegas, right now, at some sort of karate tournament. She's stayin at the Sahara and, if you want to know, I haven't even seen her. Now, if you're satisfied, let's talk about you. What have you done to your hair?"

Whoa. I was rocked back on my heels by his flippant tone. And I *wasn't* satisfied. But I must have been even more insecure than I was dissatisfied, because I reached up and touched my hair when I responded.

"Do you like it?"

The look on his face made it plain that he didn't. I had dared to change from the style with which he was so enamored.

I watched his eyes roam over my dress and, though it elicited no comment, I knew it could not have met with his approval, either.

But there were plenty of diversions, plenty of people there to take his mind off my show of sartorial independence. Soon, court was in full swing, but for once, being called on to corroborate and embellish the fulsome, exaggerated, self-aggrandizing stories of the Presley myth did not divert *me*. Neither from pondering the questions I had raised to myself while dressing, nor from the painful awareness that my stomach was still bothering me. There even came a point when, right in the middle of Elvis's saying, "Janice was there, too, wasn't she, Joyce? Can ya believe she has an identical twin sister?", I got up without answering him and started for the bar to get myself another medicinal ginger ale.

"Sit down, Joyce." He stopped me in my tracks. "Relax," he whispered, patting my knee.

I endured it, sick stomach and all, until the very end when, without even a thought of discussing anything with him, I swallowed my pills and dreamt of Priscilla marching up from the Sahara and bursting into the bedroom, declaring that I was an imposter trying to impersonate her. I was still yelling, "I've changed . . . I've changed . . ." when I woke up.

Late that next afternoon, after breakfast which, for me consisted of another ginger ale and a slice of dry toast, I was curled up at one extreme end of the sofa, trying not to feel sorry for myself and painfully aware, as I watched Elvis sitting at the other end, drum his fingers maniacally against the sofa arm, that we had so far barely exchanged a kind, let alone loving, word since I arrived.

As if sensing my discomfiture and determined to intensify it, he shifted his gaze from the middle distance to me.

"You'd tell me if you were goin' out datin' somebody, wouldn't ya?" he asked cooly.

I was staggered, just as if he had struck me with one of the karate blows he was always throwing onstage. My thoughts went back to the time he had warned me that he would know if I ever saw another man. What was uncanny was the fact that I'd had a lunch "date" with a man only days before. I immediately disclosed this, assuring him it was entirely innocent, nothing romantic, even volunteering the man's name as he was from Tennessee and happened to know Lamar. To heighten my sense of being in the middle of an old-fashioned melodrama, Lamar chose that moment to walk into the living room as if on cue.

"Lamar, do you know this guy?" Elvis mentioned my friend's name. "Joyce says he knows you."

"Oh, yeah, I know him." Lamar sat down, his enormous bulk filling an entire International Hotel chair. "Why sure. He's a really good guy. You remember him, don'tya, Elvis? He ran for governor of Tennessee. He lost, but put up a good fight. Why, I remember now that . . ."

Lamar's voice trailed off as he realized that the only response he was getting from Elvis was a cold, cold stare.

After a minute, Lamar heaved himself up out of the chair.

"Well, gotta be goin' now, gotta lotta things to do, y'know. . . ." he mumbled, probably wishing that he had kept his mouth shut.

When I looked over and saw the expression on Elvis's face, my stomach resumed the Olympic-class somersaults it had enacted the night before.

Joyce, I told myself, you better show some guts right now and stop using your stomach as an excuse for hiding what's in your head. You're practically cowering with guilt and you've done nothing wrong. In fact, it's the person glaring accusingly at you who has done something wrong.

"Elvis," I said, drawing on every ounce of strength left in my debilitated body, "if my having lunch with a casual friend bothers *you,* how do you think it makes *me* feel to have someone suddenly inform me in the ladies' room of a hotel that she . . . uh . . . that you . . . and they . . ."

"What are you talking about?"

"I'm talking about some *hooker* telling me that she and her 'friend' Shirley . . . uh . . . and you . . . to put it bluntly, that they . . . well . . . she . . . What's so funny?" I demanded.

He was laughing so hard I thought he was going to fall over. *"You're* so funny. Gettin' so excited over nothing."

"Nothing? You call not one, but *two* hookers, nothing?"

"Honey . . ." He was still laughing. "I never touched those girls."

"Elvis, please don't make it worse. I'm not a child. But if you're going to, well, you know, then you can't accuse—"

"I'm tellin' ya, you're makin' a big deal out of nothin', Joyce." He grinned. "The two of them made love and I just watched. They perform for me. Just a little innocent fun, something guys like to do, that's all."

He fluffed it all off so blithely, with such obvious sincerity, that I just sat there stunned and speechless.

"Maybe I should lie down for a bit," I said finally. "My stomach seems to be getting worse."

I got up off the sofa, walked into the bedroom and lay facedown on the bed. I could hear Elvis following me. I didn't turn around but I could tell that he first went in, and then came out of the bathroom behind me. When he came into the bedroom I didn't look up.

"Take this," I heard his voice. Then his hand was in front of my eyes with a new kind of pill, one I had never seen before, resting in his palm. "It'll settle your stomach and you'll feel better."

I had had some previous experience with Elvis's home remedies.

"Elvis, I'm afraid to take any kind of a pill right now, really. The way I feel and all, I don't think I should."

" 'Fraid I'm gonna have to insist. Don't be silly now. Here."

"I'm sorry, but Elvis, please, I just don't want to take the chance."

His voice got cold. "If you don't want to feel better in time to see my show, well, I guess that's up to you."

He turned and started toward the door.

"Is that all you're concerned about—having an audience?" I was practically snarling. He hesitated and looked at me and I could see he was startled by my tone. "Okay, Elvis, okay, give it to me. I'll take it."

He did an about-face and walked back toward the bed, the pill resting on his outstretched palm.

"Is that gonna be your solution to everything, Elvis?" I sat up and in one motion swiped it off his palm and into my hand. "Just take a pill and everything will be better?"

"Don't start that again. I don't wanta hear it. Just take the damn pill."

I slid off the bed and stormed past him into the living room and over to the bar to get something to take it with. I was still pouring the ginger ale into my glass when Sonny appeared.

"What's wrong, Joyce?"

"It's Elvis. I feel sick to my stomach and he's insisting I take this pill." I held my hand out to show him. "Do you have any idea what it is, Sonny?"

He looked down at my hand, then slowly up to me. "Don't you take that," he said, shaking his head. "Do you hear me, Joyce? Do not take that pill. Lie to him if you have to, pretend you took it, whatever."

"Sonny . . . Thanks."

I toted my ginger ale back into the bedroom where I found Elvis stretched out and staring up at the ceiling. He got up as soon as he saw me.

"Did you take it?"

"Didn't you tell me to?" I answered, indicating my ginger ale.

"Good. Now you'll see; you'll feel better."

He put his arm around my shoulders. "There's something' else I think ya should try," he said, escorting me out of the bedroom and into the sitting area next to it. "This has helped me lots of times."

I was dumbfounded. He had stopped beside the stationary exercise bike that was a fixture of the Elvis suite. It was the first time I had paid any attention to it, however. I had never seen anyone else use it, or even go near it.

"That pill and this will do it for ya, Joyce," he declared, gesturing for me to mount the bike. "It works for me."

I took a deep breath, bit my tongue, and actually got up on the damned thing.

Elvis stood there watching me pump away and nodding. "Yep, ya gotta work it out of your system. Exercise is good for what ails ya. You'll see, you'll be fine for the show."

I must be crazy, I thought. Or he is.

Nevertheless, I kept peddling, while he kept offering words of encouragement as though he was my trainer.

"I've had enough," I gasped, finally. "I'm getting off this crazy contraption." I staggered to the bed and collapsed onto it.

"Well, I'm gonna get ready for the show, then." I heard his voice behind me. "I'll be lookin' for ya down there . . ." It trailed off as he walked out of the room.

Eventually, I pulled myself together and made the show. Both shows, in fact. But for the first time, his performance left no impression on me. I was sick, not just in the stomach, but in the head, too. Worse in the head. I couldn't shake the pill incident from my thoughts no matter how hard I tried. I couldn't help wondering what was in it to make Sonny react the way he did. It brought to mind the time in Philadelphia with the needle. I sat through the festivities in the suite afterward as well, and they crawled endlessly.

By the time they ended and I was able to drag myself into bed, I had just enough strength left to down my Placidyl and sleep through the entire next day until it was time for his shows, time for me to go through my performance all over again, too.

Miraculously, by the time of the postperformance party that night, I had begun to feel slightly human again and was able to take in and keep down a little light nourishment.

And, mercifully, Elvis for once did not keep me riveted to his side corroborating his tales and anecdotes, but mingled more than usual with his guests. This left me with a certain amount of time by myself to think some things through.

I was trying to do just that, when J.D. Sumner, who sang the bass part with the Stamps Quartet, the gospel group that accompanied Elvis, came over to chat. J.D. was quite a big man in every way, not just tall, but with the kind of build you would associate with a voice as deep and powerful as his.

"You know, just looking at Elvis there," he said, gesturing across the room to where The King was holding a group of men and women enthralled, "I can't help but admire the man's power and endurance. It's a tough gig playin' Vegas, but there he is, still goin' strong halfway through his third show."

"*Third* show? Oh, you mean this one up here afterward." I nodded in agreement.

"Where, I ask myself, does the man get his energy from?"

"Mmm, I've been asking myself the same thing."

"I think you have to be up on that stage with him to appreciate just how great he is." The big bass voice boomed on. "And such an incredible voice."

"Yes." I nodded reflexively and then said, "But how about your own? Your voice is really something, too."

He explained that many years ago he had had a medical

problem which caused his voice to be altered to the very deep, rich voice he has today.

A moment later, I excused myself to go get a drink. I had noticed Elvis looking around the room and I knew it was me he sought. I still needed a further respite from my usual after-show hostessing duties and thought I might be able to lose myself in the crowd at the bar.

I was almost there when I felt his hand on my arm and his voice, gentle as his touch, in my ear.

"Joyce, honey, would you come here? Somebody I want you to meet."

The man standing beside Elvis was impeccably dressed and very handsome.

"This here's Rick Husky. He's a big-shot writer in Hollywood. Got a hit TV show goin' called, 'The Mod Squad.' "

"I'm not sure how much of a 'big shot' I am . . . Hi, Joyce. But I do know how good this guy is . . ." He raised his glass in a toastlike gesture to Elvis. "Real good."

Elvis smiled in humble appreciation and we talked for a few minutes, or Rick Husky did, mostly about what he felt were the highlights of Elvis's performance, before I excused myself and finally did get to the bar.

The night seemed to go by more quickly after that. Probably, I thought to myself as I washed up in the bathroom after everyone had left, because my stomach was feeling better.

I finished up, started to head out to the bedroom, and hesitated, my hand on the doorknob. I took a long look at the image in the mirror. The face that gazed back was still just the plain Joyce Bova I'd always known. I had not been magically transformed these past few hours by the heavy thoughts I'd been thinking or by my resolve that, this time, I would not shirk the responsibility I knew could only be mine. I walked into the bedroom.

Elvis was sitting up in bed, reading. I sat down on the other side from him, still needing to gather my strength and courage.

He looked up from his book. "C'mon, Joyce, now, come over here. What's wrong? I thought you were feelin' better?"

"I am.

"You see? I knew you'd be all right. I told you that pill would do it."

"And the exercise. Don't forget the exercise."

When he made no response, I realized my sarcasm had been lost on him.

"What about you, Elvis? How are you feeling? You seemed kind of fidgety tonight."

"Naw. Just havin' lots of people in, dealin' with 'em all and everything, you know."

"Sure. And they all love you, don't they? They kind of make a thing of it, but . . ."

"But what?"

"Ah . . . I don't know. You just have a way with them, I guess. They can't help responding to you."

I was treading water, searching for some kind of lead-in that wouldn't make him defensive, that wouldn't make him close his mind to what I had to say.

"That's just it, Joyce. People do listen to me. That's because I know what they want and need. Like you. You should listen to me more. All you have to do is listen to me. I know what's good for you, baby. One day they'll all listen."

"Who? Who will listen, Elvis?" I asked.

"People." He waved his hand in a kind of all-inclusive gesture. "The world."

"Well, they do now, don't they?" I was glad he was in a philosophical mood, bringing out the things he truly felt.

"I mean to my *message*. What I really have to say. I'm not just good ol' good-time Elvis with his wild 'Memphis Mafia.' I'm a serious man and I have a serious message for the world. I can help people. I have a vision, a purpose. D'ya hear me, Joyce? Can you understand?"

"I'm trying to. I'm just not sure what purpose you mean, you know? You've touched on this before, but you've never really explained it to me."

"There have been times you've been full of criticism, Joyce," he said. And then, as if he was clairvoyant and had grasped my state of mind, he went on. "You still want to criticize me. Because you have not understood fully."

"It's not criticism, Elvis, it's just that—"

But he had picked up another of his books and was reading from it. " 'What is yours, what *I* have given you.' "

He shut the book and looked at me. I had no response to that short and rather cryptic message.

"What I have already been tryin' to give, what I try to give to everybody, is understanding. 'Understanding solves all problems.' That's Roy Hamilton."

I recognized the name of the singer but my mind was preoccupied with getting the conversation back on track.

"But the disillusioning thing of it is, what people don't understand is understanding." He smiled. "Y'see, I understand so much now."

He put the book back on his nightstand and picked up another one. He didn't open it, though, just held it in his hand as he continued. "We all have divinity inside us, Joyce; that's a fact. Some of us just understand it more. That is, the God inside us. It's just that almost no one can face that. It's hard for people to accept. . . ."

I took the plunge, "Elvis, if we're gods, or at least have this 'divinity' in us, why do we need drugs?"

"Silence is the resting place of the soul. It's sacred. And necessary for new thoughts to be born. That's what my pills are for, Joyce, the ones I share with you. For me to get as close as possible to that silence."

"But you feel that you can be a . . . a 'prophet,' that you have a vision. What about that vision being induced or altered by drugs? I don't deny you know a lot about drugs," I added hastily, "but there are so many side effects always being discovered . . . That's why I worry—"

"Pretty women shouldn't worry," he said, cutting me off. "I hire people to do the worryin'."

He was so serene and composed, it was almost frightening. I had broached the subject of drugs and he hadn't blown up. True, he'd ignored my concern, but he hadn't gotten angry. I was encouraged to keep at it. "How can you reach out to the multitudes," I said softly, "if that's your 'purpose,' when you can't control your own life without drugs? I'm not talking only about sleeping pills. What about the stuff those doctors shoot into you, the stuff that gets you 'up' in the mornings? The stuff that makes your legs quiver like pneumatic drills sometimes, that makes you fidget and your fingers drum. There's times when I'm in your arms, Elvis, that I can hear you practically humming inside, like something's been revved up too high and it's running faster and faster until finally, it just flies into pieces."

"Honey . . ." He leaned toward me and spoke more directly, more conversationally, not so much like he was lecturing or delivering a sermon. "You have no real awareness yet. You've only begun to glimpse things. It's not your fault. We haven't been together long enough yet. Even *I'm* still in a . . . state of transition. What you see going on around you, or think you see, is only temporary. And this, too, shall pass."

"*Everything* in life is only temporary," I argued. "That's why it's so important to deal with what you can *while* you still can."

"Help me, Joyce," he said. "Don't stand in the way of my vision. Join me in it."

"Don't you think I want to help you? But you—"

"You haven't even given me an answer about coming to Graceland to be with me."

And I still didn't have any answer to that one. I looked down at the thick green carpet and then quickly back at him and the oddest thought leapt into my head. Behind Elvis, I glimpsed the thick, heavy green velvet drapes. For no rhyme or reason at all it suddenly occurred to me they weren't real velvet.

Finally, I said, "Elvis, I've got to tell you, part of me wants desperately to be with you and help you in your search for what you're looking for. But another part of me is looking to get out. To escape. I'm scared, Elvis—and so are you. The difference is that I'm scared by what you're doing . . . what *we're* doing. But what you're scared of . . . well . . . whatever it is, exactly, it's what makes you do it all, take the drugs."

"Why do you fight me?" He was shaking his head. "I don't understand it."

"You *must,* Elvis. That must be why you chose me. Remember how in the beginning I was always asking you, 'Why me?' I think you picked me because at some level you knew I could be an independent person, a person unto myself who wasn't just something of your creation. *You're* the one who fights it now, but you must have *wanted* a person who had an identity separate from you or I wouldn't be here now."

"Those things . . . your career, your life in Washington . . . Congress . . ." He dismissed them with a wave of his hand. "They're just outside things. I'm looking for what's inside. Things of the spirit. Real life is inside people. Don't fight me on this."

"But I've earned the right to," I declared. "I've learned about life inside, Elvis. I've learned the hard way. It's you who doesn't know. You don't even know that . . ."

"What? What don't I know?"

"You don't know . . ." But I couldn't tell him of the life inside me that had been lost. It was too late, anyway; what good would it have done? I watched him reach over for the Placidyl. He took his and handed me mine. And I took them, damnit. Damn him and damn me, I took them. As I swallowed I experienced a horrible, suffocating feeling, as though I was caught in the eye of a firestorm, a place where all the air and all the life had been sucked out.

Once again, as if he could read my thoughts, he said, "We all start out free, Joyce, then we turn our lives into prisons. When all we have to do is accept our freedom. And act on it."

"But you've made that into an excuse to justify anything," I said, suddenly remembering the image of self-indulgent excess and control that had come to me while listening to his music the night before I'd come out to Vegas.

He reached over and put the book he'd been holding back on the nightstand. "I have to experience everything, Joyce. The experience has to be in my voice for people to feel it, to be touched and moved by it."

"Even if it means losing me?" I asked boldly. "Is it that you really need the love and adulation of masses of people more than you really need me?"

"The people who are close to me," he said, his voice serious, "who really understand me, would die for me."

I was silent for a moment before replying. "Unless it's going to be the other way around."

He didn't answer. The pills were taking effect. He was starting to slip away.

"Elvis," I pleaded, "listen to me. Here I am, high above the Vegas strip in this hotel suite lavish beyond my wildest dreams, where you entertain all kinds of famous and glamorous people—here I am with you, the superstar of the century, the man I love as I thought I could never love anyone . . . and my heart is breaking . . ."

But it was no use. He was gone.

He was still asleep when I woke the next afternoon.

After I had showered, dressed, and packed, I walked over to the bed and looked down at him. The room was cold. It was always cold, he insisted on that. But that day, the chill seemed to penetrate to the bone. I shivered and thought back to my last words to him. The words he never heard. So that's the way it ends, I thought. Not with a roar, but with a whine. ". . . my heart is breaking . . ." Before I walk out, walk out of your life forever, there's one thing I have to do.

I was holding the ring in my hand, the lovely gold ring with the tiny diamond that he had given me when we first met . . . a lifetime ago. The ring I promised I would always wear until we no longer loved each other. Well, I still love you, Elvis, I thought but I love you too much to watch you kill yourself. I laid the ring on the nightstand and leaned over and kissed his cool cheek.

I walked out of the bedroom and then out of the suite. It wasn't until the elevator doors closed behind me that the tears came.

What a small, dull, shitty way for it to end, I thought, when the elevator doors opened and I stepped out. It should at least be dramatic, I should at least be hearing his great, golden, once-in-a-lifetime voice in a way that no one else could, in a way that I would hear it always, from then on, in my heart. But the truth was that there was only silence, and it was too late for anything but the truth.

Epilogue

For many long and painful months, I stuck to my guns and tried to rid my heart, mind, and soul of Elvis Presley. The love affair had ended. It had to. In spite of the hurt, in spite of the great emptiness inside, I knew I was right to have left him. His was a love that could destroy the very object of its desire. I had made one of the most terrible decisions a woman in love could make. It had cost me the greatest and most impossible love of my life. But it had gained me back my independence. It had gained me back a future.

It was the Elvis satellite special from Hawaii on April 4, 1973 that pierced the armor of denial in which I had shielded myself. I watched it. I had to. The final strains of its closing theme still echoed through my living room when I picked up the phone and called Charlie Hodge. Seeing Elvis again, even on a television screen, had seared my soul to the quick and I had to tell someone who would understand how much it meant to me. I knew, however, that to keep my vow I didn't dare speak to Elvis himself.

I hate to admit it, even all these years later, but when Charlie announced triumphantly that the Hawaii show would be the most watched event in human history, seen by one and one-half billion people, I couldn't help myself from thinking that now, I was only one of that number. Just one of a vast audience, no longer *the* special one with whom The King shared his most intimate needs and innermost desires. Not anymore. I got off the phone as quickly as I could.

The call from Elvis came not too long after that. As soon as I realized it was "his phone" that was ringing, my palms began to sweat. I was afraid he would say those things that would bring it all back, that I would be overwhelmed with love, that I would crumble . . .

But he was sweet, just sweet, asking how I had been, wanting to know if everything was all right, asking when I was going to come see him perform (which was so like him!)—and then surprising me by asking me to send him another copy of the photograph taken of the two of us in the suite in Vegas. As I was saying goodbye, he surprised me again by interrupting to declare that he really missed me and wanted me to meet him in Los Angeles. "Call me in a couple of weeks," he added. "Yes," I said without hesitation or thinking and, for a fleeting second, I meant it.

I sent him the photo, but I didn't call. Nor did I ever speak to him again. This fact is terribly poignant for me, even more so than might be imagined, because I did actually *see* him one more time.

By then, rumors about the deterioration of his performance and his appearance were rife. I finally reached a point at which I knew I had to see for myself if there was any truth to what was being said. I was not motivated by morbid curiosity. I honestly expected to see the rumors dispelled by the evidence of my own eyes. So, I traveled to Las Vegas in August of 1975.

The man spotlighted onstage only remotely resembled the Elvis I had known. He was almost grotesque, ballooned to a pathetic caricature of his former self. With the crowd around me still yelling and cheering for more of this awkward, pitiful parody of former greatness, I stood up, and wiping the tears from my cheeks, walked sadly up the aisle and away.

On August 16, 1977, Elvis Aaron Presley died. He was forty-two years old.

Elvis Presley had a profound effect on my life. The memory of him and of what we had together is something I will forever cherish in my heart.

Elvis now belongs to the ages. There are many people who feel that certain, less glamorous aspects of his life should be held sacred. I think that Elvis, with his self-deprecating sense of humor, would only be amused by this. The silver-throated, swivel-hipped truck driver from Tupelo was indeed soul-searching, but he was also fun-loving; he embraced all of life in his own, uniquely voracious way. Through his music, he shared all of himself, everything from his earthly passions to his deep religious yearnings.

I have tried to be true to the essence of this man as only I knew him, in those glorious years of his musical comeback. Elvis had the gift of giving of himself, and he did this lavishly, even to the end. On the day he died, those who hadn't even been born when he seemed to re-invent rock 'n' roll, wept. On that day, those who remembered knew for sure that their youth had died as well.

I lived for a while in the heat and glow of this star and I believe that for me, his light will never dim.